Making History, Drawing Territory

Making History, Drawing Territory
British Mapping in India, c.1756–1905

IAN J. BARROW

OXFORD
UNIVERSITY PRESS

OXFORD
UNIVERSITY PRESS

YMCA Library Building, Jai Singh Road, New Delhi 110 001

Oxford University Press is a department of the University of Oxford. It furthers the
University's objective of excellence in research, scholarship, and education
by publishing worldwide in

Oxford   New York

Auckland   Cape Town   Dar es Salaam   Hong Kong   Karachi   Kuala Lumpur
Madrid   Melbourne   Mexico City   Nairobi   New Delhi   Shanghai   Taipei   Toronto

With offices in

Argentina   Austria   Brazil   Chile   Czech Republic   France   Greece   Guatemala
Hungary   Italy   Japan   Poland   Portugal   Singapore   South Korea   Switzerland
Thailand   Turkey   Ukraine   Vietnam

Oxford is a registered trademark of Oxford University Press
in the UK and in certain other countries

Published in India by Oxford University Press, New Delhi

ISBN 0 19 565546 5

Typeset in Baskerville, 10.5/12.5
By Eleven Arts, Keshav Puram, Delhi 110 035
Printed in India at Roopak Printers, Delhi 110 032
Published by Manzar Khan, Oxford University Press
YMCA Library Building, Jai Singh Road, New Delhi 110 001

To my parents, Yvonne and George, with all my love
For Dana, my love

Contents

List of Figures

Photographs: Megan Battey

Acknowledgements

The research and writing for this book took place over several years in a variety of locations around the world. It is now a great pleasure to be able to thank my family, friends, and colleagues for their support, inspiration, and suggestions. Their good advice has helped me immeasurably, and my debt to them can hardly be repaid with words of gratitude.

This book began as a doctoral dissertation at the University of Chicago. My heartfelt thanks to Bernard Cohn, Ronald Inden, Carol Breckenridge, and Richard Barnett for their thoughtful guidance, and to Susanne and Lloyd Rudolph for their encouragement and interest in my projects.

The research for this book was funded by grants from the American Institute of Indian Studies, the J.B. Harley Research Fellowship Committee, the University of Chicago, and Middlebury College. I am grateful to these institutions and funding agencies for their generous support. I am also indebted to the staff at the National Archives of India, the British Library's Oriental and India Office Collection and Map Room (and, in particular, to Andrew Cook and Tony Campbell), the Public Record Office, the Royal Geographical Society's Library and Map Room, the Regenstein Library at the University of Chicago, and the Starr and Armstrong Libraries at Middlebury College.

In writing this book I have been inspired by friends whose readings of drafts or discussions of ideas have helped me clarify my own thoughts. My thanks to Vivek Bhandari, Toby Dodge, Pika Ghosh, Manu Goswami, Philip Gould, Ruhi Grover, Douglas Haynes, Walter Hauser, Bernardo Michael, Sumathi Ramaswamy, Mark Rogers, and Sudipta Sen. Megan Battey very kindly photographed the maps, for which I am deeply grateful. I also thank my colleagues in the Department of History at Middlebury College who have encouraged me in both my writing and teaching. An anonymous reviewer at OUP provided helpful suggestions, and my editors at OUP have expertly steered the book to publication. My thanks to all of them.

My final and greatest debt is to my family, to whom this book is dedicated.

Introduction:
Territory, History, and Legitimacy

In viewing colonial maps of India we read a history of possession. That history is displayed in many ways—as the rapid spread of the colour red across the map of British-controlled India, as the naming of a Himalayan mountain, as the disingenuous transformation of revenue land into British territory. It is seen in the political changes that are evident in two maps of the same area published a century apart and it is apparent in the titles and dedications of the maps. Maps present history and contain history; they explain what has happened and they show differences and similarities across time. Maps and history are interlinked, and this book is an examination of how the past is presented, used, and imagined in maps.

The map makers who figure here were conscious that the land they depicted had histories of ownership and occupation and that, if carefully crafted, their maps could portray those histories in an effective and seemingly direct manner. But they were also aware that they could make their maps more appealing, authoritative, and beguiling if they used maps as a way of incorporating the past into the present. In other words, map makers would not only show how the present political situation was derived from what had occurred previously, they would also invite their readers, through a perusal of the symbols, juxtapositions, and wording of the map, to relive and once more participate in those moments in the past which made the present possible. The history that they wrote and drew into a map was dynamic and imaginative; it encouraged the map viewers to place themselves in the crucial formative moments of the past.

The argument of this book is that colonial British map makers often constructed maps to justify territorial possession. Maps were, and indeed still are, made to have multiple uses. They could be used for utilitarian purposes such as the construction of roads and railways, the determination of revenue, or the movement of troops and goods. We tend to be most familiar with these kinds of uses for a map. Yet, maps also express perspectives that may range from the political and the religious to the economic, but which are made to seem as natural and as self-evident as the land depicted. What is particularly interesting about this intended use for a map is that, during the British colonial period in India, maps were among the most effective resources the British could turn to when they looked for their legitimacy as a colonial power.

This book, then, is only tangentially about the history of the colonial mapping of India. It is more fully a study of the histories of British possession and territorial legitimacy that are contained in colonial maps. It examines the articulation and manipulation of the past using cartographic perspectives and idioms. It focuses on various strategies used by map makers and surveyors to embed a past into their narratives, and it concludes that maps were used both to demonstrate a history of territory and, importantly, to justify the possession of land.

These cartographic efforts to make colonial rule legitimate are evident in maps that date from as early as the eighteenth century to as late as the twentieth century. Throughout this period colonial British authorities and independent British cartographers published maps that helped to bolster a British sense of entitlement to overseas power. Good examples from the mid-nineteenth century are provided by John Tallis whose *Illustrated Atlas and Modern History of the World* included several maps of India (Tallis 1851). The maps showing India are accompanied by a text that explains how British power had extended over South Asia. The maps' most noticeable features are little vignettes depicting emblems, such as the seal of the East India Company, and views, such as that of the Government House in Calcutta (now Kolkata). The map which shows all of India in one plate is entitled 'British India', thus reinforcing the idea that India is

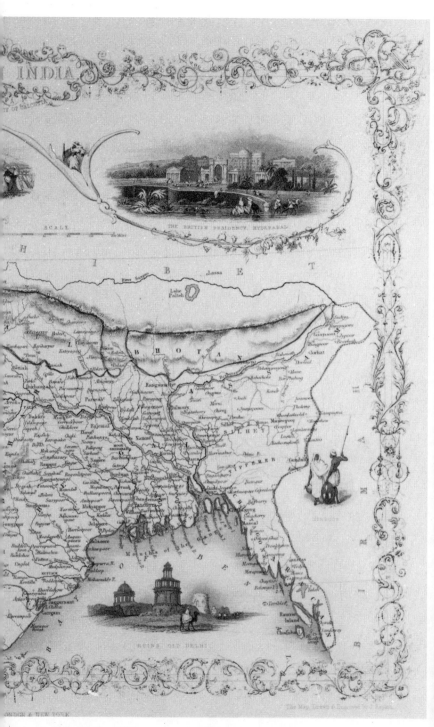

Published by John Tallis, 1851.

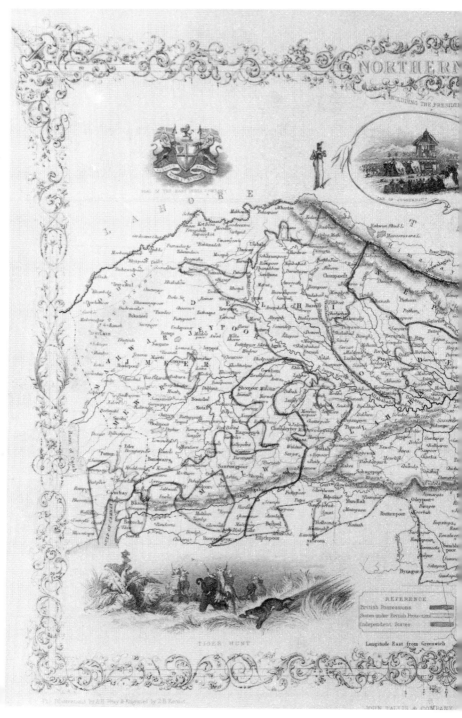

Fig. 1. *Map of Northern India, p*

a possession. The map of northern India has a reference indicating by a colour scheme which territories are 'British possessions', which are 'states under British protection', and which are 'independent states'. In addition to the Company's seal, the map also shows the British Residency at Hyderabad, a Company soldier, a tiger hunt, ruins in Old Delhi, the car of Juggernaut, and Hindoos. The insinuation of the symbols of British power into an Indian landscape suggests the naturalness of that power.

John Tallis' atlas is only one of many colonial-era atlases and maps that combined a depiction of the land with a history of possession. Such a combination goes to the heart of the cartographic practice of legitimating the Company and, later, imperial rule. However, the methods and perspectives the map makers adopted changed over time. In the eighteenth century, for example, route surveys and copper-plate engraving were routine, while at the end of the nineteenth century trigonometry and lithography were common practices. Just as importantly, map makers found that they had to adjust their conceptions and uses of history so as to present an explanation for colonial rule that suited changing political contexts and needs. This book is a study of how British map makers drew territory into creation and how they suffused history into those maps, all with a view to justify colonial rule.

Each of the five subsequent chapters, which cover the period from the mid-1700s to the early 1900s (from the beginning of British rule in Bengal to the end of Curzon's tenure as Viceroy), focuses on a different way history was incorporated into the depiction of territory. But, before turning to these chapters, several questions should be asked to help define the key concepts of the book. Our first concern is to determine how powerful maps are in formulating ideas, manipulating opinion, and reinforcing perspectives. The effectiveness of colonial cartography is based, in part, on the power of maps to shape understandings and influence policy. That power, in the colonial Indian context, was derived from specific conceptions of territory that were formulated as a way both to include India within an empire and to justify that inclusion. The second question to be addressed follows from the first in that it asks how land was depicted as territory. What were the connections between perception, land, and ownership? The third question examines how that territory was placed within a history of possession, again with the intention of explaining ownership. The fourth question focuses on how British conceptions of a history of territorial possession may be characterized as 'colonial', while the final question extends our analysis to a consideration of how the notion of possessed Indian territory contributed to the creation of British national identity.

The Power of Maps

This study of British cartographic attempts to legitimate colonial power is predicated on the idea that maps have power. It makes little sense, for example, to suggest that British cartographers could contribute to the ongoing process of colonial self-legitimacy if their notions of the past and their depictions of land had little resonance with British viewers. It is important, therefore, to explain how maps do indeed have the power to define perspectives and legitimize practices. Thus, we may begin by asking two apposite questions: How powerful are maps and what does 'power' mean?

In recent years numerous scholars in cartographic history have addressed these questions at some length. In fact, interest in cartographic history has been largely preoccupied with the ability of map makers to direct and influence public opinion. Many of these studies are indebted to the pioneering work of J.B. Harley (2001). Since my own understanding of the beguiling nature of maps is so influenced by Harley's work I will outline his arguments below and indicate how my conceptions regarding the intentions and effects of colonial cartography are derived, in part, from his ideas of power. I will then turn to a leading historian of colonial cartography in India, whose work is also indebted to Harley, and explain how he views the power of maps in the colonial Indian context. Finally, I will suggest how Harley's approach has been variously used or echoed in studies that have ranged from those of German nationalist maps to mapping practices in Australia. The purpose of referencing these works is twofold—to explain the extent and the meaning of cartographic power.

In a series of essays on how to read maps, Harley has turned scholarly attention away from a narrow examination of style, provenance, date of drawing or printing, and the map maker and

for the Diffusion of Useful Knowledge, 1842.

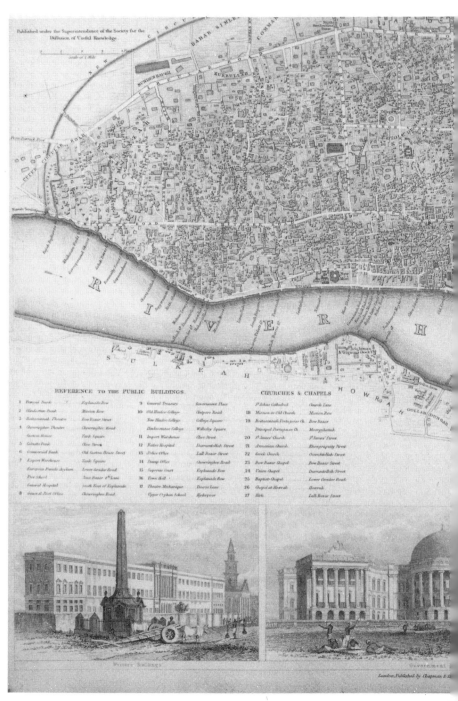

Fig. 2. *Map of Calcutta, published by the Socie*

towards a critique of the map as an expression of political, economic, or religious interest. He views a map as a text, subject to the same distortions, silences, exaggerations, and lies that may exist in all historical documents. According to Harley, maps present arguments; a cadastral map, for example, might recognize a particular form of ownership, an estate map might highlight the name of the landlord, an empire map might distinguish overseas lands that are controlled. These arguments may be conveyed by such subtle means as cartouches, colours, names, or projection. Although each of these perspectives may be contested, the power of the map lies in its seeming naturalness. If the cartographic convention is to label India as 'British India' then it is easier to recognize the country as possessed rather than consider it as independent.

Harley is also as eager to notice absences in a map as he is to find meaning in what is visible. Thus, the extrusion of indigenous peoples from colonial maps or the lack of any reference to temples or mosques in Indian city maps, such as the plan of Calcutta published in 1842 by the Society for the Diffusion of Useful Knowledge (SDUK), are ways that maps may dissimulate. The SDUK plan is noteworthy because it contains a reference and a series of illustrations.[1] The reference lists the names of public buildings, such as the Bengal Bank, the Custom House, and the police office, and the churches and chapels that appear in the plan. The scenes at the bottom of the plan are of the Writers' Building (including what appears to be the Holwell Monument to those who died in the Black Hole of 1756), the Government House, and Esplanade Row, showing a number of palanquin porters relaxing. The architecture, the choice of what buildings to include, and the depiction of Indians as servants existing outside the gates of power together suggest that Calcutta was a British city set in an exotic landscape. Apart from the depiction of Indians as porters or peasants, there is little indication in the map that Calcutta was an Indian city inhabited by Indians.

The reasons for dissimulation or for presenting a misleading argument about possession are as varied as the contexts that produced the maps. Much of the thrust of recent scholarship on cartographic history has been to examine why maps present political, economic, or social arguments. Nevertheless, Harley's point is that maps are not neutral, value-free presentations of the world. As he says, 'maps are preeminently a language of power, not of protest. ... Cartography remains a teleological discourse, reifying power, reinforcing the status quo, and freezing social interaction within charted lines' (ibid.: 79). The scientific-cum-artistic practices of surveying and map-making are avenues for the expression of social, political, and economic relations.

Harley's assertion that maps have tremendous power to influence perspective, opinion, and policy has not gone unchallenged (see, for example, Lemann 2001: 131–34). It is certainly true that maps may have a limited audience, that they are often reflections (and not just manipulators) of social opinion, and that it is difficult to prove a causal relationship between the viewing of a map and subsequent action. It is important to remember that some maps are poorly made, some viewers may misinterpret the meaning of a map (if there is ever a single meaning in a map), and some maps may be too expensive or too difficult to find to present much of an engaging argument at all. The challenges for a historian of cartographic history are, first, to place a map within a social and political context that can indicate the map's significance and, second, to not endow maps with excessive powers to transform perspective or policy. Most maps reinforce opinions that are already held and most maps are themselves the products of convention.

Harley's insight that maps are as much, if not more, the result of the mind's eye than the theodolite's aperture, notwithstanding the caveat that maps are never all-powerful, contributes to my understanding of how British colonial maps had consequence and influence. We should remember that maps are social products. If well constructed and published or released at an opportune moment, maps can be effective tools in presenting a perspective or contributing to a larger debate. The surveyors and map makers that I examine here used their skills in mathematics, perspective, and drawing to convey their ideas of the significance of land.

Turning to South Asia, there have been a number of recent and valuable studies on colonial cartography, providing a narrative of events (Kalpagam 1995, Madan 1997), a description of practices (Styles 1970), or a catalogue of maps (see, for instance, Gole 1983). However, the most important cartographic work on India that incorporates Harley's arguments of power and maps has been Matthew

Edney's (1997) *Mapping an Empire: The Geographical Construction of British India, 1765–1843.* Edney argues in his book, and in several articles on colonial surveying (1991, 1994), that the extensive trigonometrical mapping conducted throughout much of southern and central India in the first half of the nineteenth century encouraged the British to believe that they knew the real India. Whereas earlier route surveys had supplied information that was only partially reliable, trigonometrical surveying, with its emphasis on pin-point mathematical accuracy, was thought to render a thorough and precise representation of the land. Trigonometrical surveyors would throw a 'web' of triangles over the land, fixing locations and permitting large-scale topographical surveys. Edney's point is that even though the practices and results of the Trigonometrical Survey were, in truth, far from adequate (their surveys were expensive, often delayed, and frequently beset by numerous difficulties and troubles), the Company's heavy investment in it was judged to be justified because the Survey represented an Enlightenment ideal. The ideal of scientific precision, rational thought, and accurate depiction contrasted with the behaviour of Indians and of the non-elite British, who were caricatured as ineffectual and incapable of sustained rational thought and practical purpose. The ideal also enabled the British to believe that they could capture a true and complete knowledge of India.

For Edney, the power of trigonometrical mapping in India is that its seemingly objective and scientific nature permitted British surveyors and bureaucrats to indulge in the fantasy that accurate cartographic knowledge would both demonstrate British superiority and lead to better control over the land and the people. Indeed, the control exercised by the British over Indians would mirror the control surveyors exercised over the map—it would be totalizing, all-seeing, and rational. The map, therefore, depicted more than land; it represented an approach to complete knowledge and effective power. As Edney (1997: 36) notes, *Mapping an Empire* 'is a study of the creation of a legitimating conception of empire, of political and territorial hegemony, mapped out in a scientistic and rational construction of space'. The British constructed maps that revealed their penchant for systematic order.

It should be mentioned that there has been a recent challenge to

Edney's interpretation of the way late eighteenth- and early nineteenth-century maps were made. In an essay in a volume on 'society and circulation', Kapil Raj argues that too little attention has been paid to the 'hybrid', almost Company art nature of early colonial maps (Raj 2003: 23–54). These maps, according to Raj, were influenced by indigenous sources and knowledge and were therefore not direct expressions of the European Enlightenment. Raj correctly shows that there was not only a long tradition of map-making in South Asia before the establishment of British power, but that when the British began to map they relied upon Indians for information and labour, facts that even the surveyors themselves documented. The resulting maps, he claims, were much more Indian than has been appreciated.

However, Raj overstates the way in which published colonial maps were the products of both European and Indian cartographic traditions. Certainly, Indians made maps, even for Europeans, and were clearly employed in a number of ways by British surveyors. But the maps produced by the Company, and especially its published maps, were primarily intended for European audiences, steeped in European political traditions and familiar with particular sets of signs, symbols, and perspectives. Moreover, however reliant early British surveyors might have been on Indian labour, information, even perspectives, they did not claim, and probably would not have thought, that their work was hybrid in nature. In fact, as the first chapter of this book suggests, the opposite appears to be the case: that British map-makers tried to draw their maps in such a way as to conform to recognized European cartographic traditions.

This said, Raj's assessment of the involvement and influence of Indians in the colonial map-making process does open up new approaches to the study of colonial mapping. It not only forms part of a body of scholarship that seeks to identify the reliant, collaborative, and co-constitutive nature of colonial science (Arnold 2000), it also might inspire studies on how cartographic literacy was developed in India during the eighteenth and nineteenth centuries. Still, Edney's argument that British colonial mapping was *seen* as a scientific, rational, Enlightenment practice is compelling and informs my understanding of the power of colonial cartography. He makes an insightful point when he suggests that the East India Company trigonometrical surveys and maps had the power to unify India as an empire in a conceptual manner. How successfully that power was exercised over people is, of course, a different matter. Nevertheless, that the British constructed their notional empire according to their Enlightenment principles is significant because it helped to shape British attitudes, policies, and practices. Thus, following Harley, we may suggest that maps may have the power to project political perspectives and, following Edney, note that Company maps may have contributed the political idea of an Indian empire that, through minute scrutiny, could be known and fully controlled.

Although indebted to Edney's history, this book differs from his in several significant respects. First, I examine two aspects of the colonial mapping of India that he does not comprehensively address—ideas of the past and the construction of territory. Turning land into territory and then establishing a history of possession are core reasons why cartography was in the vanguard of arguments justifying colonial rule. There was more to the legitimating project than the trigonometrical surveyor's claim that the precise use of accurate scientific methods would reveal knowledge about India and mirror a comprehensive and penetrating form of rule. Second, I use a variety of cartographic practices and projects, both official and semi-official, to explain how map makers used five different historical approaches over the course of a century and a half in order to adapt the legitimating arguments to changing contexts and circumstances. Finally, a main thrust of my argument is that the mapping of India and the creation of a colonial territory helped to build British national identity and cement India's ties to Britain. The conquest of India and its transformation into a colony were integral to the making of the British nation. Mapping played an important part in this co-constitutive process of Empire- and nation-building.

Harley's re-conceptualization of cartographic power has been so influential that scholars have used it to examine maps in a variety of different contexts and eras. Several of these scholars' formulations of cartographic power have been particularly helpful for this study. Guntram Herb's (1997) work on cartographic propaganda in Germany between 1918 and 1945 is a good example of how 'suggestive' maps can be when constructing a national identity. One of Herb's arguments is that German propaganda maps from the Weimar period 'prepared' the public for later Nazi expansionism and national territorial obsession. Following the definitions of G.S. Jowett and V. O'Donnell, he distinguishes between propaganda and rhetoric.

Propaganda tries 'to shape perceptions, manipulate cognitions, and direct behaviour' in a deliberate and systematic way (Herb: 8). Rhetoric, on the other hand, is more 'neutral' in that it conceals and restricts less information. What is especially useful about Herb's analysis is that he reveals two important principles about German cartographic propaganda: that Weimar-period maps had long shelf-lives and that propaganda was not necessarily a wholly state-sponsored endeavour. Weimar cartographers, many of them independent of the state, projected onto maps their views of the breadth of German national territory that were later politically expressed by the Nazis. As he notes, 'German propaganda cartography was pioneered long before the Nazis came to power and by a variety of groups and individuals ...' (ibid.: 183).

Colonial cartography may also be characterized as propagandistic, in that it attempted to manipulate and direct ideas and policy. It should be remembered, however, that colonial surveyors and map makers believed that their maps were, first and foremost, utilitarian rather than ideological. Nevertheless, we find in colonial cartography echoes of Herb's insight that non-state directed Weimar maps contained perspectives that were acted upon years after their publication. Maps of India were published by a wide variety of institutions, firms, and individuals, many of them connected to the East India Company or the subsequent state, but many of them semi-independent or fully so. If their perspectives cohered it was partly because of the power of cartographic convention (for example, the use of red or pink to designate British Empire territories by atlas makers in the nineteenth and twentieth centuries), but it was also because earlier maps were successful in suggesting how India could be conceived and depicted as British territory.

The suggestive nature of maps has made them the friend of imperial history. Aided by a political context, colonial era maps may well be read and interpreted as texts of imperial power. And yet, surveyors themselves might have experienced their travels in ways that may be poorly conveyed in their own maps. Surveyors' journals are frequently full of their interactions and communications with people, their killing of tigers, or their periodic illnesses. What finally appears on the map, especially in the nineteenth century, is a landscape that is increasingly devoid of reference to the journeys that were necessary for its construction. This point is well made by

Paul Carter in *Road to Botany Bay* (1987). Although not a protégé of Brian Harley, Carter shows how the meandering travels of an exploring surveyor are codified and placed within a discourse of fact and location that can rob the land of its own meaning. As noticed by D. Graham Burnett (2000: 10–12), Carter identifies a tension in colonial surveyors between the need to satisfy their employers and represent places that conform to standardized symbols and the desire to portray a land that is varied, lived in, and full of character. What is particularly interesting is the suggestion that a transformation may take place in how land is first experienced by a surveyor and how it is then represented for a reader who is not present.

The power of maps is that they may conceal personal experiences or interactions with land and people only to reveal an imperial perspective. This detached, location-driven, and totalizing point of view has proven to be a powerful instrument of modern and colonial states. Between 1756 and 1905, the vast majority of published and manuscript British maps of India presented a state-centric perspective. The reasons for this conformity include the monopoly of geographical information by the state (surveys were expensive and were usually only conducted by the state), the way by which cartographic symbols were standardized and recognized (meaning that notes or unconventional symbols were gradually elided from the map), and the process of 'objectification' whereby a distance was placed between the viewer and the India conceived of as a geographical fact. Thus, it may be concluded that eighteenth- and nineteenth-century cartographic conventionality became the handmaiden of colonialism.

The Making of Territory

Any examination of colonial cartography must include more than a suggestion that maps have certain powers of persuasion. It must also address the question of the cartographic meaning of land. In the second half of the eighteenth century, the East India Company became a territorial power. Through a variety of ways—military force, bribery, deception, alliance—the Company was able to exert its control over increasingly large areas. As the Company expanded its power into and over India, it had to explain the basis of its supposed sovereignty. The concept of territory was key to that explanation. If the British hoped to bring both legitimacy and sovereignty to their rule in India, it was crucial that land be transformed into territory.

My ideas of the interwoven nature of history, territory, and national identity draw on the work of Thongchai Winichakul. In his book, *Siam Mapped: A History of the Geo-Body of a Nation* (1994), Winichakul introduces the neologism 'geo-body' to describe the modern creation of a bounded and enforced territory that became the basis for Thai national sentiment and attachment. Part of his argument is that during the late nineteenth and twentieth centuries, a new and foreign-derived conception of a Siamese, or Thai, nation supplanted long-standing indigenous understandings and meanings of territory. The new Thai geo-body was imagined by means of European-inspired mapping and then reified by subsequent maps. As he notes, the common assumption is that 'a map merely represents something which already exists objectively. In the history of the geo-body, this relationship was reversed. A map anticipated a spatial reality, not vice versa. In other words, a map was a model for, rather than a model of, what it purported to represent' (ibid.: 130).[2] In mapping the nation's geo-body, Thais came to believe that certain pre-modern boundaries that no longer existed were nevertheless essential if the country was to be whole: 'a geo-body which had never existed in the past was realized by historical projection' (ibid.: 152).

Winichakul's study helps explain the constructed nature of modern Thai nationality. His focus on the making of territory and the ostensible historical nature of an essential and complete geo-body have their parallels in the construction of both a British Empire in India and Indian national identities. As Edney has shown, the Company's cartographic projects, and especially its trigonometrical surveys, were instrumental in identifying and delimiting an Indian territory. And, as Sumathi Ramaswamy has argued, the importance of (lost) historical territory has featured prominently in nineteenth- and twentieth- century Tamil national movements (1999, 2000).

My study of cartographic uses of territory and history is indebted to Winichakul's idea of a geo-body in that colonial map makers helped to define territory as an essential attribute of the colonial state much in the same way that the European and Thai cartographers insisted on the importance of Thai territorial boundaries. However, this book differs in several respects from Winichakul's examination of a geo-body. I do not address the question of how modern mapping contributed to the imagining of an Indian nation. Nor do I examine the processes whereby an essentialized nation may have been projected into the past as a way of buttressing Indian nationalist agendas. Instead, I focus on how colonial cartography depicted histories of British territorial possession in India and how those histories helped the British to make themselves legitimate as rulers while also reinforcing the construction of a British sense of national identity. Hence, this book is not about the construction of an Indian geobody, but about the making of a British colonial territorial state.

Territory is a key term in our examination of the power of colonial cartography to justify British rule. We should recognize that not all land is territory and that a process of appropriation is involved in turning land into territory. The word 'territory' is derived from the Latin *terra*, meaning earth or land, and the suffix, *torium*, means belonging to or surrounding (Gottmann 1973: 16). But, although the root meaning is descriptive, the term, over time, has come to suggest land that is possessed. Robert Sack (1986: 19) has labelled the possession or control of territory as territoriality: it is the attempt 'to affect, influence, or control people, phenomena, and relationships, by delimiting and asserting control over a geographic area'. Territoriality was crucial to colonial map makers and officials who wished to facilitate the control over people, goods, and land by fixing borders and locations.

Territoriality does not just occur and territory itself is not just empty space. For land to be turned into territory it needs to be inhabited, appropriated, or recognized in some form. For territory to become part of the state, that habitation does not necessarily have to be by the state's subjects but must be by the *state* itself. Habitation may mean sending a representative to plant a foot on an island, hoist a flag on a hilltop, or establish a law court in a village (Gottmann 1973: 1–15). Alternatively, habitation could mean traversing the land, examining it with a theodolite, and then mapping it. In any of these ways the state may lay claim to land, helping to turn it into territory. Thus, the processes of surveying and mapping may be crucial components in the transformation of land into territory.

Jean Gottmann suggests that land's transformation into territory is further aided when land becomes accessible and controllable. 'Accessibility in space is organized, at all times in history, to serve political aims, and one of the major aims of politics is to regulate conditions of access' (ibid.: 9). Maps may be invaluable tools, therefore, in ensuring that territory is made both accessible and orderly. Moreover, this process is also facilitated when land is delimited and depicted in a fashion that highlights the limits of political control. In identifying and showing boundaries, maps clarify ownership and establish rights of access.

In sum, land may be considered territory when it is accessed, inhabited, and possessed by a state and when that possession is circumscribed and made explicit. The East India Company and, later, the British government in India used maps to delimit and depict territory and to help control access to it. The benefits that it derived from turning land into territory included the generation of wealth and, just as importantly, the establishment of sovereignty.

Such a movement towards the association of sovereignty with territory was not unusual in the eighteenth and nineteenth centuries. James Akerman has shown that by the mid-seventeenth century sovereignty moved from meaning a control over people to a control over territory. Political territoriality, to use his phrase, also became a concern of map and atlas makers. They delineated regional boundaries and hierarchies in increasingly precise but consistent ways (Akerman 1995). The East India Company, coming out of a European cartographic tradition that valued political territoriality, understood its own colonial space in terms of territory. For the Company, territory meant bounded and discrete lands made amenable to measurement, made knowable because of the power of rational and systematic surveying techniques, and, ultimately, rendered governable due to their nature as possessed lands.[3] This perspective on the colonial state's need for bounded space is reinforced by the recent work of Bernardo Michael. In an in-depth study of the Anglo-Gorkha war of 1814–16, Michael has shown how the East India Company's boundary-making efforts along India's border with Nepal helped quash indigenous notions of overlapping territory while highlighting the power of delimited territory in the making of the modern state (Michael 2001).

Even though the British embarked upon a territorializing project almost from the moment they were able to exert their influence and power over large areas of India, we must bear in mind that at no time during colonial rule was there a single kind of territory. Rather, there were a variety of territories in India. Some were governed directly by the Company and, after 1858, by the British colonial state. Other territories were ruled indirectly through treaties and alliances. There are plenty of examples of maps that indicate the varieties of territory in India during the eighteenth and nineteenth centuries. C. Smith, for instance, a cartographer who styled himself 'Mapseller extraordinary to His Majesty', published in 1822 a map of Hindoostan (a common nineteenth-century name for India). In the map's 'Explanation' Smith provides the key to colour-codes that identify British Possessions, Countries under the Protection of the British, and Independent Powers. He also includes an interesting paragraph explaining that some of the boundaries on the map are no longer valid due to the 'fluctuating nature of political power in India'.

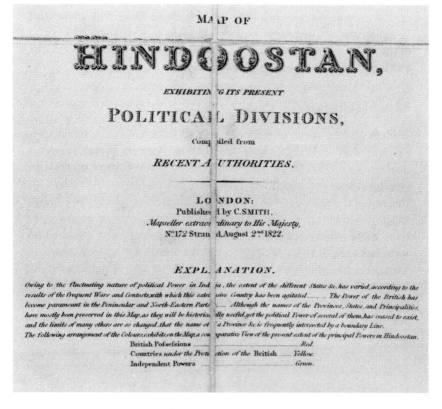

Fig. 3. *Title of a Map of Hindoostan, by C. Smith, 1822. The map has been cut and pasted on linen.*

In addition to the fact that there were always different kinds of territory in colonial India, there were also a number of mapping projects. These ranged from the Company's topographical and trigonometrical surveys and the Atlas of India scheme to the independent map and chart sheets published in London. However, what all these territories and cartographic projects had in common was that the land depicted was progressively made accessible, inhabited, and delimited by the colonial state. Finally, it could be considered owned land.

By the mid-eighteenth century a solid cartographic tradition had been established which placed considerable emphasis on showing political divisions. The advantages to the political territorialization of Company land, and eventually all of India, were that the British could then explain their presence and claim legitimate ownership by referring to a history of acquisition. The very creation of territory allowed the British to speak of a history of lawful possession. In making territory, then, map makers also inserted a past.

The Making of the Past

Clearly, the concept of territory was useful for the Company in its efforts to ensure legitimacy as a ruling state in India. However, authority could only be fully established if the Company was also recognized as the legitimate possessor of that territory. Outlining a history of possession could prove invaluable to that endeavour and maps, once again, could help document and show how and when possession was established. The meanings of territory and history, together with the uses of maps to justify colonial possession, changed over time, in almost protean fashion. It is only recently that scholarly attention has turned to the history that is contained in atlases and maps (Black 1997), but it is evident that such an investigation reveals one way that maps make their subjects, perspectives, and agendas seem natural and acceptable.

Although there may be many reasons to depict the past in maps, British attempts to show a history of legitimate possession in India are particularly germane to this study. I wish to concentrate on five approaches to the past that eighteenth- and nineteenth-century map makers frequently resorted to: associative history, progressive history, reverential history, romantic history, and, finally, nostalgic history. I should also note that each of the next five chapters focuses on one of these historical approaches.

The first approach places territory within a familiar tradition of ownership. Late- eighteenth-century map makers frequently suggested that India was possessed by the British in a manner similar to the way a landlord possessed his domain in Britain. I call this associative history because these map makers, the most notable being James Rennell, employed a variety of well established and recognizable cartographic techniques to indicate the supposed parallels between territorial possession in India and Britain. The introduction of dedications and cartouches, for example, associated Indian territory with particular British individuals whose inclusion in the maps reinforced suggestions that India was like a country estate. What makes this a historical approach is that the association with both individuals and a style of ownership was based upon the idea that a landlord had a legitimate right and historical claim to delimited land.

An example of associative history may be William Faden's 'A Map of Bengal, Bahar, Oude and Allahabad with part of Agra and Delhi exhibiting the course of the Ganges from Hurdwar to the Sea by James Rennell, F.R.S. late Surveyor Genl in Bengal.' The map was published in 1786 and was based on a manuscript map first drawn by James Rennell. It was re-issued by the firm Laurie & Whittle in 1794 (see Gole 1983: 195).

The Faden map is of interest as associative history because of the dedication it contains. In it we find allusions to the past deeds and the then–present position of a man called John Stables: 'One of the Supreme Council of Bengal.' Stables fought in a series of campaigns in northern India from 1759 up to his retirement in 1769, including as the commander of a battalion during the battle of Buxar in 1764. He subsequently became a member of the Supreme Council, where he opposed Warren Hastings (Buckland 1969: 398–99). By associating the map with the name of a conqueror-turned-councillor, not only is the map made more authoritative and trustworthy but a history of legitimate possession is also established.

The second approach is based on an idea held by many early-nineteenth-century trigonometrical surveyors. In devising ever more scientific and seemingly accurate surveying techniques these cartographers linked precision with knowledge and knowledge with possession. They believed that by privileging trigonometrical surveys over astronomical or traverse surveys the resulting map of India would certainly be rendered more reliable. But the map would also aid in the accurate display of Company territory and, as Matthew Edney argues, encourage the thought that the British could rule India (the land and the people) with the same order and control that they exercised over the map.

Maps also tell a history of possession by identifying land with an honoured individual. This third approach to the incorporation of the past may be termed reverential history. Although the Survey of India usually refrained from naming mountains, rivers, or other physical features after a person, it did do so on occasion. Its most famous naming was of Mount Everest, in honour of the former Surveyor General, George Everest. By associating the name of a retired and revered member of the survey department with the highest mountain in the world, the Survey hoped, among other things, to suggest that possession was justified because of the principles of advancement, progress, and dedication embodied in the figure of Everest.

The fourth technique used by cartographers to persuade viewers that India was legitimately possessed concerns the deliberate re-implementation of antiquated surveying methods. In the second half of the nineteenth century, the Survey employed Indians to map routes and rivers in Tibet and Central Asia in ways that were reminiscent of the first years of Company surveying in India. The romance of the Survey hinged on the idea that among the benefits of British rule was the fact that Indians could now be taught rudimentary surveying practices.

Finally, I examine what may be termed original moments, or momentous history. By the end of the nineteenth century map makers often depicted those moments in the past when British power was thought to have been established or consolidated. Maps were published, for example, that showed the locations of British military successes in Bengal in the mid-eighteenth century or in northern India during the Mutiny of 1857–58. There was a nostalgia about and a desire to recapture a time when it was thought that

Britain, in either a buccaneer or a righteous manner, fought its way to becoming the pre-eminent power in India. Following Janet Abu-Lughod's work on the 'remaking' of history, and inspired by William Sewell's concept of 'eventful temporality', I suggest that colonial map makers pursued a reverse teleology whereby they sought to display moments in which British control over territory originated. The remembrance of those moments produced nostalgic history. Abu-Lughod makes a small but trenchant point in an essay recapitulating her argument in *Beyond European Hegemony*. Among the methodological difficulties confronting historians who wish to remake history is the common practice of constructing narratives backwards. This tendency is particularly true of British colonial historians, whether professional or amateur. At the turn of the twentieth century, writers and even map makers saw history as emanating from specific events in the past.

William Sewell has also theorized the significance of past events (1996a, 1996b: 245–80). Whereas Abu-Lughod focuses our attention on how historians have constructed genealogies to trace actions back to specific sources or events, Sewell addresses the transformative power of events. He argues that an occurrence becomes an event 'when it touches off a chain of occurrences that durably transforms previous structures and practices' (1996a: 843). Momentous events of a time both reveal the underlying political, economic, and social structures of a land and alter those structures in such a way that new perspectives and modes of life are made possible. Sewell makes no claim that an event will necessarily lead to a specific outcome (no teleology is implied), only that it causes a rearrangement of patterns of life and behaviour. In fact, Sewell is at pains to contrast his eventful temporality with a 'teleological temporality', arguing that events promise no set direction.

Many colonial maps of India published at the turn of the twentieth century reveal an interest in and a nostalgia for original moments. These moments were thought to have encapsulated the reasons and disclosed the justification for British political predominance. Much in the same way as Abu-Lughod theorizes reverse teleology, turn-of-the-century maps often privileged specific moments in the past. Also, in a similar vein to Sewell's argument that events can be seen to have momentous consequences, colonial map makers regarded certain events as being pregnant with meaning and possibility. However, in contrast to Sewell's idea of eventful temporality, a colonial original moment was considered consequential because it both revealed character and explained and initiated subsequent occurrences, whose genealogy could be traced back in time to a particular *telos*.

Between the late eighteenth and early twentieth century, cartographers justified the possession of extra-national or colonial territories by resorting to these five interpretations of the past. The use of these approaches during different periods of colonial rule reflected the ever-changing political context and, thus, the changing needs of how rule was to be explained and justified to the British public. Yet, even though I have outlined how map makers infused the past into their maps I have so far taken it for granted that the power these maps reflected and projected was 'colonial'.

The Making of the Colonial

The Company's efforts to provide legitimacy for its rule, by depicting a history of possession, contributed to the ongoing and considerable historiographical debates on the making of 'colonial' Company rule. There is no clear consensus within scholarship as to when the colonial emerges in India.[4] For our purposes, however, we may tentatively and rudimentarily define the colonial as British control over Indian land and people, either in a hegemonic or dominant manner. Of course, both the purpose and manner of that control are contentious issues. Moreover, a possible characteristic of the colonial in India is that it may be associated with the introduction of the 'modern' state. James Scott has noticed that the government of the modern state administers by means of 'typifications' and 'schematic categories' that make society legible while creating a distance between the state and society. 'If we imagine a state,' he writes, 'that has no reliable means of enumerating and locating its population, gauging its wealth, and mapping its land, resources, and settlements, we are imagining a state whose interventions in that society are necessarily crude' (Scott: 1998: 77). Given this initial definition of colonialism as an expression of the modern state I would suggest that the Company's rapid adoption of traverse or route surveying techniques, coupled with its uses of the past and a conception of territory as owned and delimited land, are compelling indications that profoundly new ways of projecting and justifying power had been introduced to South Asia by the beginning of the fourth quarter of the eighteenth century. Although novelty does not necessarily equate with the colonial, the fact that a non-indigenous power claimed territory in India and made its possession by writing a history of ownership would seem to signify the beginnings of the colonial.

Yet, scholars continue to debate when 'full-blown' colonialism first emerged. This debate is summarized well by Partha Chatterjee (1993: Ch. 2) and Sunil Khilnani (1999: 219–23). Following their characterizations, it may be said that disagreement often centres on whether colonialism appeared at the beginnings of Company rule, in the mid-eighteenth century, or at the end of Company rule, in the mid-nineteenth century.[5]

One approach has been to argue that the establishment of the Company state introduced newfangled and 'colonial' practices. Sudipta Kaviraj is one political scientist who argues that the Company's state was distinctly colonial from its inception and 'did not emerge out of the internal logic of evolution of earlier Indian society' (1994: 28). On the contrary, he states, the Company imported European practices and ideas that contrasted with what had existed previously. It would appear that much of the appeal of this perspective on the introduction of colonialism rests with the fact that, as supported by some historians such as Sushil Chaudhury (1995), the Company's actions may be interpreted as being particularly destructive and overly extractive.

However, this argument about the early appearance of colonialism has proven unsatisfactory to some historians of the eighteenth century. They indicate that although the Company state may have been distinct from indigenous polities in many ways, the Company adopted much of the pomp and circumstance of political power that was a hallmark of previous regimes. It also made numerous accommodations regarding Indian religious observances, social mores, and political rituals. Recently, leading historians of the eighteenth century have noted that the weight of scholarship over the last twenty years or so has tended to move away from describing the century as one of decline, disruption, or revolution. Instead, it is now commonly argued that what happened in Bengal should not be confused with all of India; that in many parts of India there is evidence of a flourishing economy; that the so-called successor states to the Mughal empire were also successful states; and that many continuities in governance, economy, and religion are apparent (Marshall 2003: 1–49, Barnett 2002: 11–29). Historians have also noticed that the Company was in a precarious position at the time, financially and militarily, and that it needed to rely upon Indians and adhere to Indian forms of governance, trade, and social interaction in order to ensure its survival. Its rule, therefore, may be seen to be an odd amalgam of European and Indian ideas on all manner of issues, ranging from trade and revenue to the army and diplomacy. This amalgamation of approaches, styles, and ideas does not contradict the fact that the Company could be ruthlessly acquisitive, extractive, and duplicitous. (see Bayly 1983, Perlin 1985, Stein 1985, Stokes 1973, Washbrook 1988).

Historians have also presented another perspective on when a distinct colonialism was formed. For them, the focus is on the mid-nineteenth century when the East India Company was removed from power and the British Crown assumed direct control over India. The argument is that a sharp break in British–Indian relations occurred during and after the Mutiny-rebellion of 1857–58. Those who have written for a generalist audience have often remarked on the fact that not only was the Company displaced by the British Crown but there were also thorough-going changes in the army, the introduction of policies that were increasingly informed by racial typologies and hierarchies, and that 'progress', in the form of railways, for example, was introduced on an unprecedented scale. Other changes include Victoria's adoption of the title 'Empress' and the late-nineteenth-century transformation of India into an exotic tourist destination (see James 1997: 296–98, Stein 1998: 239–83, Wolpert 2000: 239–47). Historical monographs also indicate that a 'high' colonial form of rule was initiated as a result of the restoration of British control in northern India (see Hutchins 1967, Metcalf 1964, Nandy 1991). All of these characterizations of colonialism have at least three aspects in common. The first is that the new state is said to have begun to intrude upon and refashion many indigenous economic, social, and caste structures (see, for instance, Cohn 1987). The second is that after the mid-century mark, European capitalist engines of progress

were fired up with gusto (see Kerr 1997). The third aspect common
to analyses of the late nineteenth century is that they notice a widening
gulf between British soldiers, administrators, and businessmen and
Indians of all classes. Thus, even though a form of colonialism may
have been in evidence before the mid-nineteenth century, drastic
and remarkable changes occurred as a direct result of the mutiny.

These three approaches to the moment when the colonial is
evident are not necessarily mutually exclusive. It may be the case that
while the Company sought to accommodate itself to Indian political,
economic, and social ways, it also introduced new and colonial ideas
of rule that were themselves altered over time, most noticeably in
the mid-to-late nineteenth century. Colonial cartography, with its
emphasis on fashioning arguments for the legitimate and historical
possession of territory, may be considered a colonial form of
knowledge and practice. Moreover, embedded within its history of
justified territorial possession was a narrative of British national
identity. Through their control of Indian territory the British were
not just benefiting materially, they were also making their own sense
of national purpose and community. What could be more colonial
than claiming ownership over another's land and then feeling
stronger and more whole, and more alien, as a result?

The Making of a British National Identity

The final characteristic of colonial cartography to be considered is
its contribution to the construction of a British sense of national
identity. Why was the ownership of conquered land so vital for any
sense of being British, and how did the mapping of India generate
both a loyalty to and a history for a British nation? It would be
reasonable to infer, based on the work of such scholars as Matthew
Edney and Sumathi Ramaswamy, that the British cartographic
creation of a bounded and geographically united India aided
eighteenth- and nineteenth-century Indian nationalists to imagine
a similarly bounded, but independent India. The 'cartographic
anxiety', to use Sankaran Krishna's phrase, that the post-1947 Indian
state has exhibited owes much to its late colonial predecessor, which
was equally preoccupied with establishing and maintaining India's
territorial integrity (Krishna 1996: 193–214). The links between

Indian nationalism and colonial cartography are important and only just being uncovered but I would like to steer our attention to the even less frequently discussed idea that British national identity, attachment, and belonging was fashioned, in part, through the mapping of the Indian empire.

Establishing a preliminary definition of British national identity during the late- eighteenth and nineteenth century is a challenging proposition. The main questions are how to indicate that empire played a part in the making of British identity at home and how to account for the fervent expression of nationalist sentiment among many British who lived overseas, especially in the colonies. In other words, what role does the creation and governance of empire play in shaping British national identity?

Some of the principal political theorists of nationalism and national identity provide only partial answers. Their models tend to focus on populations who either live within territorial boundaries, within cultural zones, or are ruled by foreign powers. Of course, the British in India were themselves the rulers, living beyond the territory of Britain, and yet, for many, their attachment to Britain and to British identity was heightened by their experience as imperialists.

Ernest Gellner (1983), for instance, tends to focus his theory on how nationalism accompanies and springs from the transformation of an agricultural society into an industrial one.[6] For him this change from one stage to the next is associated with such developments as universal literacy, the loss of hereditary occupations, the dissemination of an increasingly pervasive high culture, political centralization, and state control over education. In fact, it is the linking (or its lack) of the state and culture that defines the industrial stage and lies at the core of nationalism. Although Gellner identifies key factors for the emergence of many nationalisms, especially in Europe, his emphasis on the need for the 'congruence' of political and cultural boundaries does little to further our investigation as to how empire helped to create nationalism at home and in British men and women living in the colonies. He does discuss diasporic nationalisms, such as Jewish nationalism, but his definition, focusing on minorities who have special occupations and who must either assimilate or discard their specialization in order to become a state, is not supple enough to explain how the empire seemed to make arch-nationalists.

An alternative theoretical perspective on the rise of nationalism and national identity is offered by Anthony Smith (1991). In outlining two models for the development of national identity (one being civic-territorial, bureaucratic, and associated with Western Europe; the other being ethnic-genealogical, rooted in vernacular mobilization, and associated with non-Western European lands) Smith recognizes that one model alone is insufficient. He also offers several requisites for national identity. These include a sense of a historic territory or homeland, the sharing of common myths and historical memories, and the expression of a common mass culture (ibid.: 19). Whereas Gellner sees the need for a state, Smith argues that none is required or even necessarily desired for the emergence of national identity.

Smith's focus on a homeland and common historical myths and culture, together with his suggestion that a national identity need not find final expression in the creation of a state, may help us to understand how the British, when overseas, developed strong attachments to their homeland and history. Nonetheless, these overarching models or theories, although identifying elements that are likely to be evident in many cases of nationalism and national identity around the world—and thus enabling comparative studies— are not quite adequate. For additional help we can turn to historians of eighteenth- and nineteenth-century Britain, especially those who have been influenced by Benedict Anderson's (1987) notion of a nation as an imagined community brought about as a result of such factors as the growth of printing. In recent years, historians have begun to examine anew the events and processes by which men and women living in Scotland, England, Wales, and, to a certain extent, Ireland, became Britons (see Murdoch 1998). A crucial glue in the process was empire.

The 1707 Act of Union has often been considered the instrument that created Britain, but it took at least a generation for many men and women to express a sentimental or political allegiance to Britain. According to Linda Colley (1992), the new British nation's sense of purpose and stature in the world was 'forged' as a result of seemingly interminable wars with France, the re-affirmation of Protestantism, and the creation of an empire. As she notes, British identity was derived from 'conflict with the Other', the Other being 'militant Catholicism, or a hostile continental European power, or an exotic

overseas empire' (ibid.: 6–7). Aided by factors such as rapid
urbanization, the extension of free trade throughout Britain, and a
flourishing and politically-attuned press, Britain's wars and its
extension of power overseas, especially as a result of the Seven Years'
War, affected the composition of the aristocracy and enabled those
who had previously been derided as infra dig, the Scots and the
Irish in particular, to vigorously participate in both the defence of
Britain and the extension of the empire (ibid.: 369). It has been
shown, for example, that between 1775 and 1785, 47 per cent of
the new writers sent to Bengal by the Company, 60 per cent of the
free merchants, and 52 per cent of the assistant surgeons were Scots
(Bowen 1996: 164). Despite resentment and opposition by some in
England, such as John Wilkes and Edmund Burke, who remained
suspicious of Scottish motives, political involvement, and character,
empire afforded an avenue of social and economic advancement
for Scots while helping to cement their ties as Britons.

Colley's analysis demonstrates the constructed and contingent
nature of British identity—that there was no primordial or long-
standing sense of Britishness or British culture before the eighteenth
century. Even 'Englishness' may be a relatively recent phenomenon,
dating back only to the sixteenth century (Helgerson 1992). But of
central concern to us is Colley's insistence that British national identity
emerged partially out of its eighteenth-century imperialist ventures.
There has been some debate as to how important Britain's so-called
first and second empires were to ordinary men and women in Britain,
and historians, in the past, have even been reluctant to incorporate
the empire into their studies of Britain or England. Indeed, in his
otherwise excellent study of English nationalism, Gerald Newman
admits to excluding any discussion of the empire as one of English
nationalism's defining features (1997: xxi). Such is the general lack
of interest in the role of empire in British national development that
David Armitage can conclude that there has been a 'general
indifference towards empire' among British historians. To explain
this indifference he cites P.J. Marshall who notes that historians have
generally regarded empire as performing a 'reflexive rather than a
transforming role' (Armitage 2000: 13).

Fortunately, this lacuna in British history is being addressed.
Armitage not only places Britain at the heart of empire, he fixes the

empire at the heart of Britain (ibid.: 15). Other historians have joined this recent and rising chorus expressing the close links between imperial and British history (see Burton 1998, MacKenzie, J. 1984).[7] H.V. Bowen, for instance, reveals the extent to which metropolitan elites, especially in the eighteenth century, participated in funding imperial expansion to such a degree that this overseas trade 'acted as a major agent of change within Britain itself' (1996: 13). Kathleen Wilson also provides good evidence to conclude that a surprisingly large number of Britons were involved and interested in the empire-building. Empire was, in her words, 'integral to shaping (English people's) own patriotic and nationalist identities' (Wilson 1998: 23). By the end of the nineteenth century, the connection between empire and nationalist and patriotic sentiment became even more evident. Jingoism trumpeted aggressive imperial intervention and, as Thomas Metcalf (1995: 64) indicates, the patriotism that fuelled the need to express and defend British character and interests also 'deepened the hold of empire over the British people'.

If the empire was so integral to British national identity, it remains for us to consider what it was about empire that helped to build that identity. Ideas and people did not just flow out into the empire. Cash, goods, plunder, ideas, and foreigners made their way to Britain (see Burton 1998, Mahomet 1997). Of course, not all that arrived was considered healthy. The return of improvident and politically-minded 'nabobs' threatened to disrupt political balances and introduce dangerous ways (see Lawson and Phillips 1984). 'It was thought that misrule,' Bowen writes, 'corruption, greed, vice, and arbitrary government would not remain confined to India but might serve as corrosive agents and weaken traditional liberties, values, and virtues within metropolitan society' (1996: 531). And, indeed, we find that in 1773 Horace Walpole asked: 'What is England now?' and answered: 'A sink of Indian wealth, filled with nabobs and emptied by Macaronies!' (quoted in Newman 1997: 59). Throughout the second half of the eighteenth century there were murmurs of disquiet and fears that Britain was being misshapen under the influence of its empire.

But there were also more constructive aspects of identity that the British received from imperialism. In building their empire the British generated and reinforced, in at least three ways, myths and seeming-certainties about their national identity. Empire allowed the British to assert a special character, past, and territory.

Conquest and imperial rule helped to establish among the British a sense of superiority.[8] The late eighteenth century saw the beginnings of a widespread expression of racial difference and of ideas of British character as being exceptional. These ideas only became more entrenched in the general British population during the nineteenth century. Many British interpreted the acquisition of their empire as proof of moral, physical, and political strength and advanced racial theories to buttress claims of innate superiority (see Trautmann 1997). British pluck and sangfroid, British rationality and foresight, were character traits that were often used to explain British pre-eminence in the world. From the late eighteenth century until well into the twentieth century, British identity was intimately bound with their status as imperialists. British character, then, grew up hand in hand with the British empire.

Despite its importance, the relationship between British national identity and the empire was more than the development of character. The empire also helped to create a national past and a national homeland and territory. Although Anthony Smith's analysis perhaps places too much emphasis on the need for a single historical culture for it to be wholly applicable to the British context, where a variety of cultures and peoples forged a nation that still retained distinct English and Scottish traits and loyalties (see Tidrick 1992, Wilson 1998), he nevertheless makes a valuable point when he suggests that nations derive much of their power and legitimacy from the sharing of common memories and the identification of a common homeland. I have already hinted that British historians believed that the nation's intrepid ways brought about an empire.

An early map that shows how national identity was beginning to be forged as a result of war in India is Thomas Jefferys' 'The Seat of War on the Coast of Choromandel'. The map faces the first page of Richard Owen Cambridge's *An Account of the War in India between the English and the French* (1761). It shows the south-east coast of India, also known as the Coromandel Coast, and identifies the roads, rivers, and places that feature in the book's account of the history of English campaigns. The map also notes which towns were Danish, English, French, Dutch, and Portuguese.

As books such as Cambridge's encouraged the British to pay greater attention to their growing eastern empire, the past was increasingly invoked as a way of reinforcing national identity. At first that identity was English, but it rapidly became British after the 1750s. The narratives of Robert Clive, tales of Tipu Sultan's defeat, and, much later, reminiscences of the Mutiny of 1857–58, all served to bond the British together. These and other well-known examples of British military success heightened pride in Britain and contributed to a common belief that as a nation the British had proved themselves both capable and superior. British imperial history offered the promise (or illusion) that the British were destined for greatness.

The memory of a British homeland was often expressed by those living and travelling overseas. The nostalgia for 'home' remained a constant topic of conversation for the British in India, prompting them to build such communities and structures as cantonments, hill stations, and churches in the style of home. By transforming their club or graveyard, and by strictly maintaining British codes of conduct and etiquette, especially in the nineteenth and the early twentieth century, the British were doing more than placing social and physical barriers between themselves and Indians. They were also actively creating an 'imagined' Britain. Even if the Britain that the colonialists imagined was more religious, more patriotic, more devoted to its monarch than might have been the case within Britain itself, and even if the imperialists' Britain was not remembered as a nation preoccupied with issues of class or economic relations, that imagined Britain was as tangible and apparent as those conceived by aristocrats and labourers living in London. The nostalgic conception of a homeland that was protective, motherly, mighty, and forever welcoming of her tired sons and daughters returning from their duty serving in the Empire was a powerful phenomenon of empire.

The final way that the empire shaped national identity is that it gave meaning to British territory. What was Britain without its colonies? Colonies lent Britain international stature and wealth. As Gottmann notes, 'territory became the physical and legal embodiment of national identity' (1973: 49). India, as a colony and as part of an economic, military, and administrative empire, was 'possessed' by Britain, and yet India was not in Britain. India was, therefore, in a curious relationship with Britain—being of Britain but not *part* of

Britain. Colonial maps of India had to suggest India's possession and incorporation within an empire, but not its subsumption within Britain. This cartographic sleight of hand helped to establish a British national identity by helping to build a sense of who the British were (martial, rational, intrepid, loyal subjects) and contributing to the idea of Britain as both a locationally fixed but imaginatively moveable homeland that was the opposite of its Indian possessions.

The love of Britain, which was evinced by most nineteenth-century British writers was, thus, as much a result of colonial experiences as it was a product of internal European events. A sense of Britishness was closely linked to the eighteenth-century appropriation of conquered land and its transformation into owned territory. So important was the belief that Britain was Britain because of its colonial empire, that any study of Britishness has to have as a focus the manner in which non-British lands were incorporated into an expanding British imperium. In mapping Indian territory, East India Company surveyors were contributing to a sense that newly conquered Indian lands belonged to, and were indeed integral to, a British nation.

An Overview of the Chapters

Beginning soon after their military conquests in Bengal and extending well into the twentieth century, the British sought to legitimate their rule in a variety of ways. From the Governor Generalship of Hastings to that of Cornwallis, physiocratic and Whig principles of a 'rule of property' and law, agricultural improvement, and balanced government were enacted in Bengal (see Guha 1981). The assumption was that Indians would reconcile themselves to and even support a foreign power that was proving itself to be the very antithesis of an Oriental despotism. Later in the nineteenth century, British ideologies of difference, such as those based on racial typologies or civilizational hierarchies, would predominate and serve to reinforce the arguments justifying their rule (see Metcalf 1995). As racial superiors, as technological instructors, and as religious mentors, it was thought that only the British could marry paternalistic and straightforward government with material improvement and progress.

Colonial cartography was another means by which the British continually buttressed their claims to legitimacy. The manner in which British map makers tied a particular understanding of the past with a perspective of land allowed them to graphically demonstrate Britain's supposed right and need to hold an empire. Each of the subsequent chapters illustrates a phase and a historical aspect of colonial cartography. Chapter One focuses on associative history and argues that the initial mapping of Bengal was conducted less for utilitarian purposes and more for reasons of propaganda. Throughout the late eighteenth century, the East India Company came under severe criticism by both ex-Company servants and malcontented politicians and it felt that it had to win the sympathy of the British public and parliament. The maps published by the Company were designed to evoke the sentiment that Bengal was administered by the Company as if it were a landlord's domain. The fact, however, that Bengal was not Company property—the Company had only won the right from the Mughal emperor to collect the revenue and administer justice—did not hinder the Company from projecting itself as a responsible and enlightened landlord. Moreover, the manner of depicting the land, although conditioned by traditional cartographic techniques, was novel in the Indian context: in trying to make foreign land seem familiar and owned, a new perspective or 'language' of territory was articulated. By focusing on James Rennell's 1781 *Bengal Atlas*, with its twenty-one beautiful, beguiling plates, I argue that it helped to launch a second and sentimental conquest of Bengal and articulated a notion of territory that became the language of colonial history. Surveyors noticed that Indian land was important, neither for its product nor for its traditional association with the Mughal emperor, but for its possession by the Company. The importance of this cartographic associative history is that it enabled the Company to encompass Bengal, now regarded as legitimately possessed territory, within an emerging British Empire.

Chapter Two examines the gradual emergence of a progressive history of surveying. Most Company surveyors of the eighteenth century, such as James Rennell, used descriptive narrative and the conventions of the picturesque to transform what might otherwise have been threatening and unknown lands into a settled and inviting picture. Their maps had a meandering quality which reflected their perspective of the land. Using trees, mountains, temples, or cities as signs, these early colonial surveyors constructed maps which described safe journeys. This manner of viewing and representing the land may be called a 'hydrographical perspective' because it relied upon the techniques of observation often used by marine surveyors. By contrast, nineteenth-century trigonometrical maps were considered by surveyors to be the pure expression of an idea and the summation of an empirical methodology—they were based upon efforts in what C.A. Bayly aptly calls 'Newtonian triumphalism' (1999: 307). The switch to trigonometrical mapping as the pre-eminent form of surveying may be characterized as a progressive history in that the surveyors believed that the introduction of new and more precise scientific instruments and techniques would improve the Company's knowledge of India, contribute to more esoteric goals such as the exact shape and size of the earth, demonstrate the superiority of British science, and thus strengthen the Company's claims to colonial legitimacy.

Although the desire to capture a true and correct perspective remained important throughout the nineteenth century, cartography also incorporated a reverential aspect. By revering the name of a former surveyor, the Survey Department hoped to strengthen its reputation and indicate that British scientific approaches were beneficial to India. Chapter Three, then, focuses on the controversies over the naming of Mount Everest. In the mid-nineteenth century, the Surveyor General of India decided that a certain peak in the Himalayas, known to the Trigonometrical Survey as Peak XV, had in fact no 'native' name. Without instituting an inquiry into the matter, and contravening his own stated policy of not importing foreign names, Andrew Waugh decided that he would honour his predecessor, George Everest, and thus ensure that the mountain, which had just been calculated to be the highest in the world, would become familiar and pronounceable to Europeans. The choice of name ignited a controversy over cartographic truth which lasted well into the twentieth century. Waugh's choice of the name Mount Everest, despite much evidence of the existence of up to half a dozen Nepali and Tibetan names for the peak, was considered appropriate by the Survey and the Government of India because the mountain's discovery and identification conformed to a method which, if properly followed, could lead nowhere but to the truth.

Chapter Four examines why, during the second half of the nineteenth century, the Survey of India and the Royal Geographical Society injected romance into Indian cartography. They were convinced that by employing Indians to map Tibet and Central Asia in an antiquated and semi-secret fashion, the profile and value of the department among British elites would be enhanced. Moreover, the use of Indians who were trained in rudimentary surveying techniques and willing to risk their lives for 'science' and the defence of British India suggested loyalty and implied the continued need for British expertise and control.

Chapter Five argues that by the end of the nineteenth century a mawkish and nostalgic approach to the past was evident in maps of India. Maps were increasingly deployed as tools for recovering original moments, moments which came to define the course of all subsequent history. My primary example is the late-Victorian nostalgia for the Black Hole of Calcutta, which occurred in the summer of 1756. It was alleged that 123 Company soldiers and civilians were suffocated in a prison in the Company fort known as the Black Hole. Together with the Mutiny of 1857–58, the Black Hole was an original moment, universally known and believed to contain within its story the rationale for British conquest and the legitimacy for continued British rule. The historical treatment of the Black Hole in the late nineteenth century exemplifies late-Victorian historiography regarding India. Attempts to 'map' the Black Hole, both on paper and on the pavement of Calcutta (delineating the old prison with brass lines, for example), were cartography's attempt to derive its own legitimacy by buttressing a historical preoccupation. More generally, maps were drawn to supplement a historical didacticism aimed at recovering those original moments which were of particular nostalgic significance.

Notes

1. For a fuller discussion of the maps of the SDUK see my forthcoming essay 'India for the Working Classes: The Maps of the Society for the Diffusion of Useful Knowledge' in *Modern Asian Studies*.
2. Compare with Frank Popper's (1993: 175) remark, in a different context: 'What is simulated is no longer the territory, an original substance or

being, but a model of the real. ... From now on it is the map that precedes, and thus generates the territory.'

3. For regional studies, see Barbara E. Mundy 1996 and J.K. Noyes 1992.

4. Shankar Raman is one scholar who pushes the colonial back long before the British conquests of India. He argues that changes in medieval cartographic perspectives as a result of the rediscovery of Ptolemaic geography, the impact of Copernicus' astronomy, and European travels to the East all helped to produce a 'colonialist space' by the beginning of the seventeenth century (2001: 17–18, 89–152).

5. The argument in this section has greatly benefited by my conversations with Douglas Haynes.

6. Gellner provides his own historical geography when explaining the differences in these stages. He contrasts a 'map' of an Oskar Kokoschka painting with one by Modigliani.

7. For an excellent account of how the study of geography in English universities during the sixteenth and seventeenth centuries helped to make an early English imperial ideology, see Lesley B. Cormack 1997.

8. See Kathryn Tidrick 1992 for a study of how empire shaped English character.

ONE

Sentimental Conquests and Evocative Histories in an Atlas of Bengal

In a presidential address before the Royal Society in 1791, Sir Joseph Banks referred to *A Bengal Atlas*, which had been published a decade earlier by his friend James Rennell, a surveyor and geographer for the East India Company. 'I should rejoice,' Banks noted, 'could I say that Britons, fond as they are of being considered by surrounding nations as taking the lead in scientific improvements, could boast a general map of their island as well executed as Major Rennell's delineation of Bengal and Bahar' (Markham 1895: 96). Thus, according to the leading scientific authority of the late eighteenth century, Bengal was better mapped than Britain.[1] Perhaps even more astonishingly, most of that mapping occurred in less than thirty years. From the time it appointed its first Surveyor General in 1767, the East India Company spent increasing amounts of time and money in mapping its new territories. Indeed, such was the need for good maps that many of the most famous names in colonial history were surveyors—James Rennell, of course, but also James Tod, Colin Mackenzie, and George Everest, for whom the Himalayan mountain was named. An important question arises when considering the Company's early surveying activities: Why did the British map Bengal so vigorously in the second half of the eighteenth century?

This chapter argues that although there was a pressing need for accurate geographical information to help the movement of goods and troops and the collection of revenue, another compelling reason for the mapping was that the East India Company wished to project a positive image of itself to the British political and financial worlds. The Company at that time was rocked by a series of scandals and parliamentary inquiries and needed to re-establish its good name, so as to ensure confidence in its monopoly privileges, fiscal acumen, and administrative capabilities. The chapter will focus on James Rennell's *A Bengal Atlas* (1780 and 1781) and will examine how the inscriptions or dedications on the plates were designed to make the province unthreatening and familiar. By making Bengal seem familiar Rennell was inviting his readers to indulge in a second and, this time, safe sentimental conquest. He was also evoking histories of possession that helped to render British rule over a foreign land legitimate.

Rennell's Atlas

A Bengal Atlas is one of Rennell's most important publications. As Andrew Cook has noted, the significance of the atlas 'lay in the large scale of its maps and the unprecedented accuracy of its details' (1978: 5–42). Rennell is well known for his 1782 map of Hindoostan and the accompanying memoir, which appeared in several editions. The map and memoir reinforced and enhanced his reputation as a cartographer of international calibre and opened professional-cum-social doors for him within the scientific community in London.[2] Such was his reputation at the time of his death in 1830 that he was buried at Westminster Abbey, with a bust in his honour by Hagbolt placed in the chapel under the north-west tower (see Phillimore 1945: 377). Although the significance of his map of Hindoostan and the accompanying memoir are undeniable, much of his reputation as the foremost geographer of India in the second half of the eighteenth century must be attributed to his atlas of Bengal. The atlas was the direct result of over a decade of surveying and was published soon after his retirement from Company service in India and his return to London in 1778.

Rennell began his career in India when he arrived in Calcutta in 1764, having spent some time in the navy. Three years after his arrival he was appointed Surveyor General of Bengal, a position that seems to have been created for him. During the previous twenty years the East India Company had sponsored coastal surveys by marine surveyors such as Bartholomew Plaisted and John Ritchie.[3] However, it was only after assuming the right to collect the vast land revenues of Bengal that the Company turned its attention to mapping the interior of the province. Rennell chose Dhaka as his headquarters and at first was instructed to survey only major river systems. He was aided by small teams of British, Bengali, and Armenian surveyors, and their surveys were rapidly expanded beyond river sketches to include road surveys and topographical plans.

The surveying of Bengal occupied much of Rennell's time. Some indication of how he worked is provided by journals that he wrote between 1764 and 1767, while surveying the Ganges and Brahmaputra rivers (Rennell 1910). For his first survey in May 1764, for instance, he set off by boat from the new fort at Calcutta with one assistant surveyor, three other Europeans, eleven lascars, eleven *motias* (or porters), eleven sepoys, and one interpreter—thirty nine people in all, including himself (ibid.: 10). His object, as explained by a letter written by Henry Vansittart, the Governor, was to discover 'the shortest & safest Channel leading from the great River to Channel Creek or Rangafulla' which would enable year-round river traffic between Calcutta and Eastern Bengal (ibid.: 9). The Governor also instructed Rennell to note 'the Appearance and Produce of the Countries thro' which you pass; the name of every Village, & whatever else may seem remarkable.' The resulting journal is often a day-by-day account of the journey, including information on the weather, the accuracy of a map of the inland navigation by Captain Polier, and such incidental information as when their boat sprung a leak. The journal also contains notes on the breadth and direction of rivers and whether they were navigable throughout the year. At this stage, Rennell's object was clearly to gather as much practical information as possible to assist travel.

In these early surveys, then, Rennell is not yet thinking of representing the land as familiar and pacified. In fact, he includes in his journal for February 1766 an incident that nearly cost him his life. While he was surveying the northern boundaries of Bengal, he participated in a battle with armed ascetics, whom he calls 'Sanashys' (ibid.: 73–74). In the skirmish that resulted, Rennell states that he 'had the misfortune to be surrounded by the Enemy, & received several Cuts from their broad Swords, one of which threatned [sic] my Death' (ibid.: 74). In another account of the fight, Rennell described his injuries in more detail, writing that a sabre had cut through his right shoulder bone and had laid him 'open for nearly a Foot down the Back, cutting thro' and wounding some of my Ribs. I had besides a Cut on the left Elbow wh^{ch} took off the Muscular part of the breadth of a Hand ...' (Yule and Burnell 1984: 872).[4] Rennell supposed that the long-term effects of his injuries were that the forefinger on his left hand would be almost disabled and that he would never recover the full use of his right arm.

In another incident involving armed local opposition, this time in December 1770, Rennell came up against 'Caddar Beg, a Mogul & Zemindar' of a district north of Murshidabad (Rennell 1910: 137). Rennell had been surveying roads when the zamindar (landowner) appeared with 'a very great Rabble, some of them armed with Matchlocks, and the rest with Pykes and Swords, etc.' Rennell shot at the zamindar, missing him but killing one of his supporters. Eventually the zamindar retreated, but not before sending messages to Rennell containing 'hints of his Independence, together with Orders for me to depart.' It appears that as a surveyor Rennell was less than welcome, a fact that he himself acknowledged in a letter to his guardian, saying that 'the Inhabitants ... are very jealous of me, so that I am forced to have a pretty large Escort to protect me.'[5] Elsewhere, Rennell observes that 'the Country People in general desert the Villages on our approach, so that 'tis with difficulty we can find an old man or woman to tell us the name of the Villages'.[6] Local mistrust of British surveyors, from a fear of either higher taxes or the loss of land, would become a recurring motif in colonial surveying literature.

Violent incidences, such as the ones described by Rennell, were to find their way into his *Bengal Atlas* in the symbol of crossed swords, for example, although the immediacy of the danger he and other Company servants faced was transformed into a depiction of victories or a testament to their gallantry. There is little indication in the atlas of the precariousness of British rule within Bengal. Instead, as we shall see, Bengal was shown to be pacified, and only threatened by external, Maratha forces.

Yet, even as Rennell was battling sannyasis (ascetics) and zamin-
dars, he was constructing his maps of Bengal. As early as September
1764 he mentions that he is 'correcting the Geography of the
Kingdom of Bengal, a work never attempted before the present
Governor (Mr. Vansittart) came here'.[7] In January 1767 his surveying
and mapping efforts were boosted when he was appointed Surveyor
General of Bengal and was given four assistant surveyors (Rennell
1910: 86). In March 1772 he writes that he has made 'considerable
Progress in this Work, and shall completely finish it in a twelvemonth
now. ... Besides the Maps there are compleat tables of Roads, and
Directions for navigating the Rivers'.[8] However, it was not until he
returned to England that he was able to persuade the Company to
underwrite the publication of his manuscript maps as an atlas.[9]

The atlas was published in 1780 and again, in an expanded form,
in 1781. Andrew Cook (1978: 5–42) has carefully documented the
publication record of the atlas and has shown that, contrary to
previous opinion, the atlas was not first published in 1779. He also
notes that the Company's Court of Directors had hoped to recoup
its advances towards the cost of publication by selling to servants in
Bengal the atlases in folio and quarto, for 16 and 14 rupees. However,
the atlases were lost when the ship carrying them was captured by
the Spanish (ibid.: 22–23).

Though Rennell's surveys were initially intended to aid the
Company's consolidation of its power in Bengal by facilitating troop
movement, the collection of revenue, and the transportation of
merchandise, the atlas was constructed and embellished in such a
way that it would appear that Rennell had more than just utilitarian
purposes in mind when he prepared the maps for publication.
Besides, despite their importance as the first detailed maps of Bengal,
they were sufficiently imprecise for a later Surveyor General to
determine that the maps 'can be of little or no use, to the Magistrates,
and Collectors, or for Military Purposes'.[10] It would appear that the
atlas was an attempt to ensure legitimacy for Company rule in Bengal
by inviting armchair bibliophiles to conquer the province in a
sentimental fashion and by evoking histories of rightful possession.
Rennell's maps were influential, perhaps even instrumental, in
fashioning opinion, policy, and perspective. And as such, they were
not simply mirrors of but tools for change.

The Significance of the Atlas

A *Bengal Atlas* was more than a simple map of the land. It contributed to the debates in England concerning the rights, privileges, and power of the East India Company in its affairs with India. In seeking to justify Company rule Rennell introduced three important perspectives—he made Bengal a territory that was possessed by the British; he asserted that it was the British people, and not just the Company, who were the real beneficiaries of Company rule; and he gave Company rule a colonial character, suggesting that the Company was interested in governance and improvement and not just in conquest. These perspectives were made possible by Rennell's decision to dedicate all the major plates of his atlas to individuals associated with the recent history of Bengal.

As noted, the atlas appeared at a time when the Company was facing political and financial difficulties and it was crucial for the Company to secure favourable attention in Britain so as to ensure continued Crown patronage, buoyant stock prices, and healthy recruitment. A series of scandals had severely tarnished the Company's reputation in Europe, including the yearly return of extravagantly wealthy nabobs, the 1772 parliamentary enquiry into Robert Clive's alleged avaricious activities, the Rohilla War of 1774 that many found distasteful because of the use of British soldiers to protect Awadh, the extraordinary circumstances surrounding the 1776 imprisonment and death of the Governor of Madras, George Pigot, and the factional disputes (and duels) between the Warren Hastings and Philip Francis camps on the Calcutta Council. Moreover, a number of pamphlets and books published by returned and disaffected Company servants added evidence to accusations of gross mismanagement and corruption.[11] The publication in 1772 of the scurrilous *Considerations on Indian Affairs* by William Bolts (1772) contained such inflammatory charges against the Clive and Verelst administrations in Bengal that the Company backed Verelst's vigorous response entitled *A View of the Rise, Progress, and Present state of the English Government in Bengal: including a reply to the misrepresentations of Mr. Bolts, and other Writers* (1772).[12] Verelst himself died in Boulogne, impoverished by litigation challenging his actions in Bengal, while Bolts, unable to withdraw his large fortune from Bengal, was forced to fight numerous lawsuits brought against him by the Company. Alexander Dow was also emboldened by Bolts' publication to bring out a third edition of his *History of Hindustan* which was more critical than the previous two editions had been (see Sutherland 1962: 221). Horace Walpole summed up the mood of the country when he wrote that

> The oppressions of India and even of the English settled there under the rapine and cruelties of the servants of the Company had now reached England and created general clamour here. Some books had been published, particularly one by Bolts and Mr. Dow, the first a man of bad character, the latter of a very fair one, which carried the accusations home to Lord Clive; and the former represented him as a monster in assassination, usurpation, and extortion, with heavy accusations of his monopolizing in open defiance of the orders of the Company. ... To such monopolies were imputed the late famine in Bengal and the loss of three millions of the inhabitants. A tithe of these crimes was sufficient to inspire horror (ibid.).

The political public was not the only section of British society that was becoming alarmed by the Company's affairs. Parliament, itself, was taking more of an interest in the financial health of the Company. The debt crisis of 1772 prompted the government to pass the Regulating Act the following year, which granted a loan to the Company but restricted the dividend it paid its stockholders and placed limits of tenure on the Court of Directors. Among other terms placed upon the Company, the government also appointed additional members to the Bengal Council, among them Philip Francis, who acted as a voting bloc against Hastings and Richard Barwell. Throughout the rest of the decade directors and servants were wary of further government encroachment on the administrative and mercantile business of the Company.

The Company itself was not quiet in the pamphlet war. Many of its servants, such as Alexander Dalrymple, the Company's hydrographer, published tracts which reminded readers that the Company's trade to India had resulted in great financial benefit to Britain. For instance, Dalrymple noted in one work that his readers must be alarmed to see the Company on the verge of ruin 'from the narrow views of skin-deep Politicians who have dreamt that they are Statesmen ... and of Men who having acquired much in the Service of the Company apply their accumulated wealth in endeavours to make a property of their parent' (1777: 1–2).' Nevertheless, despite such attempts to assert the Company's legitimacy and continued independence from parliamentary interference, constant disputes and scandals eroded the public's goodwill, spurring parliamentary censure and debate, and encouraging attacks on the Company's monopoly status. Adam Smith's *The Wealth of Nations*, for example, first published in 1776, vigorously criticized the Company's monopoly rights, arguing that such privileges permitted high prices, inordinate private gain, and administrative corruption. Smith argued that the monopoly and mercantile character of the Company prohibited it from acting in its new self-proclaimed role as a disinterested Indian government. 'Such exclusive companies,' he noted, 'are nuisances in every respect; always more or less inconvenient to the countries in which they are established, and destructive to those which have the misfortune to fall under their government' (Smith 1976, Book IV: 158).

It was in this poisonous political atmosphere that *A Bengal Atlas* was published in 1780 and 1781. The contemporary reception given to the atlas, however, is difficult to gauge. Certainly, the Company was willing to underwrite its publication, give Rennell a pension, and, based upon his reputation, call upon him periodically to state his opinion on important surveying matters. Prominent men such as Joseph Banks praised his work but there appears to have been few reviews of the atlas itself.[13] Nevertheless, he was one of very few Company surveyors who superintended the publication of his own survey maps, which, together with the comprehensive nature of the atlas, would have added authority to his work. Contemporary writers, particularly historians, did refer to or use his other maps. Edward Moor, for instance, in *A Narrative of the Operations of Captain Little's Detachment* (1794) and William Robertson in *An Historical Disquisition* (1809) were effusive in their praise for and reliance on Rennell's maps and writings. Robert Orme accompanied his second volume of *A History of the Military Transactions of the British Nation in Indostan* (1778) with a map by Rennell. Orme, who had written his own 'Geography of Indostan',[14] was, according to Rennell, hoarding 'all the geographical materials in order to extract such particulars only, as to serve the purpose of illustrating his History. I probably may either lose my eyesight, or drop into the Grave, before he has done with them'.[15] Clearly then, Rennell's maps were valuable sources, no doubt because of his use of appealing calligraphy, his ability to lend his maps an ambling quality, and the novelty and seeming reliability of the information presented. For all our uncertainty as to how the atlas was received, its manner of construction, the wording of the dedications, and the heated environment in which it appeared all indicate that Rennell's atlas was a timely political statement. Thus, following the work of Brian Harley (2001) and W.J.T. Mitchell's arguments regarding landscape (1994: 5–34), the atlas should not only be seen as a 'genre' but also a 'medium' of representation. In other words, the apposite question is not what is the atlas, but what does the atlas do? The significance of the atlas is, therefore, not limited to its illumination of the geography of Bengal. It should also be read as an intervention in a vigorous debate on the financial acumen of the Company, the appropriateness of its monopoly privileges, and the effectiveness of its rule in parts of India.

Sentimental Conquests

Both the 1780 and 1781 editions of the atlas contain twelve plates with dedications.[16] The dedications in the atlas appear as part of the titles of the maps which together form what may be called a cartouche, although a cartouche often comprises a pictorial embellishment as well. The twelve maps with dedications represent all of Bengal and Bihar, and even territories extending up to Delhi, divided along both geographical and political boundaries. The dedications form a prominent component of the maps, and their examination has been overlooked in previous treatments of the atlas. The dedications serve to explain the meaning, context, and importance of each map. As G.N.G. Clarke (1988) has reminded us, a map's 'cultural meaning' may be apparent in its 'visual calligraphy'—in its lettering and symbols and cartouche. Rennell's dedications helped to give a semblance of legitimacy to Company territorial rule.

How were these dedications to be read? How did they legitimize Company rule? By associating a person with the land depicted they suggested that Bengal was possessed and governed appropriately. Yet, the Company did not own Bengal; it only had legal rights to the collection of revenue and the dispensation of justice. The dedications created the semblance though of the Company as indeed the possessor, the rightful owner, of the territory of Bengal. And, in suggesting parallels with British landlords, they confirmed the legitimacy of Company territorial rule. Semblance was therefore a crucial aspect of any sentiment conjured up by the beguiling atlas.

Furthermore, the dedications may have lulled a potentially hostile reading public into believing that it had a 'sentimental' involvement in the recent conquest and ongoing pacification of Bengal. The sentiment was the appreciation, after viewing the atlas, that the Company embodied and exhibited the administrative and proprietorial functions of a landlord, when, in fact, the evidence coming to England suggested to many that the Company was ruthlessly extractive and financially irresponsible.

A potential difficulty Rennell may have faced was that Bengal was too remote and unknown for many in Britain to develop the sentimental attachments and historical identifications that were suggested in his dedications. After all, years before, when referring to Bengal, even Rennell had said that 'I have long since forgot myself so far as to imagine that this is no part of it (the world), but only a separate part of the universe'.[17] The challenge, therefore, was to make Bengal seem relevant to British interests. Part of the solution was to dedicate each plate to a well-known Company servant.

All the dedications are to individuals who had an association with the land depicted. The men who are honoured include administrators and soldiers as well as Rennell's friends. The following is a list of the twelve men to whom the maps are dedicated, in order of appearance, together with a partial listing of the territory represented, written according to Rennell's spelling: Francis Russell (the Delta of the Ganges); Brigadier General Richard Smith (the Jungleterry District); Sir Hector Munro (South Bahar); Brigadier General John Caillaud (North Bahar); Hugh Inglis (the Northern Provinces of Bengal); Thomas Kelsall (the Low Countries Beyond the Ganges); Harry Verelst (the Provinces of Bengal ... on the west of the Hoogly River); Jacob Camac (The Conquered Provinces on the south of Bahar); Warren Hastings (Bengal and Bahar); John Cartier (Oudh and Allahabad); Edward Lord Clive (Cossimbuzar Island); Brigadier General Sir Robert Barker (the Doo-ab).

Plates III and IV provide two examples of the association between men and territory. Plate III, 'A MAP of SOUTH BAHAR', is dedicated to Sir Hector Munro (1726–1805). In October 1764, Hector Munro defeated the Nawab Wazir of Awadh, Shuja-ud-daula, and Mir Kasim (Qasim) at Baxar (Buxar), while earlier in the year he had suppressed a sepoy mutiny at Patna.[18] Rennell drew a sword each at Baxar and Patna and included the relevant dates, which, in conjunction with the dedication, clearly established the connection between Munro and the map. Similarly, Plate IV, showing 'A MAP of NORTH BAHAR', is dedicated to Brigadier General John Caillaud (1724–1812) and includes the scenes of his victories over the Mughal emperor's son in 1760. Caillaud is also of interest for his involvement in deposing Mir Jafar and replacing him with the seemingly more pliable Mir Kasim, but since that 'revolution' in government only resulted in further struggles—see Plate III for Munro's victory over Mir Kasim— it is no wonder that Rennell should pay tribute to the victorious, and not the scheming, Caillaud. It should be noted, therefore, that through a process of deliberate inclusion, association, and exclusion, a history of Company success is presented to the reader.

The organization of the maps, while systematic, is perhaps not immediately evident—the maps' sequence is not from east to west, north to south. Instead, the first three maps follow the Ganges from its mouth (and including Calcutta), up past Murshidabad, to the area surrounding Patna. Then, the next three maps reverse direction and depict northern Bihar and Bengal, progressing from west to east. The seventh and eighth maps show south-western Bengal and the areas surrounding Chota Nagpur. The ninth map depicts all of Bengal and Bihar, the tenth focuses on the area between Plassey and Murshidabad, and the final map with a dedication represents the lands lying between Bihar and Delhi.

Of all the map plates in the atlas, Plate IX is the most impressive. Its dedication is one of the longest and most informative, and its subject is a comprehensive view of Bengal and Bihar. It is dedicated to Warren Hastings, one of Rennell's patrons and a powerful, controversial man, as much maligned as he was adored. Rennell's decision to dedicate this most important map to Hastings may indicate a desire to enter the debates over the character of Company rule by demonstrating that these vast territories were governed legitimately and competently.

The full inscription for Plate IX is as follows: 'To the HONORABLE
WARREN HASTINGS ESQR. GOVERNOR GENERAL of the
BRITISH POSSESSIONS in ASIA: This MAP of BENGAL & BAHAR
(Comprehending a Tract more extensive and populous that the
BRITISH ISLANDS) Is respectfully Inscribed: In testimony of his
DISTINGUISHED ABILITIES; And in Gratitude for Favours
Received; By his obliged h[umbl]e Servant J Rennell.' The dedication
contains several key phrases that occur in other maps. The term

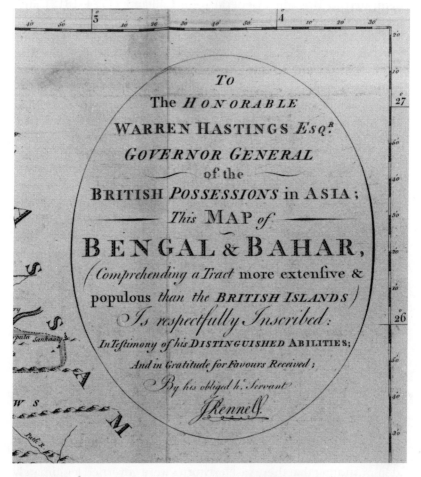

Fig. 5. *Title of Plate IX of* A Bengal Atlas, *by James Rennell, 1780.*

'British possessions' also appears in Plate X, dedicated to John Cartier, while 'abilities' may be seen in Plate XI, dedicated to Edward Lord Clive. In addition to these phrases, the Hastings dedication has an intriguing conclusion—'in Gratitude for Favours Received'. These three phrases—British possessions, abilities, and favours received—together are an indication that Rennell worded his dedications in such a way that they presented as positive an image of the Company as possible while suggesting that Bengal was ripe for a second, sentimental conquest.

In November 1778, Rennell told Hastings that he would 'take the liberty to inscribe one of the general maps' to him.[19] Hastings was an obvious choice. As the most powerful Company figure in India he was particularly well known, while the reference to his position added a cachet to the map. Despite his controversial nature, appending his name was a way of signalling that Rennell believed his practices conformed to accepted norms of governance. Moreover, apart from being a form of judicious flattery—in a deferential world Rennell would have been keen to be appropriately obsequious and ingratiating—his dedications were among the most evident techniques Rennell used to make the land familiar and give his maps additional authority. Indeed, one of the advantages of including the name of Hastings was that, when coupled with the phrase British possessions, it may have reinforced a reader's impression that all of Bengal and Bihar was now British territory.

Dedications were part of an established cartographic tradition acknowledging proprietorship. At least since the sixteenth century, land surveys were associated with establishing or reinforcing ownership over domains. Landlords in Britain would traditionally employ a surveyor to construct a map of their estates, in order to indicate the extent of their ownership and to locate villages or fields (see Buisseret 1996: 2). P.D.A. Harvey (1996: 57) notes that estate maps often presented the best aspects of the property; what cannot be found on the maps 'are the ruts and boggy patches in the roads, the sorry disrepair of the bridges and gates, the derelict outbuildings, the dung heaps'. Moreover, only the property of the landlord was surveyed and presented; other estates, even if they were adjacent to, or even within, the property, were often extruded from the representation. These estate maps would invariably contain a cartouche of the sponsor's name and, perhaps, the coat of arms. Rennell's maps were also part of the convention which emphasized, by means of dedications, the connections between the land and its proprietor. It is true that Warren Hastings, for example, did not legally 'own' Bengal, yet the appearance of his name on the Bengal and Bihar plate indicated that if he, himself, did not exercise proprietary control, he represented others, including stock-holding viewers of the map, who were beginning to regard this productive and vast land—'more extensive and populous than the BRITISH ISLANDS'—as somehow belonging to them. There are no 'boggy patches' in the map, no indication that Bengal had recently suffered a catastrophic famine, nor is there any sign at all that the Company had a tenuous hold over Bengal and that even surveying was a contentious and dangerous occupation. In fact, the use of the word 'possessions' suggests quite the contrary—that Hastings and, by implication, the Company, were the uncontested and supreme power. Moreover, this sense of domination and ownership is buttressed by key symbols in the map, representing fortresses, roads, and fields of battle.

But the map presented more than a conquered and pacified land. In transforming undifferentiated land into a 'territory', or in making owned land discrete and recognizable, it may have permitted the British viewer to share, perhaps at first only vicariously or imaginatively, in the land's ownership and appropriation for personal pleasure and exploitation. This is not to suggest that viewers would necessarily actively participate in the control of Bengal, but that, in recognizing the name in the dedication, and believing that Bengal was owned in the manner of a British country estate, they might well identify with those who were administering the province. Furthermore, by virtue of being British, or because they had sent a son to serve the Company, readers might imagine that they were passive participants in the acquisition and governance of Bengal. Theirs was a mental feeling, or sentiment; whether they felt jealous of those who returned from Bengal, unimaginably wealthy, or whether they felt pride in the establishment of British rule, viewers could well indulge in a sentimental conquest of Bengal. Rennell's maps were an invitation to participate in the enjoyment of a possession.[20]

The inclusion of the words 'Distinguished Abilities' in the map dedicated to Hastings may have signalled that Rennell envisaged the atlas as providing an opportunity to redress negative opinions regarding the Company's activities in India. By projecting the Company's highest representative in India as enacting the principles of an improving government the implication might have been that the Company was not abusing its proprietorial responsibilities at the nation's expense. Indeed, there was a tradition of thought in the late seventeenth century and throughout the eighteenth century that not only was property made legitimate when labour was expended upon it, but also that sovereignty was best established through the extension of cultivation (see Locke 1955). That Bengal was depicted as being in a flourishing state might have conveyed an impression that the territory was the Company's legitimate property because the Company's servants, such as the able Hastings, were labouring as a landlord would labour over his estate. Moreover, with physiocratic notions of wealth beginning to take root in both Europe and Bengal, it may have been Rennell's intention to suggest that the prosperity of Bengal was conditioned and maintained by the improvement of its agriculture, and that the Company was, through its industry as a landlord, its legitimate possessor.

The term distinguished abilities might also be read as an effort to portray the Company and its servants as recognizably competent, both politically and financially. The great disquiet in England about the evident malfeasance of Company servants was, in part because it was disrupting traditional political balances in Parliament, but also because it raised questions about the role and nature of government both in Britain and in India. Samuel Johnson, for instance, when discussing with James Boswell an accusation against a man for 'supposed delinquencies in India' remarked that he did not know what foundation there might be for such an accusation, but was sure that the man would not be caught. 'Where bad actions are committed,' he said

at so great a distance, a delinquent can obscure the evidence till the scent becomes cold; there is a cloud between, which cannot be penetrated: therefore all distant power is bad. I am clear that the best plan for the government of India is a despotick governour; for if he be a good man, it is evidently the best government; and supposing him to be a bad man, it is better to have one plunderer than many. A governour, whose power is checked, lets others plunder, that he himself may be allowed to plunder; but if despotick, he sees that the more he lets others plunder, the less there will be for himself, so he restrains them; and though he himself plunders, the country is a gainer, compared with being plundered by numbers (Boswell 1978: 464–65).

Whether or not Johnson was being facetious, the passage indicates that at the time the atlas was published (Johnson's remarks were made in 1783), there was some debate as to how best to rule India. Rennell may have wished to portray India's new rulers as able, not delinquent, and suggest that since Hastings' abilities were distinguished (meaning recognized) there was no 'cloud' obscuring his actions.

Finally, the use of the phrase 'in gratitude for favours received' alerts us to the eighteenth-century truth that patronage was one of the privileges of power. The fact that Bengal was 'possessed' by Company servants with 'distinguished abilities' conferred upon them the right to 'favour' the less powerful. The recognition in the map of such a relationship serves to demonstrate the supposed or seeming exercise of legitimate power. By invoking the familiar language of patronage Rennell was able to yoke together Hastings' public accomplishments with his personal loyalty and thus present an image of the Governor General at once master of the great affairs of state and conversant with the Company servants' petty needs. Rennell did indeed have good reason to be grateful to the man he termed 'a Hindoostany Patriot'.[21] Hastings had given Rennell a large rupee pension, which the Directors had reduced to the still 'handsome' sum of £400 a year.[22] By publicly declaring his gratitude to Hastings, Rennell was underscoring the Governor General's administrative greatness.

An examination of phrases within the cartouche of Plate IX, therefore, provides a plausible argument that Rennell hoped to elicit in his readers the sentiment that Bengal was rightfully owned as property and ably governed. Apart from a sentimental response to the atlas however, histories of possession could also be evoked, showing the need for and appropriateness of British rule in Bengal.

Evocative Histories

Dedications were able to evoke histories and associations with the land that may not have been immediately apparent in the map itself.

Not only did some of the dedications refer to the past, they also explained its relevance and meaning to late eighteenth-century readers. The primary way Rennell evoked a past was to dedicate particular maps to men associated with military victories within the area depicted. Thus, whereas the map dedicated to Hastings (Plate IX) focused on the credibility of British rule in Bengal, suggesting that that rule was neither louche nor wanton, other plates, particularly Plate XI, highlighted the history of conquest within Bengal. The history Rennell inserted into the dedications and maps presented the conquest of Bengal in three ways—as the culmination of battles fought in the 1750s and 1760s; as the reflection of British national behaviour; and as the beginning of legitimate colonial administration. The emphasis in these maps is on the British nation, not the Company—a rhetorical sleight of hand that might have made it possible for critics of the Company to applaud the continuing transformation of Bengal into a colony.

Rennell's interest in depicting the history of territorial possession was part of a new trend of British writing on India. Books and essays were written which, as Ranajit Guha has observed, 'were conspicuous by their interest in the historical aspects of the land' (1988: 8). Guha suggests that these histories comprise three types: political histories, exemplified by Alexander Dow's *The History of Hindostan* (1772); histories of political economy, such as James Grant's *An Inquiry into the Nature of Zemindary Tenures in the Landed Property of Bengal* (1791); and unpublished official reports. All three were concerned with examining the connections between history, land, and wealth, and attempted to describe systems of revenue administration which provided reliable alternatives to the supposed fabrications of Indians.[23] As part of a growing number of Company servants who were curious about the connections between past and present control of land, Rennell mapped a history of military success and colonial control.

The themes of historical victory, British national character, and colonial rule are most apparent in Plate XI, 'MAP of the COSSIMBUZAR ISLAND. In Testimony of Respect to the MEMORY of that GREAT MAN To whose Abilities the British Nation owes The SOVEREIGNTY of BENGAL, This MAP is Inscribed To the RIGHT HONORABLE EDWARD LORD CLIVE BARON of

PLASSEY, By his Lordship's most devoted Serv[an]t J Rennell'. As with Plate IX, this map contains key terms—'Memory', 'British nation', and 'Sovereignty'—that signal the legitimacy of Company rule.

One of the most noticeable features of the map is that it contains an inset sketch, entitled 'BATTLE of PLASSEY, Gained by COLONEL CLIVE June 23^d 1757'. The sketch shows the positions of the two armies before the battle. The course of the battle is both described with the help of a legend and shown by means of ruled lines, indicating the direction of British cannon fire. The success of Robert Clive's army against what appears to have been a far larger force is indicated by the fact that no enemy's cannon fire is shown and by numbers inserted into the sketch that refer to the legend. The legend itself reads as follows:

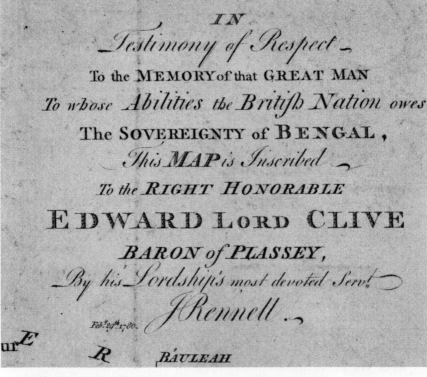

Fig. 6. *Title of Plate XI of* A Bengal Atlas, *by James Rennell, 1780.*

A. Position of the **British Army** at 8. in the Morning.
B. Four guns advanced to check the fire of the **French Party** at the Tank **D**.
C. The **Nabob's Army**.
D. A Tank from whence the French Party cannonaded till 3 in the Afternoon, when part of the **British Army** took Post there, and the Enemy retired within their Entrenched Camp.
E & F. A Redoubt and Mound taken by Assault at $\frac{1}{2}$ past 4 , and which completed the Victory.
G. The Nabob's Hunting House. The dotted Line **B E** shews the encroachment of the River since the Battle.

Together, the legend and the sketch are forceful reminders of how British power was advanced in Bengal. They add drama and interest to a map that otherwise may not have been included in the atlas, since the area shown was already depicted in the top left corner of Plate I, although on a smaller scale. The sketch also reinforces the military nature of the conquest and the fact that British power in Bengal was the result of a war that was won. After all, the title of the atlas is '*A BENGAL ATLAS: containing MAPS of the THEATRE OF WAR AND COMMERCE on that side of HINDOOSTAN*'. While the map dedicated to Hastings suggests that legitimate commerce was possible in a now-pacified Bengal, this sketch of Plassey reminds the viewer that military genius and might was necessary in the first place.

A closer look at the sketch also reveals two arguments that bolster the claim that the British were legitimate rulers. The first argument is that in the sketch of the battle, emphasis is placed on the idea that the battle was not just between the Nawab and Clive, but also between the French and the British, with the enemy's defeat seemingly precipitated by the retreat of the French. The explicit reference to the British army not only diverts attention away from any association with the aggrandizing or belligerent tendencies of some of the Company's servants (and thus away from remembrances of controversial exploits such as the Rohilla War), but it also concentrates attention on the absorbing and long-running antagonism between two newly emerging nations.

The second argument for legitimacy contained within the sketch is the suggestion that it was not the Company's army that was victorious, but the British army. Thus, the past that is represented is

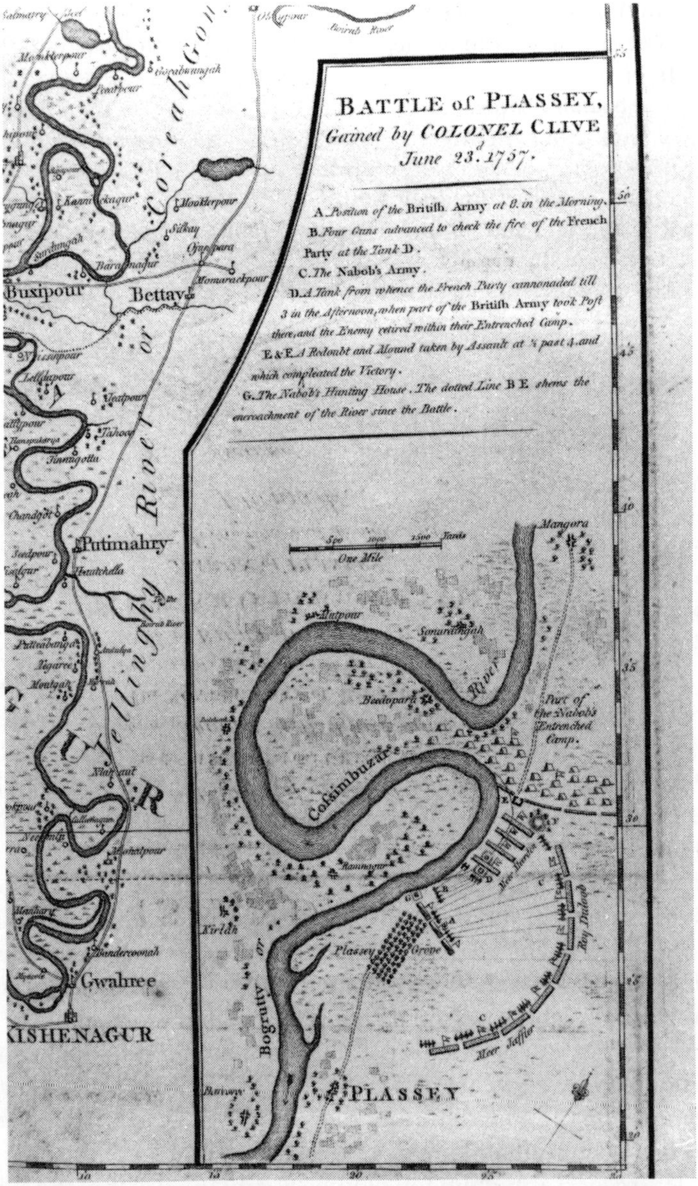

Fig. 7. *Detail from Plate XI of* A Bengal Atlas, *by James Rennell, 1780, showing the sketch map of the Battle of Plassey.*

not merely the Company's past, but the *nation's*. The key question is: Where is the Company in these maps? The Company is almost elided from the atlas itself. It only appears once, as a sponsor on the title page—'published by Order of the Honourable the Court of Directors'; the Company as a ruling force is clearly eclipsed by individuals acting as and on behalf of the British nation. Thus, the allegiance of the reader is not jeopardized but reinforced by the atlas; at a time when the Company was poorly perceived, Rennell's maps remained unthreatening, uncontroversial, but definitely patriotic. The implication was that it was the British nation, and not really the Company, which had ennobled and enriched itself from the conquest of Bengal. By jogging the reader's memory concerning Clive's fundamental role in the acquisition of one of Britain's Eastern possessions, the atlas might have been able to appeal to a Briton's sense of history, self, and community; to view the map meant to appreciate, and perhaps sentimentally participate in, the honourable overseas endeavours of the British nation. By drawing the British nation into his maps of Bengal, by evoking the nation's history in Bengal, Rennell may have wished to imply that the Company's and the nation's efforts were one and the same.

In private, though, Rennell had less flattering words for Clive. In a letter to his English guardian, dated 10 March 1767, Rennell complains bitterly of an order issued by Clive that reduced the pay of most officers. He claims he lost 15 shillings a day for seven months, and that Clive had promised to reimburse him 'but lo! he deceived me', Rennell writes, saying that one day he may remind Clive of his promise, 'but that must be when I am independent; for had I told him unwelcome Truths when he was Governor of Bengall, and as absolute as Harry the Eighth was, I should in all probability have been sent home to England, as some others have been for defending their liberties'.[24] However, after his return home, still dependent upon the Company for patronage and a pension, Rennell masked any lingering disaffectedness. Instead, a fond memory of Clive served his purpose of turning the Company's victories into national achievements.

It was also the national character of the conquest that allowed Rennell to claim that it was to Clive that 'the British Nation owes The SOVEREIGNTY of Bengal'. The implication of this statement is that the kind of control that was exercised was colonial; the rule was British and not just Company in nature and the object was more than a simple conquest. It was also the long-term administration of the territory. Moreover, the juxtaposition of the terms 'British nation', 'sovereignty', and 'Bengal' reflect late eighteenth-century trends that saw empire as one of the important building blocks of the new British nation. The allusion to Clive helped Rennell inject national pride into not only the conquest of Bengal but also its continued control.

If 'colonial' is defined, in this late-eighteenth-century context, as being a national endeavour animated by a struggle against France, a desire to not just engage in trade but to rule and administer non-national territories, and a tendency to justify that rule by invoking a rhetoric of historical legitimacy, then Rennell's maps provide additional evidence of colonial control. A further examination of Plate XI, for instance, reveals a curious anomaly. All the other dedications in the atlas are to men directly associated with Bengal. What is of particular interest in Plate XI is that the dedication is not to Robert Clive, although the inscription alludes to him, but to his son and heir, 'the Right Honorable Edward Lord Clive', the Baron of Plassey and later Governor of Madras.[25] Rennell's decision not to dedicate his map to Robert Clive was probably due to the fact that Clive had committed suicide in 1774 following years of public scrutiny and inquiry into his conduct while Governor of Bengal. However, in then dedicating the atlas to Clive's relation and titular successor, Rennell might have wished to stress the legitimacy (and not the near bankruptcy) of British rule by demonstrating that Bengal was continually possessed of and, in all likelihood, would continue to be British territory.

This history of succession, from Robert to Edward, mirrors another form of succession that is nestled in the map itself. The map, as we know, is of 'Cossimbuzar Island' and contains a sketch of the Battle of Plassey. What is missing in the title is any reference to what had been the seat of power in Bengal prior to Plassey—the city of Murshidabad. The city does appear on the map, and the size of the lettering and the area represented show it to be heavily populated, but its political significance is diminished by the prominence given to the battle and to the victor at Plassey. Rennell could have titled the map 'PLAN of the ENVIRONS of the CITY of MURSHIDABAD', as he did with Dhaka in the next plate (Plate XII). Instead he chose to tell the history of a political revolution within a map that, at first sight, purports to be about the geography of an island. Moreover, the fact that the map's prime meridian is centred on Calcutta, and not on Murshidabad, only increases the political insignificance of the former capital and further illustrates a dramatic history of political change.

If we turn to another map in the atlas, Plate VIII, we may find further illustrations of recent political change. As with the representation of Plassey and Murshidabad, the history in Plate VIII bolsters British legitimacy by inviting a contrast between what had been and what existed in 1780.[26] The full title of the plate is: 'The CONQUERED PROVINCES on the south of BAHAR; Containing RAMGUR, PALAMOW, & CHUTA-NAGPOUR, with their dependencies. Inscribed to Major JACOB CAMAC, By his most obed(ien)t Servant J. Rennell.' As the commander of the 24th Bengal Infantry, based at Ramgarh, Camac was involved in the conquest of these territories and was responsible for the defeat of a Maratha army under Scindia in 1779, thus justifying his name's appearance on the map.

The area depicted, according to Rennell's definition in the title, is beyond the territory of Bihar. Why, then, should Rennell have included this map in an atlas of Bengal? Similarly, why include Plate X—'A MAP of OUDE, & ALLAHABAD: with part of AGRA & DELHI: Including the Course of the GANGES to Hurdwar; and the MAHARATTA FRONTIER: Inscribed to JOHN CARTIER ESQR: Late GOVERNOR of FORT WILLIAM, and of the BRITISH POSSESSIONS in BENGAL, By his obliged, and affectionate Friend J Rennell'? Neither map shows Bengali territory.

Both maps represent the frontier of the Company's power and both refer, one explicitly and the other implicitly, to the Company's most potent adversary in northern India—the Marathas. These were vulnerable regions, with much of the area represented not under the direct rule of the Company. Although their indirect or direct control was undeniably important for an uninterrupted administration in Bengal, there is no clear indication why Rennell included these maps in the atlas. However, word associations within both maps might provide some clues. In Plate VIII, the title is balanced with the words 'conquered provinces' and 'dependencies'. In Plate X, mention of the Ganges is followed immediately by the Maratha frontier. In both maps, then, a certain military and economic vulnerability is revealed; on the one hand, dependencies require defence and military strength, while on the other, the Ganges, a major thoroughfare for trade, needs protection. If Rennell were indicating the need for a robust and vigilant military policy towards the Marathas it would suggest that Rennell's atlas was using a history of 'war and commerce on that side of Hindoostan' to argue for further military and administrative involvement in eastern and northern India. And, if Plate XI, dedicated to Clive, is any indication, such involvement would only redound to the British nation's benefit.

Finally, the evocative strength of the history within Rennell's maps is suggested by yet another plate—Plate XVIII of the 1781 atlas. It depicts the Brahmaputra river and also includes a sketch of the southern view of Dalimkote fort in Bhutan, inscribed to Captain John Jones, who captured it in 1773, and, as Rennell says, 'soon after fell a sacrifice to the unwholesome Climate of Coos Beyhar'. Such is the power and permanence of the inscription that these same words appear in the Dictionary of Indian Biography under Jones' entry. Thus, the atlas contributed a written and visual language of Company history—identifying battlegrounds, evoking a remembrance of heroic deeds—but couched it as an expression of national fortitude and genius.

Conclusion

This chapter began with a deceptively simple question: Why might the East India Company support the surveying and publication of an atlas of Bengal? The question is deceptive because the answer seems self-evident. Increased and more accurate geographical knowledge would enable the Company to collect revenue and transport goods in an expeditious manner. These are undeniable and logical reasons for the heightened mapping activity during this time period. Yet, an examination of James Rennell's Bengal Atlas reveals that the publication may also have been undertaken in order to contribute to and advance a more positive perspective on Company rule in Bengal. It was imperative for the financial health of the Company that it be well regarded in Britain and, so, one of the ways Rennell sought to present a semblance of legitimacy was to suggest that the Company was fulfilling its new, dual role as improving private landlord and responsible national custodian. Rennell employed traditional cartographic techniques, such as recognizable symbols, stylized calligraphy, and, especially, dedications to men associated with the land depicted, in an effort to make the province seem familiar and non-threatening. Such familiarity enabled Rennell to transform a foreign land, still legally the sovereign property of the Mughal emperor, into territory putatively possessed by the British nation and governed by able men. What is significant, then, about the atlas is that it contributed to both the construction of a national colonial state and the imagining of that state in Europe. The manner of publishing of Rennell's maps, and the inclusion of dedications to officials (even to men such as Verelst and Hastings, who had been accused of despotic behaviour), suggests that Rennell wished to project the Company as a government that was both enlightened (mapping for the benefit of more efficient rule) and conservative (spending its resources on activities that were poles apart from the supposed dissipation and lethargy of 'country' courts).

Controlling the first perspective or impression was a valuable asset for a Company seeking understanding and support. Through the use and the particular wordings of the dedications the atlas helped to usher in a second and sentimental conquest of Bengal. It evoked histories which made that sentimental conquest legitimate and intimated that if Bengal were defined as British territory and felt to be a part of a British military past and commercial future, it was a place which required Britain's continued attention. The maps suggested that British sovereignty was the logical and seamless successor to Mughal rule, that the province had been pacified successfully, but that enemies lurked on the boundaries. Thus, by making a British territory of Bengal, by building a British national identity through the sovereignty of Bengal, by giving British control of Bengal a colonial character, the maps made it seem both natural and patriotic to support the Company's rule in Bengal.

Notes

1. Rennell (1976: ix) himself claimed that 'the first maritime nation in the world, has no good chart to direct its fleets towards its own coasts ... the

soundings on the coast of Bengal, are better known that those in the British channel.'
2. Michael Bravo (1999: 162–83) uses Rennell's work to explore the connections between scientific precision and imperialism.
3. The French also employed surveyors during the eighteenth century. For a selection of their manuscript maps and plans see Jean-Marie Lafont 2001. Susan Gole has published a copy of a manuscript atlas of Mughal India by a French officer who, when French power in India was effectively halted after 1759, took refuge in a succession of Indian courts (1988).
4. A full account can be found in the typescript of Rennell's letters (30 August 1766), Oriental and India Office Collections (hereafter OIOC) MSS EUR. D. 1073.
5. OIOC MSS EUR. D. 1073, 30 August 1766.
6. OIOC Orme MSS 7, p. 6, 'Journal of an Expedition from Telingee ...'
7. OIOC Orme MSS 7, 1 September 1764.
8. OIOC MSS EUR. D. 1073, 15 March 1772.
9. British Library (hereafter BL) Addl MSS 29210, p. 298, Rennell, 'Proposals for a New Set of Maps of Bengal, &c'.
10. National Archives of India, Dehra Dun Volume List (hereafter NAI, DDn Vol. List), Old No. SGO 53 (A), Sl. No. 81, p. 83, Colebrooke to Richard Parry, 13 May 1807.
11. For a discussion of nabobs see Lawson and Phillips 1984.
12. For a full discussion of the debates see Kate Teltscher, 1995: 158–59.
13. Andrew Cook has identified one review—*Göttingische Anzeigen von gelehrte Sachen*, Vol. 3: 1523–24, 1783. See Cook 1978, 26, note 85.
14. OIOC, Orme MSS 176, pp. 32–52.
15. James Rennell, BL Addl MSS 29147, pp. 191–92, Rennell to Hastings, 26 January 1781.
16. The 1780 editions have a title plate that is left undedicated, as is Plate XII—the 'PLAN of the ENVIRONS of the CITY of DACCA'. The 1781 editions have eight new numbered plates, plus a map of the inland navigation. These new plates are left undedicated, except Plate XVIII, which includes an inset containing a southern view of Dellamcotta fort, inscribed to Captain John Jones.
17. OIOC MSS EUR. D. 1073, Rennell, 'Letters', 20 April 1763.
18. Much of the information on individuals comes from C.E. Buckland (1969).
19. BL Addl MSS 29142, p. 75, Rennell to Hastings, 20 November 1778.
20. This argument is similar to the notion of 'anticonquest' articulated by Mary Louise Pratt (1992).
21. BL Addl MSS 29193, p. 516, Rennell to Hastings, n.d.

22. BL Addl MSS 29140, p. 343, Rennell to Hastings, 1 May 1778.
23. Rennell wrote *A Description of the Roads in Bengal and Bahar* (1778) in order to counter the Company's guides, who often misled 'through ignorance or interested motives'.
24. OIOC MSS Eur. D. 1073, Rennell, 'Letters', 1758–85, 10 March 1767. In the same year Clive wrote to Robert Orme about his efforts to curtail the rush for 'independency', the very condition Rennell was seeking: 'I call it licentiousness and a struggle whether the immense Revenues of Bengal, Bahar and Orissa shall go into the pockets of Individuals or the Company.' BL Addl MSS 44061, (p. 11), Clive to Orme, 5 February 1767.
25. In 1784, Edward Clive had married the sister of the Earl of Powis, and in 1804 he succeeded to the title. In 1955 Sotheby's sold a number of manuscript maps by Rennell which had been in the library of Powis Castle, and presumably had been the (illegal) private property of Robert Clive. See Baker 1963: 139.
26. Rennell also used the technique of contrasting the past with the present in his 1782 Map of Hindoostan. The accompanying memoir states: 'These modern divisions are not only distinguished in the Map by the names of the present possessors; but the colouring also is entirely employed in facilitating the distinctions between them. So that the modern divisions appear, as it were, in the *fore ground*; and the ancient one in the *back ground*; one illustrating and explaining the other.' Rennell 1976 (1793), p. ix.

TWO

From Route Surveys to Trigonometrical Maps: A Progressive History of Surveying

In 1786, William Faden published a map by James Rennell depicting 'Bengal, Bahar, Oude and Allahabad with part of Agra and Delhi exhibiting the course of the Ganges from Hurdwar to the Sea'. The map was dedicated to John Stables, a commander at the Battle of Buxar in 1764 and later, between 1782 and 1787, a member of the Supreme Council of Bengal. As with Rennell's atlas of Bengal, the dedication on this map reveals a history of possession. But, unlike the atlas, the Faden map attaches this dedication to a splendid cartouche. The scene depicts a Neptune or Poseidon-like figure sitting nestled in lush vegetation, his right arm resting on the head of a cow. A trident made of rushes or grasses appears from his hidden left hand, and at his feet lie a crocodile and what seems to be a tiger. The cartouche may contain traditional Hindu iconography and allusions. The figure, for example, may be a stylized version of the Hindu god Siva, whose hair was said to have caught the Ganges as it fell from the sky. Similarly, the Ganges itself was said to issue from a boulder shaped like the head of a cow, perhaps explaining the latter's inclusion in the map. Behind the figure towers a rock on which the dedication is written, and on the other side of the water (presumably the Ganges) are four additional figures. These figures seem to depict a Company soldier, a woman holding a lit lamp over a kneeling Brahmin, and a turbaned Muslim man. They are all looking up the river from their position in Bengal.

The cartouche may be read in many ways. One interpretation may be that it contains a plea for an extension of British control along the whole course of the river. The main elements of the cartouche tell a story of opposites—wild nature vs cultivated landholdings; the mythology of Siva vs the rational map below; the

Fig. 8. *Title and Illustration of William Faden's Map of Bengal, 1786.*

river's mysterious source vs the well-known delta. However, it is also a story of the danger of those opposites, since the evident reverence shown to the river and to Siva by the Indians (Muslim as well as Hindu, men as well as women) seems to present a challenge or alternative to British power. One of the map's messages may be that if the Company wished to dispel the power of the river, i.e. of the Indian, and consolidate its rule, the river must be surveyed and controlled right up to its source. This reading is certainly not the only possible interpretation. The cartouche could also be an early Orientalist illustration, showing the supposedly superstitious nature of India. No matter what the interpretation of the cartouche may be, it certainly reveals one of the preoccupations of Company surveyors in the late eighteenth century. Not only is the Ganges river a central feature of the cartouche, the map itself presents the viewer with a sweeping view of the river from its source in the mountains to the Bay of Bengal.

Rennell and his contemporaries were usually route surveyors, following the course of rivers, roads, or mountain ranges, and using bearings to remarkable rock formations, peaks, or permanent structures as the bases for their maps. The maps that resulted, as exemplified by Faden's publication, have a journey-like quality that leads a viewer from a starting point to a destination, 'from Hurdwar to the Sea'. They focus on particulars, notice incongruities, convey the excitement of exploration through tactile and sentimental maps. A map made by Charles Reynolds in the late eighteenth century, for example, was so large (fourteen feet by ten) that viewers were obliged to wear silk stockings and gloves in order to crawl over it (see Welsh 1830: 243–44).[1]

These maps, being largely based on route surveys, were quite different from those drawn and published a generation or two later. Early-to-mid-nineteenth-century maps increasingly incorporated information that came from trigonometrical surveys. Their character was less rambling and they contained fewer narratives that were readily apparent. The use of illustrated cartouches diminished rapidly and maps lost their interest in showing political divisions without also including contiguous areas. Instead, the maps became more focused on the geographical grids made by lines of longitude and latitude. The transformation of the map (in its content and presentation) is similar to Sumathi Ramaswamy's characterization of the modern science of Geography—'through direct observation, classification, and comparison, the earth was tamed, and progressively rendered nonmysterious, unwonderous, disenchanted' (2000: 579). The change in surveying approaches in India also heralded an era in which maps were seemingly more objective in their perspective and more systematic in their construction. The vagueness and unreliability of route surveying was often contrasted with the rock-solid certainty of triangulation. With regard to trigonometrical surveying, a colonial official noted in 1817 that 'there is no other solid basis on which accurate Geography can so well be founded'.[2] These surveyors wished to distance themselves from the subjective description of vague route surveys and replace that method with calculations which could at once explain, project, and present the only true cartographic image of the earth. Rather than focus on the singular oddities which might occur along a surveyor's path, trigonometrical mappers hoped to capture, through an emphasis on fixed locations, an abstract essence, such as area or distance, which could be viewed with disinterested attention.

The difference in the styles of the two kinds of maps is largely due to changes in surveying techniques and, to some extent, surveying technology. At the beginning of the nineteenth century trigonometrical surveying became an established practice in India, and soon it became the pre-eminent form of surveying, considered more scientific than topographical or revenue surveying. With the advent of trigonometrical techniques, route surveys were progressively regarded as obsolete.

The notion of progress, in fact, was an important factor that prompted the shift towards trigonometrical surveying. Beginning in Europe in the late eighteenth century, surveyors began to incorporate trigonometry into their surveying, believing it to be an approach that would lead to considerable improvements in the accuracy of their maps. So long as an initial base line was measured with as much precision as possible, subsequent distances, based on angles taken from the base line's two ends, would also be consistently reliable. In India, the arguments for adopting expensive trigonometrical surveying establishments were accepted by the very beginning of the nineteenth century, and its two chief exponents, William Lambton and George Everest, were thereafter motivated by a desire to provide topographical surveyors with a trigonometrical backbone. Lambton and Everest were also conscious of the fact that their surveys, which for many years followed an arc of the meridian (from southern to northern India), would be helpful to geodetic science since the surveys' data could also be used to determine the exact shape of the earth. They were convinced that their use of trigonometrical techniques placed them at the vanguard of improvement and progress, both in India and in the world.

Lambton and Everest were not the only ones convinced that trigonometrical surveying represented progress. Historians of the Survey of India, especially those writing in the late nineteenth century, also subscribed to the notion that the Survey's early adoption of more rigorous scientific techniques and procedures improved the quality of both manuscript and published maps, and enabled other branches of the government to conduct their colonial business more effectively (see Black, C.E.D. 1891, Markham 1878). Their writings are characterized by a sense of the Survey's political disinterest since its mission and objectives were purely cartographical and scientific. In their assessments, they tended to laud the Company and its trigonometrical surveyors for their contributions to geodetic research as well as for providing the 'grid' system of lines of longitude and latitude that formed the basis of topographical and revenue surveys on a larger scale.

Many of these historical accounts placed emphasis on two important themes. The first was that trigonometrical surveying made 'improvements' in geography possible. The Company's trigonometrical surveys were considered to be the most advanced and scientific approach to mapping. As such, this form of mapping represented the triumph of British science (see, for example, Walker 1870).

The second major theme in the histories of the Survey of India was that trigonometrical surveying indicated the enlightened and justified rule of the colonial government. In the 1830s, for instance, one historical account of British India celebrated the accomplishments of the Great Trigonometrical Survey's first superintendent, William Lambton. It pointed out that his contributions were not just improvements but were also 'a proof of the intelligence with which the present rulers of India have applied their power and their ample means to the promotion of geographical knowledge' (Murray 1836:

325). For colonial historians, the improvements accompanying trigonometrical surveying gave reason to colonial power.

It has been very persuasively argued, however, that Western science and colonialism were closely linked even beyond the desire to improve and increase knowledge about the shape and figure of the earth. The argument has been that science helped colonialism and colonialism helped science (see Adas 1989, Headrick 1988). In an essay titled 'Scientific Empire and Imperial Science', for instance, David Gilmartin begins by noting that 'in the eyes of many colonial administrators in the nineteenth century, the advance of science and the advance of colonial rule went hand in hand. Science helped to secure colonial rule, to justify European domination over other peoples, and to transform production for an expanding world economy.' He then continues with the observation that 'a scientific administrative "discourse" influenced significantly the forms of control that came to dominate the imperial Raj' (Gilmartin 1994: 1127). The introduction of trigonometrical surveying, which was considered far superior to route surveys, let alone any indigenous practices, was thought to be both evidence of British intellectual superiority and a sign that colonial rule was not stagnant.

Matthew Edney (1994) too, has made a powerful argument that nineteenth-century trigonometrical surveyors in India were part of a European Enlightenment milieu that saw India as a convenient location for scientific verification, experimentation, and discovery. The idea that trigonometrical surveying could embody perfection and rationality was the key reason why this most mathematically rigorous of all surveying techniques was considered the epitome of progress and an aid to both the notional and literal construction of the British Indian empire.[3]

This chapter builds upon the claims that a close connection existed between science and colonialism. The focus is a comparison between the methods and perspectives of route surveyors and those of trigonometrical surveyors. The argument is that the promise of an improvement in geography and a concomitant progress in British colonial rule were powerful inducements for the adoption of trigonometrical surveying as the pre-eminent mode of surveying in India. While topographical and revenue surveys continued to be authorized throughout the nineteenth century, and while route surveys were never fully discontinued (see Chapter Four), there was an assumption among the surveying and administrative community that the Great Trigonometrical Survey was the flagship surveying establishment, representing an advancement in knowledge and a sign of the value of having a colonial government in India.

The central question to be addressed, then, is why surveyors and the Company were convinced that trigonometrical surveys were prudent investments and superior to route surveys. Although trigonometrical mapping had been practised in Europe, notably in France, England, and, later, in Ireland, it was not adopted in many other colonies. It was considerably more expensive than a route survey and its results were not immediately available. What factors, then, prompted the colonial establishment in India to embrace an expensive, difficult, slow, and esoteric scientific practice?

The argument is threefold. First, route surveys were most suitable for exploration. They were descriptive and picturesque, and were ideal for identifying safe journeys and locating towns, fords, and impasses. They were useful for showing what could be expected, in terms of physical and political dangers, if a journey were to be undertaken. Their reliance on astronomy to fix positions provided sufficient accuracy, while their use of quick bearings ensured that the survey was cheap, fast, and effective. Second, by the beginning of the nineteenth century, the need for quick descriptive sketches of the country, while never disappearing, was supplanted by the desire to have more detailed topographical plans, greater uniformity among maps, a higher scientific profile in Britain, and a visible sign of the prudence, foresight, and enlightenment of the Company's colonial government. Third, the privileged position of trigonometrical surveying in India, although seen at the time, and since, as an integral part of the colonial state, was not replicated in other colonies. It is no doubt true that science was an important component of colonialism, but its expression or manifestation was decidedly different in each colony.

A brief comparison with colonial mapping in Sri Lanka, then called Ceylon, reinforces the final point. Except for one survey operation in the middle of the century, almost no trigonometrical surveying was conducted in Ceylon until the last quarter of the nineteenth century, and then only sporadically and reluctantly. Due to the lack of trigonometrical surveying on the island, it may be suggested that this form of surveying was not necessarily an integral aspect of a nineteenth-century colonial state. The adoption of trigonometrical practices in India, therefore, may be the result of a combination of factors, including the availability of resources and qualified surveyors, the need to connect disparate surveys from all over India as accurately as possible, and the Company's desire to project itself as enlightened. Although science may have helped colonial rule, and vice versa, and although science was undoubtedly important for the projection of a 'civilized' colonial state, giving it a certain character, we should be careful not to claim that science was uniformly important in all colonial states, nor that science was implemented or practised in the same way throughout the colonies.

The Company's Route Surveys

As was suggested with the 1786 Faden and Rennell map, land surveyors of the second half of the eighteenth century, who most commonly conducted their mappings on route survey principles, understood the land and its depiction in hydrographic terms. Water was not only the means for exploring land but also a metaphor for comprehending new territorial domains within the Company's purview. By the mid-nineteenth century a shift in perspectives occurred that emphasized land over the sea and placed increasing importance on accurately positioning places on a map. In the eighteenth century, however, Europeans held the reverse view. British surveyors and travellers in India felt comfortable with coasts and rivers and used them as arteries for exploring a perilous inland. Moreover, in using rivers as a means for gathering information, the surveyor's journey was more important than fixing precise locations. After all, hydrographers were primarily concerned with ensuring safe passages. Their charts pointed the way for ships and used topographical markers and astronomical bearings as signs for a successful journey. As the Company's own hydrographer wrote, a blank space in his charts 'does not denote that there are no dangers in that Space; but only that the Dangers, in such a Space, are unknown' (Dalrymple 1806: 2). Trees, hills, even people were signs leading the traveller on to a safe arrival, and each of these signs spoke to each other for the benefit of the foreign viewer. Lands had, in Alexander Dalrymple's words, 'reciprocal Situations', a language which conveyed life-saving information to the traveller (1771: 2).[4] Charts, maps, and views provided more than mere supplements to written accounts of the land; they were the very descriptions of the land which words alone were incapable of expressing.

Traverse or route surveyors were also concerned with showing how best to move along a route. For them, the particulars of the journey, seen as if sailing to port, were of the utmost significance. Route surveys were particularly useful when new territories or little-known districts were being explored. The resulting maps were neither abstract nor disinterested perspectives but narratives which conveyed a wealth of detail allowing travellers to journey successfully. Thomas Jefferys' map of the East Indies, with the roads, for example, may have been constructed with the aid of a few route surveys because of its focus on travel. The second edition of the map was published in 1768 and furnishes details that would have been very helpful for a traveller; the part of the map that shows northern India, for instance, names not only the provinces—Bahar or Bengal—but also the men who controlled the land, Sujah Dowlah or Shah Alum. Even the nearly blank spaces in the map, where few geographical features are drawn, warns the potential traveller that the 'Rajahs and Poligars (are) little known and in a manner independent'. This is a map meant for travel and even an armchair map reader is swept across the map along boundaries, roads, and rivers.

Another example of a published map that certainly incorporated information derived from route surveys is William Faden's 1800 map of the peninsula of India. The title cartouche explains that the map includes 'several Roads which have been Measured by Captain Pringle ... (and) Capt. Douglas' together with a road followed by British prisoners after their release. Faden also states that the map was '*COMPILED chiefly from Papers communicated by the late* SIR ARCH[D]. CAMPBELL, *the SURVEYS of* COL. KELLY, CAPT. PRINGLE, CAPT. ALLAN, &c.' Route Surveys were one of the primary ways cartographers were able to improve their maps and add new information on historical events, the location of places, and the topography of the land.

Late-eighteenth-century route surveyors were fairly uniform in the manner they conducted their surveys, described their journeys, and constructed their maps. For example, they would often accompany armies on their marches, would submit a descriptive day-by-day journal, and draw a map that illustrated the journey, showing remarkable or strategic points along the way. Of particular interest as well is that many of these surveyors would also adopt a picturesque perspective when describing, drawing, or mapping the land around them. Though any of a number of other aesthetic conventions might have been chosen, including perspectives that highlighted the beautiful or the sublime in the subject, it was the picturesque that was often chosen. Its advantage was that it was particularly suitable for exploration. It helped to transform and control what was terrifying, unknown, or unfrequented. It is important to discuss the picturesque at some length for two reasons. The first is that it helps to explain the character of route surveys in the late eighteenth century in India in a way that has not been fully addressed. The second reason is that it throws some light on why trigonometrical surveying superseded route surveying at the turn of the nineteenth century—rather than make unknown lands less threatening, a state of affairs that was no longer applicable to Company territory, trigonometrical surveyors wanted to inject into their work the science and rhetoric of progress.

Edmund Burke's *Philosophical Inquiry into the Origin of Our Ideas of the Sublime and Beautiful* (1756), was perhaps the most well read and important work on aesthetics in the eighteenth century. His argument, in brief, is that many have asserted that pleasure and pain are dependent upon each other; that a lessening of pain results in pleasure, while a loss of pleasure excites pain. Burke counters that there is no correlation between pleasure and pain because positive pleasure does not rely upon a lack of pain, and vice versa. Instead, an absence of pain, or rather the awareness that one is not in any danger of pain, produces delight, and the quality which induces delight is called the sublime. The sublime is an acknowledgment that terrifying horrors have been averted. In a remarkable section entitled 'power', Burke notes that terror is the 'common stock' of the sublime. He asks the reader to picture a man 'of prodigious strength', and wonders what emotion the reader may feel. Invariably, he suggests, the reader will fear that the man's strength may be used to terrible ends. Power, being dependent upon terror, is sublime when it is not controlled or only partially made subservient to our will. The strong man becomes contemptible, however, if his power is no longer his; but he remains sublime if he retains the power to terrify. 'In short,' Burke concludes, 'wheresoever we find strength, and in what light soever we look upon power we shall all along observe the sublime the concomitant of terror, and contempt the attendant on a strength that is subservient and innoxious' (1854: 96).

The beautiful, according to Burke, is characterized by the qualities of smoothness, gradual variation, and symmetry, among others, and is thought to be that which induces the pleasurable emotions of affection and tenderness. These passions must be seen as distinct from the kind of love which gives rise to lust. It is certainly possible to lose a beautiful object, but the resulting emotion is not pain, since pain cannot be the result of a diminution in the pleasure of experiencing beauty. The sublime and the beautiful, therefore, are distinct and should not be confused.

The significance of referring to Burke's argument is that it has been suggested that the rhetoric of late-eighteenth-century England with regard to India was suffused with the sublime (see Suleri: 1992). Burke and others may indeed have regarded the Company, and even India, as capable of sublimity since they were entities or areas which had the potential for unleashing terrifying and unfettered power. However, route surveyors transformed any fear of an unknown India into a managed, ordered, and comforting picture. For them India was neither sublime nor beautiful, but picturesque.

The picturesque has been defined as either a characteristic of those landscapes which look like a picture or a quality assigned to the rural and antiquarian sites and customs that were noticed by a sophisticated traveller.[5] The picturesque was also often understood by its relation to the beautiful and the sublime. Uvedale Price, for example, wrote *Essays on the Picturesque, As Compared With the Sublime and the Beautiful* (1810) in which he explained the qualities which define the picturesque. He noted that while the beautiful was defined by smoothness, gradual variation, and lack of intricacy, the picturesque was characterized by roughness and sudden variation. Beauty was, therefore, often associated with youth and freshness, while the picturesque conveyed a sense of age and decay. Good examples appear in a review of the 1810 edition of Price's book (*The Quarterly Review* Vol. IV, 1810: 372–82). The reviewer refers to the many 'low subjects' in Dutch and Flemish paintings and comments that they are always 'disgusting in the original, but not in the representation' (ibid.: 375). That which would ordinarily excite repulsion is instead transformed into both an appreciation of the painter's skill and a (possibly perverse) association with the joys of relaxation and contemplation. Towns, the anonymous reviewer writes, are full of misery, while the country is the site of contentment. The inclusion of thatched hovels or decayed ruins in picturesque paintings prompts the viewer to consider the pleasures of studied observation. A scene which contains an old male gypsy is thought to be picturesque if he is drawn with a countenance that expresses 'his three-fold occupation of beggar, thief, and fortune-teller' (ibid.: 379). In all these examples it is important that a wildness and incivility are conveyed, and that the painter uses harsh tints, extraordinary figures, and sudden variation to portray the undesired and disgusting as curious and unthreatening.

While the sublime, therefore, depends upon horror for its effect, the picturesque relies upon the management and transformation of horror into either the contemptible or the decaying. A wolf baring its fangs is sublime—its power is 'noxious' and terrifying—but an old gypsy is picturesque since the threat of his strength and cunning has been dissipated or removed. The East India Company's route surveys were picturesque in this sense; instead of regarding India as sublime, with a sense of gratitude that terror had been temporarily averted, the surveys sometimes portrayed a land of decay and impotence, where Indian power was increasingly subjugated to British will.

An example of a surveyor who incorporated the picturesque in his work is R.H. Colebrooke, a Surveyor General for the Company. He spent much of his surveying career in northern India, surveying the Ganges, but during the wars with Tipu Sultan he did travel and survey the Mysore region. In 1805 he published a set of picturesque views of Mysore, all taken from sketches he drew while he was surveying (Colebrook [sic] 1805). The plate exhibiting the eastern view of Bangalore, for instance, depicts a British flag, a flat plain, cultivators, and what looks like a small temple. It shows a calm and peaceful country. However, the account which accompanies the drawing states that it was in this fortress that Tipu Sultan had imprisoned British soldiers and treated them 'with inhumanity, rigour, and insolence'. The contrast between the serene landscape dominated by a British flag, depicting peaceful cultivation, and the torment said to have been suffered by the prisoners at that very spot, provides a glimpse of how the picturesque works to remove all anxiety from a scene which might otherwise be sufficiently terrifying to be considered sublime.[6]

A less well-known route surveyor, who was not part of the official surveying establishment but who incorporated the picturesque into his work, was the Reverend William Smith. His journal of the march of Colonel J. Upton across central India in 1775 and 1776 was a recognizable route survey.[7] One of his principal objects was to provide 'a short description of the roads, country, places, the encampment, and other incidences of the day'.[8] Such entries were standard practice for officially sanctioned surveyors although many thought such descriptions tedious and unprofitable, including Smith, who rebelled at having to perform such a 'disinteresting and insignificant' task. In an unusually blunt passage Smith complained that such 'disagreeable' descriptions must be considered 'trivial, low, paltry performances', yet he felt compelled to comply with his instructions. The practice of including such mundane information in the journal, although rarely drawn in the resulting map, provided a method for examining new territory and ensured that the surveyor remained alert and observant. This aspect of the route survey, therefore, was well suited to the problem of introducing a surveyor to new territory in a regular way and protecting him from feeling overwhelmed by new information. It also prepared him for the construction of the map of his journey.

In order to make a map, Smith's journal featured a geographical section. Here he mentioned his bearings and distances, together with the location of all remarkable or habitable places. Smith also made his account picturesque, transforming what was a potentially dangerous military experience into something akin to a jaunt. The entry on 8 November 1775, indicates that the party was near Kalpi, at a place that 'affords one of the finest rural and romantic prospects, that can well be imagined; nature seems to have lavished a rarity of beautiful contrasts of towering hills, craggy rocks, level plains, fruitful vales, elegant and rude buildings . . .'. The sudden variation, the roughness, the manner in which the prospect has been manipulated by 'nature', all indicate the picturesque. Smith retains control over the scene and turns the unknown into something 'that can well be imagined'.

Although route surveys were often picturesque, they also strove to be scientific. One of the ways in which surveyors ensured accuracy was by taking occasional astronomical observations. Smith took observations in his survey and remarked on their importance by saying that anyone who has on two occasions measured the same piece of land using either a perambulator or chain will invariably notice the disagreement of the two calculations, a state of affairs which 'puts him under the necessity of taking a little from one, and adding to another; carrying one more to the south, or farther from the west ... and patching up an agreement in the best manner he can: whereas no such embarrassments can ever happen from proper astronomical instruments'. As daily journal entries and regular bearings helped to make foreign land seem familiar and unthreatening, so astronomical observations ensured a degree of accuracy without impeding the march or slowing down the other aspects of the survey. In fact, the observations were thought of as being very much part of the journey.

One of the most accomplished Company astronomers and route surveyors was Reuben Burrow (1747–92). Burrow was a self-taught mathematician who had held several jobs, including as a teacher, an assistant astronomer at the Royal Observatory, a surveyor in southern England, and the publisher of an almanac.[9] In an undated essay on the advantages of examining the observatory at Benares, Burrow asserted that the Company's surveys were 'remarkably defective ... made up of ideal chains of mountains and imaginary woods, taken piecemeal by pretended Surveyors'. He claimed that such maps were 'a nuisance' and could only be corrected and improved if the positions of important locations were established through astronomical observations.[10] These observations, he argued, together with an examination of Hindu astronomical principles and practices, would ensure safer journeys, a greater knowledge of Hindu religion and government, and a fuller understanding of nature; 'Astronomy,' he declared, 'treats of the History of nature in its greatest aspect.'[11]

For most of his career Burrow used astronomy to fix the locations of places in terms of longitude and latitude; knowing the exact positions of towns and cities would inevitably aid travellers reach their destinations. The focus of astronomical calculations remained the successful conclusion of journeys. The Reverend Smith, Alexander Dalrymple, James Rennell, and to some extent R.H. Colebrooke, all incorporated astronomy as part of their descriptive and picturesque route surveys.

Although Burrow was an accomplished route surveyor and astronomer—most of his surveys in northern India were tied to rivers and coastlines[12]—he is representative of several men who, by the turn of the century, had begun to regard route surveys as inadequate. Two years before he died in 1792, Burrow attempted to measure a degree of longitude, and a year later he turned his attention to calculating a degree of latitude.[13] These surveys used the principles of triangulation (including the establishment of a baseline) and were intended to provide information regarding the figure or shape of the earth. The perspective was shifting away from rivers and coastlines, description and the picturesque, and towards the explanatory and the mathematical and the scientific. Astronomy was one of the bridges in this move, allowing surveyors to continue to use their technical skills, but for different ends. By the turn of the century, safe journeys and arrivals were no longer the high priority that they had been when the Company knew little about its newly conquered territories. A few surveyors began to turn their attention to solving questions regarding the shape of the earth and the best manner for improving geography.

The Company's Trigonometrical Surveys

While the line of the route survey united two points, the line of the trigonometrical map divided two areas. Although several surveyors and astronomers, including Burrow, had advocated the regular use of triangulation as a supplement to the usual traverse or route surveys, Colin Mackenzie was one of the first surveyors to propose its adoption as a standard technique.[14] Following the Company's victory over Tipu Sultan in 1799, Mackenzie had been instructed to survey the lands and assess the value of Mysore. In a letter to Colonel

Barry Close, the Resident at Mysore, Mackenzie proposed a 'Geographical and Geometrical Survey' which would encompass the 'Great Outlines' of the country, together with all the 'divisions and boundaries interior and exterior'.[15] Triangulation, the primary method of trigonometrical surveying, was to enable Mackenzie to divide Mysore into its constituent segments, which would in turn provide a basis for systematic statistical, revenue, and topographical surveys. After the turn of the century, penetrating into completely unknown territory was no longer as important as it had been. Instead, increasing accuracy in those territories that were under Company control or were contiguous became a priority, and trigonometry offered many advantages in this regard.

Just as Burrow represented a transition from route surveys to trigonometrical mapping, so Mackenzie straddled both approaches. He spent much of his time in the peninsula of India assiduously surveying, collecting coins, cataloguing Indian manuscripts, and documenting historical finds.[16] His earlier work was especially concerned with journeys and he recognized objects along the road as signs leading the traveller on to a successful arrival. His historical writing was also characterized by his use of archaeological and numismatic evidence as guides, leading the scholar back in time towards a clearer understanding of India's lost golden age. His later writings, which become increasingly bureaucratic and concerned with proper procedure (he later became Surveyor General of India), reveal an increasing and deeply held belief that the manner of historical or cartographic observation, as opposed to the quality of interpretation, was fundamental to the generation of correct views. As the Company's principal surveyor in Mysore after Tipu Sultan's defeat, Mackenzie became a staunch advocate of geographical surveys which subsumed all manner of statistical, botanical, census, and historical surveys. In both his cartographical and historical writings, Mackenzie came to view locations as important in and of themselves.

One of his collections of manuscripts, titled 'Memoranda and lists of historical and geographical information', was compiled between 1789 and 1819 and shows him at times as a route surveyor and at other times as a trigonometrical map maker.[17] Some of the manuscripts, such as 'General Directions for keeping a Route', written in 1800, are representative of an older form of surveying.

The very first instruction is for the surveyor to note the direction of the road by compass from one place to another, or to 'remark the nearest object'. Distances in *kosses*, or in hours marched, were to be recorded (presumably by perambulator) and the surveyor was to note the practicability of carrying guns along the route. River crossings, access to potable water, all impediments, descriptions of every town and village passed, remarks on the wind and the weather, the composition of the soil, the variety and health of the crops, and a sketch of the journey were all to be included in the surveyor's journal and final report. This list of tasks was typical for most route surveyors. They were also expected to produce a map of their route that exemplified their perspective. This map would show, for example, the line of the march with all remarkable objects which could be seen from the road. No grid was expected, no controlling lines of latitude and longitude were to be made the focus, no stationary observation posts were to be regarded as the necessary beginning and end of the survey. Description was privileged over explanation, a potentially dangerous journey into little-known territory was transformed into a routine genre of observation, and the journey was much more important than the identification of immobile survey points. As Mackenzie commented in one of his 'hints' for military marches, 'it is supposed that much usefull [sic] information might be obtained ... by attending to objects *as they present themselves*' (emphasis added).[18] Despite the formulaic nature of the journal, the survey retained an ambling quality and a well-articulated route-survey perspective.

A surveyor who followed Mackenzie's orders would have been able to write an acceptable memoir describing how his maps were constructed.[19] But although Mackenzie was interested in gaining a sense of a surveyor's journey, he was also eager for highly detailed and systematically arranged information on localities.[20]

Mackenzie vacillated between two different perspectives on the land. As a route surveyor he favoured the descriptive, the impressionistic, the particular. Journeys connected areas and were made memorable and depictable by the remarkable objects and places along the route. A deliberate and sanctioned manner of viewing these objects transformed them into signs leading the surveyor and his team to the successful conclusion of the undertaking. But, as an advocate of trigonometrical mapping, Mackenzie also valued the explanatory, the studied, and the universal. He regarded India as having a discrete present and past, which if understood correctly could explain circumstances and inform policy. Locations were important, not as signs pointing a way, but as depositories of the past; they contained particular information which could be compared and made universally significant.

At the turn of the nineteenth century Mackenzie envisioned establishing a baseline from which a series of triangles would stretch from east to west and from north to south. These triangles would connect well-defined stations within Mysore to the surrounding provinces and countries. The advantage of triangulation over route surveying was that whereas route, or traverse, surveying required constant measurement, by means of estimation, a perambulator, or a watch, triangulation required only the careful measurement of a baseline. Knowing the exact distance of that base, which was typically several miles in length, a trigonometrical surveyor could then determine, by means of angles, the distances to any number of other points without physically having to measure the routes. It was an economy of labour and an improvement in precision. But what was gained in accuracy was lost in the quality of description. Journeys to the trigonometrical stations were of little significance so long as the angles and distances were successfully determined. Whereas Dalrymple might have regarded areas as having a 'reciprocal' quality, a trigonometrical surveyor saw locations as being discrete. As Mackenzie wrote, his geometrical survey would help to divide Mysore 'by its Provinces, or by its natural Divisions of Hills, and one portion be assigned to each assistant'.[21]

Mackenzie's ideas regarding the utility of triangulation were shared by another surveyor attached to the Madras Presidency. William Lambton, quite independently of Mackenzie, had also petitioned the Governor of Madras for the establishment of a trigonometrical surveying team. Mackenzie, who was the most senior and well-respected Presidency surveyor, endorsed Lambton's proposal, commenting that it 'agrees with an idea I have suggested'.[22] Mackenzie's term for Lambton's technique was 'spherical survey', a characterization which indicates the nature of trigonometrical surveying. Although Lambton was surveying tracts of the peninsula, his overarching concern was geodetic; he wanted to calculate the shape of the earth. Lambton was uninterested in the picturesque and disinterested in description. His journeys were so long, they were practically neverending.

Before Lambton could begin his spherical survey, however, he had to convince the Madras government to authorize the necessary expenditures. In February 1800, he submitted a detailed report, which expanded upon a letter he had written the previous year.[23] In this report, Lambton identified two utilitarian reasons for undertaking his survey—the surveyors under Mackenzie would be spared the inconvenience of precisely locating positions and the new surveys would enable the Surveyor General to combine all the various large-scale maps into one general view. 'The utility of such a work,' he boasted, 'and the advantage and information which the nation would derive therefrom, are so clearly understood that no argument is necessary to demonstrate its advantages.'[24] Nevertheless, Lambton appended a detailed plan of his proposed survey in case the Company Directors wanted to gain the advice of 'scientific men in England'. He explained that because the earth is not a perfect sphere, it was important to determine the length of a degree of latitude since that degree would differ from that of a sphere. Such knowledge would enable geographers to compute the true shape of the earth, a computation which would serve to better locate places on the globe. Realizing that his employers might wish for material results from his labours, Lambton added that his survey would 'involve many more objects than immediately appertain to Geography'.

Although the Madras government sanctioned the survey, which was to proceed across the peninsula before beginning a line of triangles northwards from Cape Comorin, the plan did have its detractors. The most vocal of these was James Rennell. His opposition to Lambton's survey is instructive since it provides an insight into the differences between old and new perspectives.

Rennell, whom a later Surveyor General termed 'the Father of Indian Geography',[25] balked at the idea of a separate survey establishment. He thought that the plans forwarded by Mackenzie and Lambton meant that their surveys would consist only of astronomical observations which would be used to correct the ongoing route surveys. He wondered why an astronomer was not simply attached to regular survey parties and termed the new idea as 'one of the most extraordinary things that has been heard of'.[26] Rennell, an exponent of an older school of surveying, misunderstood Lambton's survey. The purpose of triangulation in providing a known grid within which topographical and revenue surveyors could operate in concert, and the reason for measuring an arc of the meridian (or a degree of latitude) were not addressed by Rennell. Instead he only argued that an astronomer should accompany the surveyor and that there was no need to determine special observation points—the astronomer could conduct his work as part of the survey journey.

When Lambton received news of Rennell's criticism, he wrote to a friend in London and complained that 'the good old man' could not have read his paper, and asked him to convey to the Directors 'the magnitude and importance' of his undertaking.[27] Magnitude was indeed a good word to describe his survey. Lambton thought of his work as totalizing, subsuming all other forms of surveying. He was convinced that his surveys would enable the Surveyor General to 'exhibit under one view' all the detailed maps of the revenue surveyors. Lambton wanted to understand the shape of the earth and to establish known and incontrovertible locations on the earth which would serve as the basis for more detailed survey work and map compilation. He wanted to furnish 'permanent data' in the most 'unexceptionable manner' in order to improve the geography of India and the earth. 'For a project of such magnitude,' he wrote, 'no country in the world is so well adapted as the Peninsula. The mountains run in ranges nearly North and South. Between those ranges are vast extended plains interspersed with hills of a size to be seen at a great distance, and are mostly accessible.'[28] Lambton's approach was scientific, explanatory, permanent, and universalizing. It was also to produce the perfect and unique image of the earth, a 'Map without a parallel [sic]', as a punning high government official labelled the expected map of India.[29]

Parallels, or lines of latitude, were, of course, necessary for all trigonometrical maps. Yet the atlas maps of India which were contemplated and begun in the 1820s, and which were dependent upon the geographical data forwarded by Lambton, were indeed without an eighteenth-century rival (see Edney 1991). They were based upon distances and angles determined by triangulation, and were divided into large square areas. Little or no consideration was given to the topography of the land when deciding how to divide the maps of India into an atlas, and the data projected had none of the older descriptive and picturesque qualities. When the idea of constructing an atlas was first broached by the Company Directors, Rennell was asked his opinion on how best to conduct the necessary surveys. His memorandum, written in February 1828, two years before his death, was a plea for an older form of surveying. Rennell's celebrity among explorers and geographers was based upon his *Bengal Atlas*, which had been constructed primarily from route surveys and had adopted Mughal administrative units. In his memorandum Rennell recommended that the Company employ surveyors to rapidly map all accessible areas, paying special attention to the delineation of roads, mountains and passes, river courses, and district boundaries. While he did not advocate a rough 'military' survey, he pointedly noted that triangulation was 'out of the question'. Triangles, 'formed in a coarse way', could be used to calculate distances but were to be subsidiary to the astronomical observations and rapid surveys he was advocating. He did mention the use of squares but he did not mean the imposition onto the land of an arbitrary or mathematical category: 'For the design of apportioning the space into *equal* squares (or *any kind* of squares) does not accord with my ideas.' The squares were merely divisions to be made by the surveyors who would take topography into account. He also suggested that roads would make better boundaries than rivers, since roads were less liable to change course.

Rennell's previous objections to trigonometrical surveying and his continued enthusiasm for route surveys as a means for gathering rapid, accurate, and relatively inexpensive information, contrasts markedly with the increasingly dominant surveying paradigm. Rennell's memorandum exhibits a preoccupation with astronomy, the descriptive (how to get from A to B, rather than provide causal explanations for the length of a degree of latitude), and the picturesque (how to turn the unknown into a terrain safe for a journey). The official position, though, was written by the Surveyor General of India, V. Blacker, who, in polite terms, informed the Directors that Rennell's ideas had become unscientific: 'how unworthy of the character,

power, interests and opportunities enjoyed by the Hon'ble Company,' he wrote, 'to return to such a rude expedient, after having originated ... an operation approved by science.'[30]
Lambton's trigonometrical survey, therefore, had the mantle of science. It was explanatory (using data as a basis for determining the shape of the earth), instrumental (employing extraordinarily valuable instruments in order to further the interests of a disinterested science), and universalizing (requiring all other surveys to rely upon its results for their success). The route surveyor's supposed predilection for the rambling journey and safe arrival was precisely what Lambton and his successor, George Everest, wished to avoid.[31] Instead of being journey-like they intended their maps to be so distanced, so accurate and so scientific as to be 'the foundation of Indian geography' (Lambton 1818: 515). Rather than India as unknown and potentially dangerous, it was the trigonometrical surveyor who was the one to be feared. Everest, for instance, considered himself a 'necromancer' since it was rumoured that by the power of his theodolite he could protect his survey party from tigers, 'a notion which, of course, it would not have been politic to discourage' (Everest 1830: 40).

Conclusion: Mapping and Colonialism

Trigonometrical mapping supplanted route surveying's pre-eminence in India during the first quarter of the nineteenth century for numerous reasons. The picturesque and descriptive qualities of route surveying, although ideally suited for exploration into little-known lands and for the acquisition of trade and military information, were less appropriate to an era which was more concerned with the consolidation of power and the improvement of geographical knowledge. Moreover, there was a sense among surveyors and the Company's high bureaucracy that trigonometrical mapping would enhance the reputation of the Company as an enlightened patron because of its rigorous and scientific nature. Lambton and Everest believed their work to be a considerable improvement over the previous route surveys, and later, nineteenth-century historians of the Survey also considered the Great Trigonometrical Survey to be a sign of scientific progress. This rhetoric of scientific progress and improvement was a significant factor contributing to the character of colonial rule in India during the nineteenth century. As one of the Company's most visible and scientific departments, as a tangible sign of the supposed progress occurring under the Company's colonial rule, the Trigonometrical Survey was intimately associated with the entrenchment of colonial rule in India. The Survey not only helped the state gather information and knowledge, it also—and this was its greatest advantage over route surveys—added legitimacy to colonial rule by making it seem that this form of science in India would not only result in India's progress but would also improve geodesy.

Although science was an important component of the Company's colonial rule in India, it should not be concluded that rigorous or mathematically-based science was indispensable to colonialism more generally. The Company was fortunate that it could afford an expensive trigonometrical surveying establishment and that it had at least two accomplished surveyors (Lambton and Everest) who together spent over forty years in prosecuting the surveys. Throughout this time, there were many larger-scale, topographical surveys conducted, which were increasingly controlled by Lambton and Everest's trigonometrical stations, but which provided a steady stream of geographical information that could be more readily converted into a map. There were, therefore, particular reasons why trigonometrical surveying was supported in India.

Other colonies were not so fortunate. Ceylon, for example, had a surveying department that was woefully inadequate when compared with the Survey of India. In 1911, the Colonial Survey Committee, under the aegis of the War Office, reviewed the history of the Ceylon Survey Department and concluded that 'almost all the elements of a satisfactory condition of affairs are absent in the case of Ceylon. The triangulation is not good. There is no systematic cadastral survey ... . The topographical survey which has been in progress for three years has only resulted in the survey of 1,200 square miles of country.' The Committee traced this state of affairs to the fact that 'the Department was not originally organized on sound lines; no broad scientific principles were adopted; no general scheme which might be pursued year after year was laid down; the habit of working from hand to mouth became ingrained; the vicious system of undertaking "application" surveys has been peculiarly fatal to the efficiency of the Department; and, finally, the reports of the inspecting officers ... have been largely set aside and ignored.'[32] Yet, despite these problems and the unscientific nature of the mapping in Ceylon, the colonial government consolidated its power in the nineteenth century and survived until 1948.

The Ceylon surveys are also interesting because they provide a model for the colonial use of science and surveys that is quite different from that pursued in India. The Ceylon Survey Department was established in 1800 and by the end of the century it was one of the largest among the British colonies. Nevertheless, as the Colonial Survey Committee noted, it never instituted an island-wide and systematic trigonometrical survey; only one significant map was published in the century that was based on trigonometrical surveying, and that map was constructed by the Quartermaster General's office, not the surveying department.[33] Instead, the department faced a series of crises that rendered it ineffective as a scientific surveying department that could be compared with India's trigonometrical and topographical surveys. A lack of training and prestige for surveyors and an inundation of what the Colonial Survey Committee called 'application surveys' (more properly known as 'block surveys' in the nineteenth century), contributed to a century-long malaise within the department.

Moreover, the department was hampered by ineffective and lackadaisical leadership. From 1812 until 1833, the department was led by a Dutch officer, G. Schneider, who had remained on the island after it had been captured by the British in 1796. It appears that he spent the majority of his time tending to his seemingly more pressing duties as the island's Civil Engineer, and only drew maps of Ceylon that were copied from earlier Dutch maps.[34] The next four Surveyors General (F.B. Norris, W.H. Simms, W. Driscoll Gosset, and Charles Sim; 1833–1865) were disgraced by scandals. Norris was dismissed from his post as Civil Engineer because he failed to detect massive fraud perpetrated by his head clerk.[35] Simms was forced to resign after repeated tussles with the Governor and the Colonial Secretary.[36] And Gosset's and Sim's reputations were tarnished by their involvement in yet another embezzlement committed by the department's head clerk.[37]

The department under these heads was poorly trained and

inadequate to the task of conducting any trigonometrical survey. As Norris said about his surveyors, many of whom were Dutch 'burghers', 'such is the indolence, and the procrastinating habits of the Burgher land surveyors of this country, that it is scarcely possible to exaggerate the difficulties I have experienced in getting the most ordinary surveys from them'.[38] The greatest portion of their time was spent conducting 'block surveys'. These were surveys of Crown land, usually forest wastelands, that were auctioned in lots to villagers and to British coffee planters. The demand for Crown land was so high and the need for block surveys so pressing that systematic, or even rudimentary, trigonometrical surveys were not begun until the fourth quarter of the nineteenth century, and even then only half-heartedly.

Ceylon's experience with scientific surveys was, therefore, very different from India's. Even though both were colonies (after 1802, Ceylon became a Crown colony, when it was removed from the dual control that had seen both the Crown and the Company govern the island's maritime provinces) their use of surveyors could not have contrasted more starkly. Ceylon used its surveyors to help the cultivation of coffee; the Company in India was lucky to have both resources and talented men who wished to improve geography, further the 'progress' of India, and make a geodetic contribution to science. Thus, although the Company and the administration in Ceylon both used surveyors to facilitate colonial rule, the specifics of how that was accomplished differed in the two colonies.

Notes

1. This map was to be part of an even larger map, measuring thirty feet by twenty, but Reynolds never completed his project.
2. NAI, DDn Vol. List, Old No. 1/1, Sl. No. 64, p. 262, J. Young, Sec. to the Governor General, Mil. Dept. to Major John Craigie, officiating Sec. to the Govt. Mil. Dept., 25 October 1817.
3. These claims are discussed in detail in *Mapping an Empire: The Geographical Construction of British India* (Edney 1997).
4. For an excellent biography of Alexander Dalrymple, together with a lucid account of his publications, see Andrew S. Cook 1992.
5. See Nicholas Green, *The Spectacle of Nature*, 1990. He also points to more

specific uses of the term, noting that it sometimes referred to the private gardens of eighteenth-century aristocrats who wished to make their gardens more natural, according to Chinese or English landscape principles.

6. Other good examples of how Colebrooke used the picturesque are to be found in NAI, 'Journal of a Voyage to Pulo Penang and Sumatra', Catalogue of the Memoirs of the Survey of India, Journal 3, in which he describes how he met the king of the island which had just been ceded to the Company. Not knowing whom to expect, Colebrooke was taken aback at the fact that the fearsome king was in fact a child—'a little Fat Malay Grinning from behind a Curtain'. See also Journal 6, 'Notes on a Voyage from Calcutta to the Nicobar Island with naval Squadron. R.H. Colebrooke, 1789', especially pp. 36 and 77; and Journal 11 (M. 532), 'Journal of Col. R.H. Colebrooke in Oudh, 1807' and 'Journal of a March from Azimgurh to Allahabad, 1803–05'.

7. For an account of the circumstances surrounding Upton's march, see William Charles Macpherson 1928: 232–34. The book also includes a reproduction of Smith's map of the route.

8. W. Smith, 'A Journal of the Road, travelled by Colonel Upton, from Kalpee ... on a Deputation to Poonah ... in three Parts, Geographical, Historical, Astronomical and performed in the years 1775 and 1776'. BL Addl MSS 29213. All subsequent quotations from the journal are from this manuscript, which has no pagination.

9. For biographies of Burrow see R.H. Phillimore 1945 Vol. I, *The Dictionary of National Biography*, and E.G.R. Taylor 1966: 198–99. Burrow published a number of mathematical works in England and in India (which were included in volumes of *Asiatic Researches*), but perhaps his most entertaining publication was his almanac—*The Lady's and Gentleman's Diary or, Almanack* (Burrow 1776–79).

10. Reuben Burrow, 'Hints concerning some of the advantages derivable from an examination of the Astronomical Observatory at Benares', BL Addl MSS 29233, p. 274.

11. BL Addl MSS 29233, pp. 237–38, essay sent to Warren Hastings.

12. See, for example, his 'Remarks etc. Made in the Ganges and Burrampooter River in the latter part of the year 1787', OIOC X/520 (Map Collections—formerly MSS 5). His initial instructions for this survey were to fix the positions of the principal places along both rivers, from Hardwar to the Hugli, and from Goalpara to the Bay of Bengal. He was also required to survey the coasts of the Coromandel and Malabar, an instruction he was unable to fulfil.

13. See Isaac Dalby, 'A Short Account of the Late Mr. Reuben Burrow's Measurements of a Degree of Longitude; and another of Latitude,

near the Tropic in Bengal, in the Years 1790, 1791'—Manuscript copy in the Library of the Royal Society, Letters and Papers X 140.

14. There have been a number of excellent recent essays on Mackenzie, including 'Colonial Histories and Native Informants: Biography of an Archive', (Dirks 1993: 279–313). See also the discussion of Mackenzie's historical and ethnographic archive in Dirks 2003: 81–106. For an older biography of Mackenzie, see Mackenzie, W.C. 1952.

15. NAI, Catalogue of the Memoirs of the Survey of India, Memoir 6 (M. 130 B), Public and Official Letter Book of Supdt of Mysore Survey, 1799–1803, p. 28, Colin Mackenzie to Barry Close, 9 November 1799.

16. Of his vast and scattered collections and writings, many are in the OIOC, under the Mackenzie Collections, but the majority of his official survey writings are to be found at the NAI, under both the Catalogue of the Survey of India Collections and the Dehra Dun Volumes List.

17. OIOC, Mackenzie MSS 108, 'Memoranda and lists of historical and geographical information which Mackenzie wished to collect in various areas chiefly South India and the Deccan, but also Hindustan, c. 1789–1819'.

18. OIOC, Mackenzie MSS 108, 'Hints or Heads of Enquiry for facilitating our knowledge of the more Southerly parts of the Dekan (1800)'. Memorandum No. 5.

19. There were at least four types of account which could be written either during or after a survey. Journals and field books were usually daily diaries containing notes, angles, distances, etc., often compiled in a systematic, pre-arranged, and recognized fashion. Memoirs were commonly written after the conclusion of the survey and were intended to describe how the map was drawn. Reports were sometimes written by senior surveyors in order to arrange and explain the findings of various surveys.

20. See, for example, OIOC, Mackenzie MSS 108, 'Historical Memorandum', No. 1.

21. NAI, Catalogue of the Memoirs of the Survey of India, Memoir 6 (M. 130 B). Public and Official Letter Book of Supt Of Mysore Survey, 1799–1803, p. 29, Colin Mackenzie to Barry Close, 9 November 1799.

22. NAI, Catalogue of the Memoirs of the Survey of India, Memoir 6 (M. 130 B), p. 36, Mackenzie to Close, 6 December, 1799.

23. NAI, DDn Vol. List, Old No. 63, Sl. No. 3/1, pp. 2–14, Lambton's Letters to Government, Surveyor General, and Others, 1800–1818, 'A Plan of Mathematical and Geographical Survey proposed to be extended across the Peninsula of India under the Direction of Brigade Major Lambton. Fort St. George. 10 February 1800'.

24. NAI, DDn Vol. List, Old No. 63, Sl. No. 3/1, p. 5.

25. NAI, DDn Vol. List, Old No. SGO 58, Sl. No. 204, p. 61, V. Blacker to Lt. Col. Casement, Sec. to Government Mil. Dept., 3 March 1824.

26. NAI, DDn Vol. List, Old No. SGO 3, Sl. No. 68, p. 69, Official Letters Public and Private Orders from Government and from other Public Authorities relating to the Surveys and more particularly to the Survey of Mysore addressed to C. Mackenzie, 1799–1807, 'Copy of Major Rennell's Observations on the Plans proposed by Captain Mackenzie and Brigade Major Lambton for the Survey of Mysore'. As if this remark was not sufficiently critical, he added that a proposed plan for establishing a botanical garden at Bangalore under Mackenzie's surgeon and botanist, Benjamin Heyne, was unnecessary since all the plants to be collected 'must of course grow spontaneously in the very Country itself'.

27. Cleveland Public Library, John G. White Collection, William Lambton (1756–1823), Letters to Samuel Peach on the Capture of Seringapatam and on Trigonometrical Surveying, 1799–1802, W q091.92 L179L, 26 June 1802.

28. BL Addl MSS 13658, 'An Account of the Trigonometrical Operations carried on in the Carnatic in the years 1802 and 1803. Being a work intended to improve and correct the Geography of the Peninsula of India, by Brigadier Major William Lambton, Assisted by Lieut. Warren of H.M. 33 Regiment'.

29. NAI, DDn Vol. List, Old No. 1/5, Sl. No. 90, p. 263, 'Lambton. Letters from Government, 1800–1824', Letter J. Young, Sec. to the Governor General, Mil. Dept. to Major John Craigie, 25 October 1817.

30. NAI, DDn Vol. List, Old No. SGO 58, Sl. No. 204, p. 99, Blacker to Casement, Sec. to Government, Mil. Dept., 11 August 1824.

31. Lambton died in 1823, seven years before 'old man' Rennell.

32. Public Record Office (hereafter, PRO) WO 181/135 Document 18.

33. 'Map of the Island of Ceylon' by John Fraser and published by John Arrowsmith in 1856. See PRO CO 700/Ceylon 9. For a description of the mapping see Thomas Skinner 1995.

34. A list of Schneider's works as Surveyor General and Civil Engineer can be found at PRO CO 54/127. No. 41 of 25 February 1833. The claim that early British maps of Ceylon drawn in the island were inspired by earlier Dutch maps is to be found in R.L. Brohier 1950 Vol. II: 18.

35. PRO CO 54/270. No. 133 of 14 August 1850.

36. PRO CO 54/309. No. 57 of 21 October 1854, PRO CO 55/95. No. 88 of 4 December 1854.

37. PRO CO 54/353. No. 139 of 30 June 1860.

38. PRO CO 54/179. No. 62 of 9 April 1840, containing a letter by Norris to Skinner, 21 May 1839.

THREE

Naming Mount Everest and the Making of a Reverential History of Surveying

In 1810, James Rennell received a sketch map of a tour to the sources of the river Ganges, together with an explanatory letter, written in December 1808, by Captain Hyder Young Hearsey, although he styled himself Major.[1] He was the son of an East India Company officer and, it is thought, a Jat woman.[2] Hearsey had recently joined the Company's army having served under both the Marathas and an Irish adventurer, George Thomas, and appeared eager and able to undertake arduous military reconnaissances. His letter and map immediately attracted Rennell's attention since they seemed to answer important geographical questions which Rennell himself had addressed in his memoir and Map of Hindoostan, published nearly twenty-five years earlier (Rennell 1788).

Rennell's best source of information on the early course of the Ganges was a map published by Jean, or Johann, Bernoulli, but drawn by Anquetil du Perron from the materials of the traveller, Jesuit missionary, and noted geographer, Padre J. Tieffenthaller.[3] This map suggested that the Ganges began its journey at Gangotri, above Haridwar, a town in the foothills of the Himalayas. Tieffenthaller had visited the headwaters of the Ganges but, since he himself had not seen the source, he had to rely on a description provided by 'a *native*, of Hindoostan, we may presume' (ibid.: 354). An even earlier map was constructed by Jean D'Anville, the most respected French cartographer of the eighteenth century. This 1733 map, which was drawn for (and based upon maps transmitted by) Jesuits living in Beijing, located the source of the Ganges above Mapama lake, which was later thought to be the Mansarowar lake.[4] The problem to be solved, therefore, was that there appeared to be two possible sources of the Ganges. One was deep in the Himalayan mountains and issued out of the Mansarowar lake, a perspective depicted in numerous European maps, including D'Anville's *Carte de l'Inde* (1752), Rennell's map of Hindoostan (1782), and Arrowsmith's maps of Asia (1801) and India (1804).[5] The rival theory placed the source at Gangotri, where it appeared, to 'incurious spectators', to originate from a cavern which, according to Rennell, 'the mind of superstition' had identified as the head of a cow (Rennell 1788: 363).[6] Rennell was convinced that, despite appearances, Indians had been fooled by their incurious and superstitious nature into believing that Gangotri was the source of the Ganges. In his influential memoir, Rennell noted that 'our ignorance of this circumstance, till so very lately, is a strong presumptive proof, that there yet remains a vast field for improvement, in the geography of the eastern part of Asia' (ibid.). The ability to discriminate between credible and incredible information was necessary to successfully construct an authoritative map, and Rennell believed that not only was 'native' opinion prejudiced, but that his geographical and sociological understanding of India was sufficiently acute for him to locate the Ganges' source far beyond Gangotri. The crucial questions concerned appearance, truth, and authority—whom to believe, and why.

So when Rennell received Hearsey's letter, he immediately recognized that the map was significant—'curious' was the word he used—and he thought it merited remuneration from the Company. Hearsey was not a regular surveyor and was not entitled, therefore, to the considerable additional allowances which were given to defray the costs of a survey. Nevertheless, it was common practice for enterprising and ambitious officers to submit to the Surveyor General sketches and maps of their routes and travels. James Tod, for example, Hearsey's contemporary, drew several maps of the deserts of western India, which prompted the Surveyor General to comment that 'they will obtain you Reputation; and Wealth follows good fame as certainly as the Shadow does the substance'.[7] Hearsey no doubt hoped that Rennell would appreciate his efforts and persuade the Court of Directors to grant him a reward and publish the map. At the end of the letter Hearsey offered Rennell, as a mark of esteem, the original sheet from which copies were to be drawn.

Hearsey's letter clearly stated that the Ganges did not have its source in the Mansarowar lake, a conclusion which contradicted Rennell's map and memoir. However, Rennell thought that the map bore 'the stamp of truth' and considered forwarding it to the Directors, although he thought it 'impolitic' to publish the map, probably because of the ongoing war with France. For Rennell, the truth of Hearsey's map may have been established, in large part, by the accompanying letter, which explained the circumstances of the map's construction. In his letter, Hearsey was effusive in his descriptions of the people they encountered—the men, for example, were 'florid in their complexions, middling sized, but sturdily made'— and he was particularly sensitive to the political ramifications of the journey, noting in great detail the various hostile reactions he prompted. These seemingly accurate observations lent credibility and veracity to the map. Hearsey, however, was noticeably laconic regarding the geography of the region, presumably because he hoped the map would speak for itself, needing only a political and anthropological commentary.

Thinking the map 'a meritorious act' Rennell transmitted it to the directors. However, a problem soon arose. It appeared that Hearsey had plagiarized the map; the sketch he presented to Rennell had been stolen from Lt. W.S. Webb, the leader of the survey party, while the latter was ill after the journey. Webb was indignant when he found out and he complained that his companion had accomplished very little on the journey, having neither mathematical nor astronomical ability. Hearsey only drew three or four views, shaded a few of Webb's maps, and inserted the names of places. 'He certainly while with us never kept a Field Book, or made a single Celestial Observation.'[8] As soon as Rennell heard that he had been duped, he rushed a letter to his employers begging them to forgive his mistake, arguing that 'no Blame may attach to me, who only intended to do a just act'. But the damage had been done and Rennell, considered the world's greatest geographer of India, had been fooled.

This episode raises some intriguing questions and concerns regarding both the veracity of surveyors and the authority of maps.

What is it about maps that makes them believable? How do surveyors convince their audience that the information they present is unexceptionable, trustworthy, even true? This chapter will not detail the scientific criteria expected of cartographers and surveying organizations in order to ascertain the value of a map, although, of course, reference will be made to some of their usual requirements. Instead, the focus will be on how surveyors seek to encourage a sympathetic response and a faithful adherence to common perspectives by both writing the history of a name and appealing to the authority of a name. The creation of a reverential cartographic history during the mid-to-late nineteenth century permitted the colonial state to congratulate itself on its superior scientific approaches and demonstrate the need for and legitimacy of a British scientific presence in India. This chapter examines in detail the controversies surrounding the naming of Mount Everest in the mid-1850s, and then follows the debates around it through the 1880s and up to 1931, when the Survey of India published what it believed to be the definitive paper on the subject. My core argument is that the naming of a mountain after a surveyor, or the making of a reverential cartographic history, was an important means by which truth, recognition, and authority were established and maintained. At the same time, however, naming was also a way of hiding truth, imposing recognition, and obscuring authority.

Hearsey's journey to the source of the Ganges was one of the most anticipated Company surveys and it provides an entrée into the problems of establishing cartographic truth that will be examined closely when we turn to the naming of Mount Everest.[9] The difficulties of finding the source of the river did not end with Rennell's letter to the Directors of the Company. Hearsey had relied on a conventional narrative in order to present another's work as his own. As Rennell complained to the Directors, internal evidence did not contradict Hearsey's claim to be the sole author. That, indeed, is one of the focuses of the chapter—the beguiling manner in which surveyors or the Survey of India appropriated ownership and authority, while eliding or discounting others' perspectives. Hearsey, for example, thanked Webb for the latitudes of places, a disingenuous move since it was Webb's map which had been copied. The implication, nevertheless, was that the map was Hearsey's. Rennell might also have been inclined to think that he was being presented with an original and unique work since Hearsey noted, towards the end of his letter, that although Captain F.V. Raper, who was the third companion on the journey up the Ganges, had given R.H. Colebrooke, the recently deceased Surveyor General, a manuscript, it was likely to 'fall into Hands whose curiosity will not induce them to peruse it or indolence permit them to publish'. In addition to the fact that it was improbable that the effects and papers of the notoriously untidy Colebrooke would ever be sorted, let alone published, it perhaps seemed unlikely to Hearsey that Raper would even live to testify to the truth of their trip since he had been ordered to accompany the Company's embassy to Kabul.[10]

Nevertheless, ten years after the journey towards the source of the Ganges, Raper's account was published in *Asiatic Researches* (1979). His narrative was preceded by an essay on the reasons for the survey, written by the late Surveyor General's Orientalist brother, H.T. Colebrooke (1979). Raper's essay was a lengthy version of Hearsey's account; the geographical information in it was scarce while emphasis was placed on describing political intrigues, the customs of local villagers, religious festivals and gatherings, and the articles and manner of trade. Raper acknowledged that the survey party never reached Gangotri but instead sent 'Captain Hearsay's [sic] moonshee, a very intelligent man' to investigate. It is upon his word that the surveyors concluded that the source of the Ganges was 'situated in the snowy range' and not at some lake on the other side of the mountains, from which it was said to flow through the Himalayas and emerge through a cavern's opening, known as the Cow's Mouth. 'With respect to the *Cow's Mouth*,' he wrote, 'its existence is entirely fabulous, and that it is found only in the *Hindu* book of faith' (Raper 1979: 482). Raper's dismissal of Hindu writings but his complete reliance upon and trust in the Hindu explorer suggests that truth is more often asserted than proved. The *munshi*, by association with Hearsey, was trustworthy, but we know that Hearsey himself was hardly the paragon of honesty (see Phillimore 1950 Vol. II: 404–5 for biographical details).

H.T. Colebrooke praised the surveyors' efforts, noting that the results of the journey were 'conclusive', with no doubt remaining as to the source of the Ganges (1979: 444). As well as receiving

Colebrooke's approbation, Raper's essay also attracted literary notice. *The Quarterly Review,* for example, devoted nearly forty pages of commentary on Himalayan explorations, including an appreciative review of Raper's narrative.[11] As has been mentioned, Raper accompanied Webb and based his narrative, in part, on Webb's survey. Certainly, Webb was the officer in charge of the party and responsible for the geographical determinations—conclusions which Colebrooke, the editors of *Asiatic Researches,* and the anonymous reviewer in *The Quarterly Review,* all considered to be correct and conclusive.

Such success, however, masked the fact that the survey was hurried, incomplete, and, on the basis of the instructions given to Webb, a failure. Raper did, in fact, include in his narrative a version of Webb's instructions, although he omitted two of the ten orders and modified the wording in others.[12] Moreover, most of the instructions, even those Raper communicated to the journal, were not fulfilled. The first two instructions, for example, clearly stated that the principal object was 'to survey the Ganges from Hurdwar to Gangoutri' and there to determine whether the Ganges originated at that spot or beyond. The survey party never reached Gangotri and relied on the *munshi*'s testimony to answer the journey's most important question.

There were, however, other, less obvious problems with the survey. When the new Surveyor General, John Garstin, received Webb's field book, the protraction of the survey, and Raper's journal, he rebuked Webb for a series of blunders and amateurish practices— Webb's map sheets were not numbered; there was no general scale, meaning distances could only be guessed; it appeared as if the sheets were drawn in two different scales; there were no bearings or height calculations for remarkable peaks; and there were no barometrical observations to determine altitude.[13] All of these omissions, except the obvious need to number map sheets, had been explicitly mentioned as important tasks in the instructions sent to Webb. In his reply, Webb was contrite, regretting that his preparations 'were so unavoidably hurried' that he was obliged to set out without a chronometer, astronomical telescope, or barometer, 'supplied with which, I might have been enabled to finish something more like a correct Survey than the imperfect Itinerary I have forwarded'.[14]

Such imperfections were hardly noticeable in Raper's narrative, Colebrooke's essay, or the London review. To them and, no doubt, to a general public, the journey was an outstanding example of a successful survey; an intrepid expedition had resolved a century-long controversy by conclusively determining that the Ganges did not pass through the Himalayas and emerge through a cavern which resembled a cow's mouth. Three years later, however, two new versions of the Ganges' source were written by men who claimed to have travelled up to the point where the Ganges becomes snow. The first was by James Baillie Fraser (1820) the second by a future Surveyor General, J.A. Hodgson.[15] Hodgson waxed poetical about the landscape and asserted that the point where the river flows from under an arch of snow did indeed strongly resemble a cow's mouth. 'I cannot think of any place,' he wrote, 'to which they might more aptly give the name of a Cow's Mouth, than to this extraordinary *Debouche*.' But while Hodgson might have rehabilitated Hindu texts in the eyes of European readers, others questioned the veracity of Hearsey's *munshi*, the very man on whose testimony the whole of Webb's survey rested. *The Quarterly Review*, following Fraser, chose to shift the focus—and the blame for any misrepresentation—away from Webb and his companions and onto the *munshi*, stating that not only was his description of the cow's mouth 'pure fiction', but that his general account 'affords such a singular mixture of truth and falsehood, authenticity, and error, as to create a doubt whether he really proceeded as far as Gangotrée or not'.[16] So, while the *munshi*'s veracity was now suspect, Webb and Raper were still not suspected of incompetence; it was the *munshi*'s fault for not having reached Gangotri but it was entirely understandable that Webb had been unable to travel beyond the spot which had, to use *The Quarterly Review*'s term, 'arrested' his progress.

The point of this introduction is not to rehearse the possibilities for the true source of the Ganges.[17] The central question concerns the establishment and acceptance of geographical truth. Rennell had believed Hearsey's representations that his sketch of the Ganges was his own work, when in fact the map had been plagiarized. Raper's narrative was published in the renowned *Asiatic Researches*, the foremost academic journal on Indian affairs, and H.T. Colebrooke, a celebrated scholar, wrote a prefatory letter in which he praised

Raper's account. But Raper had based his paper on the results of Webb's survey, which not only had failed to reach the source but had drawn the severe criticism and censure of the Surveyor General, who was astonished at Webb's unprofessional conduct. Such was the authority of Raper's narrative, however, that *The Quarterly Review* published a glowing account of the journey, which never doubted the author's honesty and accuracy even when, several years later, new reports contradicted many of Raper's assertions.

This early-nineteenth-century journey to the source of the Ganges introduces questions of truth and credibility in geographical narratives and observations. These men's accounts were seen to be authoritative for a combination of reasons—the maps or journals seemed to conform to expectations of style or presentation; the authors were seemingly respectable and trustworthy; and they were thought to be good interpreters of 'native' observation. By the mid-nineteenth century the Survey of India boosted its scientific authority and public visibility by attaching the name of its retired head to a Himalayan mountain that was beyond the boundaries of colonial India. This decision to name the mountain after a trigonometrical surveyor who, it was thought, exemplified ideal principals and behaviour, reinforced colonial cultural, scientific, and political authority.

The reverence paid to Everest suggested that the mountain was a symbol of the superiority of modern scientific method. Moreover, since Everest was British, the naming of Peak XV was also a celebration of British scientific achievement and political supremacy. The reverential use of Everest aided in creating a perspective which seemed true and accurate, systematic and complete. Such certainty, however, was accomplished through the extrusion of other perspectives, other names, other conceptions of truth and knowledge. And thus, while one of the Survey of India's proudest claims was to have found true knowledge by means of robust activity, perception, and observation, it was also, like Hearsey's claim to Rennell at the beginning of the century, a charlatan's boast. The Survey's pronouncement that there were no local names for a specific peak that it wished to name after a revered man did not go unchallenged. The debate focused attention on the credibility and authority of the Survey, with the Survey claiming that its manner of observation and identification, once advocated by George Everest, made its use of a British name appropriate.

Thirty years later, when the debate over the naming of Mount Everest resurfaced, the major change that had occurred was that instead of reflecting British scientific and political success, the name was stripped of much of its national and personal connotations. Instead, the Survey of India argued that the non-local name reflected the notion that the mountain belonged to no particular nation, while many of the Survey's opponents felt that now that the name was no longer a direct celebration of either man or nation, the name Mount Everest was incongruous.

In recent years, historians have provided summaries of how Mount Everest came to be named (see Keay 2000, Phillimore 1968, Smith, J.R. 1999). R.H. Phillimore's treatment of the subject is unfortunately in a volume that has been suppressed by the Government of India and is therefore difficult to find.[18] Although he provides little analysis, the strength of his contribution is his bibliography. Two other historians, J.R. Smith and John Keay, sketch the narrative of the naming but also enter the debate with their own conclusions as to the appropriateness of the name Mount Everest. Smith, for example, ends his outline by noting that 'the time has surely come to resist more alternatives and accept "Everest" as the English language version', and argues that even if different names are used in other languages, they must not exclude the use of Everest (1999: 224). John Keay concentrates much of his attention on the character and surveying activities of both William Lambton and George Everest. He admits that during the course of his research he became 'obsessed by the sheer audacity of the (surveying) enterprise' and suggests that even if the surveyors' efforts seem remote and inconsequential now, a reader need only 'get up close ... breathe the sharp air and sense the monstrous presumption, and the Arc like the mountain soars imperiously to dwarf all else' (Keay 2000: xxi). Keay is at pains to show how Lambton's surveys and Everest's measurements were both exciting and exceptional but he devotes only the last few pages of his book to the naming of Peak XV. While he does briefly indicate that there were disagreements over naming it Mount Everest, he notes that 'when the name was again questioned, the logic of sticking with it was stronger than ever', suggesting that the name 'has a ring of permanence, an aura of assurance' (Keay 2000: 170–1). The question, therefore, has not disappeared even after one-and-a-half centuries. However, if we return to the origins of the debate, a historical context can be established to help explain why the name Everest was first proposed for the mountain and why it survived despite the appearance of other, more local alternatives.

Himalayan Discovery and British Naming

The heights of the Himalayas had long been a subject of debate. W.S. Webb, for example, declared in 1818 that 'the extreme height of the *Himalaya* is yet a desideratum', while, even earlier, Sir William Jones had been curious to measure the peaks (cited in Colebrooke, H.T. 1979: 444). Hodgson, the first surveyor who claimed to have reached the source of the Ganges, was also attracted by the Himalayas. Determining the heights of various peaks became an obsession with the surveyors, including Webb and Hodgson, who were instructed to map the newly conquered hills in northern India and southern Nepal. In fact, Hodgson was so keen to approach the Himalayas that he informed his superior of his hope to calculate the heights and distances of the mountains 'when we have possession of the Ranges of Mountains South of the Himalaya'.[19]

Hodgson's mercurial and frank nature enlivens his letters. He detested John Garstin, the Surveyor General, declaring that he was 'equally contemptible in his professional and private Character'.[20] His journals are also full of lively description and metaphor, and he never missed an opportunity to express his awe and astonishment at the height and magnificence of the Himalayas. While on his survey to the source of the Ganges, when he had passed Gangotri, he noticed before him a mountain with four peaks—'the grandest and most splendid object the eye of man ever beheld.'[21] Although the mountain, which he asserted was neither known nor named, appeared so inhospitable that 'a Pagan might aptly imagine the place a fit abode for demons', he assumed the 'privilege of navigators' and named the peaks St George, St Patrick, St Andrew, and St David. He called the mountain the Four Saints.

Naming is a parental prerogative, conveying both a sense of

ownership and an acknowledgment of responsibility. And yet, even though Hodgson wanted the East India Company to conquer the Nepalese and take possession of the Himalayas, his naming of the Four Saints was as much a gesture of humility as it was a self-referential sign of discovery and ownership. There seems to be an unresolved tension in the naming of a mountain. On the one hand, the namer asserts control and, to use Hodgson's term, privileges over the mountain, but, on the other hand, by naming the mountain after saints, for example, Hodgson intended to honour a more powerful and influential force than himself. Thus, acclaim is requested and authority is asserted by Hodgson's seemingly self-effacing naming of a 'discovered' mountain.

Such a rhetorical move implies that there is some quality to the mountain which is exceptional, or unique, or worthy of being named *in honour of someone* completely unconnected with the mountain. In fact, Hodgson believed that the physical aspect of the peaks suggested that they were hardly suitable homes for saints and yet, despite that incongruity, he nevertheless though it appropriate to name them so. Why should Hodgson have felt a need to name peaks which he assumed had never previously been seen, let alone named? Why did he think that others would agree with his choice of names? What, indeed, did it mean for Hodgson to name those 'demonic' peaks, which rise above one of Hinduism's most holy sites, after Christian saints? But perhaps the most important question is: Who or what was the subject of the naming—the saints, the peaks, or Hodgson?

Although the naming of a mountain appears to be a straightforward and immediate assertion of ownership and authority, there is little that is straightforward in the naming of Himalayan mountains. For instance, in naming the four peaks after Christian saints, Hodgson was using incongruity as a way of lauding a spiritual force. He was also deprecating and disempowering the demonic physical terrain around him, which he found so overwhelming and threatening. Last, he was also inserting his own figure into an area to which he did not belong. Unlike the naming of a child, where there is usually an intimate physical connection, Hodgson's naming gained its initial force from both his own foreignness to the location and the incongruity in his choice of names.

Although Hodgson did not name the mountain in jest, his names failed to last beyond his journey. This may have been due, in part, to the fact that he recorded his names in a journal which was never published or it may have been that his names were thought to be inappropriate and incapable of conveying the true nature of the mountain and its peaks. Nevertheless, his early attempt to name an Indian mountain raises questions that find a parallel with the later naming of Mount Everest. What did it mean, in a nineteenth-century colonial context, to give a Himalayan mountain a foreign name? How was appropriateness gauged in matters of naming? And how did the Survey of India, a scientific organization preoccupied with the principles of accuracy and verification, present its choice of names as natural and suitable?

Another reason why Hodgson's names did not last may have been because it had long been a rule of the department of survey that surveyors would assign to every location 'its true local or native appellation' (see Waugh 1857: 301). This rule, however, had been broken on previous occasions. In 1849, for example, seven years before the naming of Mount Everest, the name of Drummondgunj was chosen for a range of hills to the north of Rewah. The range had been variously called the Rewah, Kaimor, and Drummondgunj hills, but since Rewah referred to a location and Kaimor to a range, both far to the south of the hills, the Surveyor General, Andrew Waugh, decided on Drummondgunj, a market town named after an Englishman. Waugh's decision was reinforced by reports that there was no 'recognised name in use among learned native Geographers', which meant that it was difficult to describe and identify the hills properly.[22]

The one notable departure from the official policy regarding naming occurred in 1856, when Waugh decided to name Peak XV— the temporary number assigned to a large peak east of Kathmandu— Mount Everest. The naming caused considerable debate on the appropriateness of assigning a foreign name to a Himalayan mountain, a debate which lasted well into the twentieth century.

Waugh's decision to name the mountain should be placed in a historical context. Associating names with places—a form of geographical interpretation—had always been an important aspect of a surveyor's work. However, by the mid-nineteenth century, Waugh understood that a shift in emphasis had occurred following the publication of Rennell's maps. The changing military, revenue, and administrative needs, combined with a greater geographical knowledge of India, had meant that the Survey felt the pressure to insert more and more names into their maps. This change is reflected in a letter Waugh wrote to his deputy, Major H.L. Thuillier, in 1858. In the letter Waugh criticized maps of the country bordering the Great Trunk Road, which had been lithographed by Thuillier and were soon to be sold to the public.[23] Although the criticisms were not offered in a 'captious spirit'—after all, Waugh wrote, 'there are spots on the sun itself'—they were intended to impress upon his subordinates that names of villages and towns had become of greater concern to the public than the names of territories. Maps, he wrote, should not be crowded with unnecessary names and that it was unfortunate that, according to cartographic tradition, the names of provinces, zillas, districts, parganas, etc., should be 'printed in large letters, spread across the space they refer to'. He claimed that in maps where territories were of paramount significance, names interlaced with each other, crossing over the names of villages 'which are thereby either obliterated, or confused'. Waugh argued that the Survey should no longer place such emphasis on territorial divisions, which he believed were usually named after a principal town, but should instead focus on inserting into its maps as many names of villages and towns as possible. Moreover, rather than printing the names in a fashion which might, for example, follow the contours of a mountain range, he wanted all writing to conform to the map's lines of longitude and latitude, although he admitted that the names of rivers would necessarily meander. 'As this idea is an innovation on established practice,' Waugh noted, 'it will no doubt prove distasteful at first.' Yet at a time when the British were still struggling to pacify mutinous troops and tax a hostile countryside, Waugh recognized that his office had to name those very ordinary villages which were the sites of war and revenue, in such a way that they became readable, visible, even remarkable.[24]

Waugh's policies were consistent with European trends that saw the ordered insertion into maps of increasing numbers of names. Even in areas that were poorly known by the Survey, such as the Himalayan mountains lying beyond British-controlled territory, Waugh's surveyors assigned either names or numbers to peaks whose heights had been calculated trigonometrically. Many peaks were given Roman numerals by the surveyors, who.were unable to determine what their local names might be. One such peak was known as Peak XV. Peak XV was the only Himalayan mountain given a British name by Waugh. The first official indication that the mountain was to be named after George Everest occurs in a letter, dated March 1856, from Waugh to his deputy, H.L. Thuillier.[25] Soon afterwards, Thuillier informed the Asiatic Society of Bengal that the Survey had concluded that Peak XV, at 29,002 feet, was the highest mountain in the world, exceeding Kanchenjunga and Dhaulagiri, the two mountains which had long been considered the world's highest.[26] In his speech before the society, Thuillier noted that in this instance the department was deviating from its usual practice of giving an indigenous name to every geographical object since the peak was 'without any local name, that he (Waugh) could discover'. In a gesture reminiscent of Hodgson, the Surveyor General assigned to the peak

a name whereby it may be known among geographers, and become a household word among civilised nations, and in virtue of this privilege and in testimony of his affectionate respect for a revered chief ... and to perpetuate the memory of that illustrious master of accurate research, he had determined to name this noble peak of the Himalayas 'Mont Everest'.[27]

Thus, Mont Everest was named in order to honour a retired Surveyor General of India and to direct 'civilized' attention to the achievements of the Indian departments of survey. But why should the name Everest make the mountain a household word? Prior to the peak's measurement, Kanchenjunga was considered the tallest mountain in the world, yet few had known of its existence. What did Waugh see in the name Everest which would distinguish both the mountain and his department? Why not call the mountain Mont Rennell or Mont Clive, names which would have been far more familiar to Europeans than Everest? Even Everest was unimpressed with the honour; he announced to the Royal Geographical Society that his name 'was not pronounceable by a native of India'. The name could not be written in either Persian or Hindi and, as the secretary of the society wrote, 'it would be confounded with that of O'Brien, and the hill people would probably call this mountain Ob'ron'.[28] In his fear that his English name would be transformed into a parody of an Irish name, Everest was expressing a larger concern that names should be appropriate.

Despite Everest's protests, Waugh refused to rename the mountain, although 'Mont' was soon altered to 'Mount'. One of Waugh's concerns was that the new name should be recognized—understood and accepted—by Europeans. Indeed, professional and public reaction to the name was generally positive, although a former Company Resident at Kathmandu, B.H. Hodgson (not to be confused with J.A. Hodgson, the former Surveyor General), suggested that Peak XV did have Nepali and Tibetan names. Many of those who favoured Waugh's choice of name remarked that it was appropriate because it was English, and therefore pronounceable, and because it reflected scientific triumph. J.F. Tennant, for example, a young survey officer, wrote that it would be inadvisable 'to abandon this definite name, which will soon be familiar to every English or European child, for one of the—to Europeans,—unpronounceable names given by Mr. Hodgson, whose application is, to say the least, extremely doubtful, and whose misapplication would cause endless confusion'.[29] So while Everest was worried that his name would be mangled by Indians, Tennant was concerned that a local name would prove a tongue-twister to Europeans. Moreover, Tennant thought that no local name could be more appropriate than the name Everest. This sentiment was echoed by Roderick Murchison, president of the Royal Geographical Society, who argued that even though the peak may have an Indian name, 'a more appropriate name could not be given than that of Mount Everest'.[30] Even the non-scientific community voiced support; an American traveller was overheard saying that 'Mount Everest is the most beautiful name in geography, it is suggestive of perfect solitude' (Burrard 1931: 16).

George Everest was indeed a solitary figure.[31] He had been Surveyor General of India and Superintendent of the Trigonometrical Survey, and was known for his zealous prosecution of trigonometrical mapping. He was often cold, aloof, and quick to temper. In a letter to one of his assistants, for example, he complained that the valuable blue lights used for night surveying were being wasted: 'you will not abide by my orders, but—pell mell—helter skelter—foul or fair—away go to damnation and destruction the only means we have of getting through our work. You all seem to me to be right stark—staring—mad' (Phillimore 1958 Vol. IV: 434). While Everest might have been a mordant critic and exacting supervisor, he headed a department which prided itself on being a model of modern science. Trigonometrical surveying had been introduced in India in a systematic fashion by Everest's predecessor, William Lambton. As discussed in the previous chapter, trigonometrical mapping replaced the tactile and sinuous nature of the route survey map with a more rigid and mathematically precise representation. When Lambton died, Everest became both Superintendent of the Great Trigono-metrical Survey and Surveyor General of India (it was not until the 1870s that all departments of survey—the trigonometrical, the topographical, and revenue—were combined under one Survey of India department). Both Lambton and Everest understood that the advantage of trigonometrical mapping lay in the fact that locations were accurately fixed and known. Whereas route or traverse surveys enabled a map maker to depict topographical features on a large scale, trigonometrical mapping permitted accurate topographical surveys. By knowing the precise locations of fixed, visible, and prede-termined sites, a topographical surveyor could proceed to position roads, villages, or lakes within an area which was enclosed by known lines of longitude and latitude. In other words, the object of travel-ling to a place was less important to trigonometrical surveyors than the object of knowing the exact location of that place. It was Ever-est's obsession with both location and precision of vision which prompted Waugh to attach his name to Peak XV. The irony, of course, is that the reason why the name of Mount Everest was not changed was that no one could prove to the Survey's satisfaction that the many alternative local names submitted by B.H. Hodgson and others actually identified and designated Peak XV.

However, when Waugh chose to honour his former supervisor, he gave three reasons why Everest was an appropriate name for Peak XV—the name was memorable, it honoured a 'revered chief', and it strengthened the memory of a 'master of accurate research'. All these reasons had, at their base, the recognition that Everest, despite his difficult personality, embodied scientific rigour, exploration, and zeal. He had suffered long bouts of illness while engaged in making the most minute observations, and his struggles against hostile forces and elements, together with his efforts to map India in a highly specialized and intricate manner, had ensured that his name, when recognized, was always associated with British imperial scientific endeavour.

Waugh thus chose to name the peak as much in recognition of a scientific method as in honour of an individual. In his letter to the Royal Geographical Society, Waugh included the comparative tables of observations and heights for the four highest Himalayan peaks. The height of Everest, a verifiable and permanent figure, was also the benchmark by which to judge the Survey and its trigono-metrical perspective. When Waugh retired in 1861, his farewell speech reflected his pride in the achievements of the department: 'The almost impossible barriers of the greatest mountain range in the World, covered with perennial snow, has been unable to arrest the progress of the work'.[32] Mount Everest was the supreme testa-ment to the 'efforts of British energy'.

Once before, however, Everest had seen his name, or rather his title, appropriated. In 1838, thirty-eight Fellows of the Royal Society had urged the Court of Directors of the East India Company to appoint Major T.B. Jervis to the position of Surveyor General, even though Everest still occupied that post at the time. Everest wrote a blistering and embittered response (1839: 5) to the president of the Society, in which he quoted Shylock, the merchant of Venice.

Who steals my purse steals trash; 'tis something, nothing,
'Twas mine, 'tis his, and has been slave to thousands;
But he who filches from me my good name,
Robs me of that which not enriches him,
And makes me poor indeed.

Everest, impoverished once, was now to witness his name become again the subject of great controversy.

The debate over the name Mount Everest began with a question of appropriateness. Waugh himself used the word when defending his choice; in a letter to the department's chief computer, Radhanath Sickdhar (also spelled Sikhdar and Shiqdar; see Raj 2003: 42), Waugh thanked him for his support in this matter and informed him that there had been 'no alternative but to assign an appropriate name'. To have done otherwise would have created confusion and 'stamped it as an insignificant nameless peak'.[33] For Waugh, therefore, what was appropriate was that which was clear and aggrandizing. Waugh's decision received wide support. Even the Court of Directors, two years before their own abolition, conveyed their approval to the Surveyor General.[34] However, as soon as Major Thuillier had announced the new name to the Asiatic Society of Bengal, Brian Houghton Hodgson wrote a letter of complaint, alarmed by Waugh's claim that Peak XV had no local name.[35] In fact, Hodgson argued, the peak had two names, Deodhunga, or holy hill, ('Mons Sacer in Latin', as he explained), and Bhairavathan. As proof, Hodgson pointed to a paper he had submitted to the Asiatic Society entitled 'Route from Kathmandu to Darjeeling' to which he had appended a 'Memorandum relative to the seven Cosis'. In this memorandum, Hodgson had written that one of the Kosi rivers has its source at 'Deodhunga, a vast Himalayan peak, situated sixty or seventy miles east of Gosain-than ... being probably the nameless peak which Colonel Waugh conjectures may rival Kangchanjunga in height' (Hodgson 1880: 207). Hodgson claimed that his association of Deodhunga with Peak XV was further proved by a sketch map which accompanied his memorandum. In this map Deodhunga had been 'set down, eo nomine', at the peak's location in 86 East longitude. The proof provided by the map was that by following the Bhotia Kosi to its source, a reader would encounter a darkly shaded mass located east of the mountain Gosainthan. Nevertheless, Hodgson was adamant that the peak had two Nepali names, although he was not sure which name was more common. He concluded his argument with an emotional appeal that it would have been 'a strange circumstance' if such a 'remarkable' peak had escaped local notice. 'Nor would it have been very creditable to me,' he added, 'after 20 years' residence in Nepal, had I been unable to identify that object.'

Hodgson's claim that the local name of Deodhunga had already been published by the Asiatic Society contained within it an accusation that Waugh had either ignored available evidence or failed to conduct the 'exhaustive enquiry' which many assumed had been undertaken.[36] Moreover, Hodgson wished to introduce another debate into the controversy over Mount Everest. For many years he had been the Company's Resident at Kathmandu and had nurtured various schemes for the extension of European colonization; he wished to see Europeans establishing farms in the foothills of the Himalayas.[37] He had also stimulated the commercial cultivation of tea by planting his own bushes at the Residency in Kathmandu. However, Hodgson was equally well known for his staunch advocacy of 'vernacular' languages (see Hunter 1896: 310–11, also, Hodgson 1837). During the contentious debates of the 1830s, Hodgson had sided with H.H. Wilson, H.T. Prinsep, and John Russell Colvin. Together they had argued successfully against propositions made by Charles Trevelyan and Thomas Macaulay for the rapid adoption of English as the language of Indian education. Hodgson encouraged the government not to impose English as the medium of education but instead support education conducted in regional Indian languages. Hodgson had himself frequently published articles on north Indian languages and had contributed vocabularies of tribal and 'aborigine' languages to the journals of several societies.

Hodgson's involvement in the language debate twenty years' earlier no doubt informed his ideas concerning the naming of Peak XV. However, Hodgson was also known as 'the best living authority' on the geography of Nepal and had published many articles on the Himalayas.[38] He was persistent in his claim that Nepali names did exist for the peak and again pressed the point in a paper he submitted to the *Journal of the Asiatic Society of Bengal* (1856: 473–86, also in Hodgson 1880: 167–90). In the essay Hodgson introduced yet another variation on the name of Peak XV—Bhairava Langur. He explained that Nepalese embassies on their way to China reported the position of a mountain pass known by this name, which corresponded to the location of Colonel Waugh's Mount Everest. He reminded his readers that it was common for the Nepalese to 'blend' the meanings of peaks and passes, and that in this case, the peak was known by its pass, or 'langur'. Hodgson also insisted that the Tibetans designated the mountain 'Gnalham thangla', or 'pass of the plain' (of Tingri), but would often omit Gnalham, which designated the peak as opposed to the pass (1856: 479). Hodgson, therefore, was eager to demonstrate that even though the Tibetans and the Nepalese might at times place more emphasis on identifying the names of passes, they were either conflated with or derived from the names of the adjacent peaks. Finally, Hodgson threw down the gauntlet; the Surveyor General, he asserted, 'may be assured that his Mount Everest is far from lacking native names, and, I will add that I would venture in *any* case of a signal natural object occurring in Nepal to furnish the Colonel with its true native name (nay, several, for the country is very polyglottic)' (ibid.).

Indeed, Hodgson had furnished four local names for Waugh's 'unnamed' Mount Everest: Deodhunga, Bhairavthan, Bhairava Langur, and Gnalham Thangla. But who or what was to say that his names were more appropriate than Waugh's? The problem for both men was that no European had travelled to the peak. The Survey had determined its height and position based on a series of triangulations from positions outside Nepalese territory. Hodgson himself admitted that he had never visited the mountain, although he had twice approached the vicinity. Both men, therefore, had the difficulty of persuading a reading and interested European public that their interpretations and perspectives were correct. The principal forums for their debates were the journals of the Asiatic Society of Bengal and the Royal Geographical Society, and the weight and authority of each society was considered crucial for deciding the dispute. While it seemed that the Royal Geographical Society had accepted Waugh's choice and had conferred on him the Royal Award for the Encouragement of Geographical Science and Discovery,[39] the Royal Asiatic Society, on the other hand, had voted unanimously in support of Hodgson. The battle had been joined.

Hodgson's claims to the truth of his names rested on descriptions by Nepalese of a 'snowy mass' which, although visible from Nepal proper (the valley) and from Sikkim, had never been visited or observed closely by Europeans. Moreover, Hodgson also relied on testimony that this mountain peak and pass had no competitor in the immediate region, suggesting that it was fair to assume that the local names accurately designated and even described Peak XV. There are many parallels here to the earlier debate over the true source of the river Ganges. Who should the public believe, and why? Hodgson argued that his many years as Resident in Kathmandu enabled him to interpret Nepalese observations correctly. His reliance on others' descriptions of physical characteristics led him to believe that truth lay in *interpreted* observation.

Hodgson's interpretations of 'native' observations challenged the truth of Waugh's *mediated* observations. For Waugh, scientific observation, invariably involving the use of trigonometrical practices, meant the extrusion of local designations. At this early stage of the debate over the name of Peak XV, Hodgson pointed to visible characteristics as proof of identification while Waugh maintained that the verification of the peak could only be accomplished from the Survey's trigonometrical stations, located in Company territory. Since no European had visited Peak XV, identification became the key for determining whether a certain name was appropriate.

This point was reinforced in a letter Waugh sent to the Asiatic Society of Bengal in August, 1857.[40] The letter is particularly interesting since it was Waugh's attempt to refute Hodgson's claims by shifting the focus of attention away from the possibility of there being local names and towards the problem of correctly identifying the peak. For Waugh the difficulty to be overcome was that of classification—finding a principle of identification whereby each mountain could be recognized as unique, independent, and remarkable. Towards this goal, Waugh hoped to establish a method, verifiable by means of trigonometrical experiment, whereby a mountain's intrinsic qualities were clearly identified. Structure, position, and above all, height, were aspects which could be tested and would provide invariable results. 'All these data,' Waugh noted, 'are elements necessary to the identification of that mountain.'[41]

Waugh thought that Everest was an appropriate name since it reflected the principles used in the mountain's identification. In his August letter to the Asiatic Society, Waugh characterized Hodgson's claims as 'palpably conjectural, resting on hearsay evidence alone'.[42] Waugh was at great pains to make two important points. The first was that, for him, the debate was not over whether Everest should be used in place of Deodhunga, or any other 'true native name'—Waugh admitted the principle of assigning a local name over a foreign name—but whether Deodhunga was, in fact, the correct 'native' name for that particular mountain. The second point was that the 'physiognomical contour' of a mountain, as reported by 'natives unable to determine the actual height of a mountain', was a poor proof of identification. In other words, Waugh attempted to turn the tables on Hodgson; instead of admitting that Everest was inappropriate, especially since those who lived near the mountain had reported several names for both the peak and the pass, Waugh asserted that the name Deodhunga was itself inappropriate since it most likely referred to another mountain in the vicinity. Waugh even went so far as to suggest that the name might be attributed to the Survey's Peak XIII, located a little to the south-east of Peak XV. In dismissing Hodgson's proof as hearsay evidence, Waugh ended his letter with a statement that the 'reckless' adoption of the name Deodhunga would 'violate every principle of accuracy and precision laid down by my predecessor'.[43]

Waugh wrote with such confidence and authority because he had just received four letters from subordinate officers in his department, all supporting his choice of Everest—or, rather, all dismissing Hodgson's identification of Deodhunga with Peak XV. In April 1857, Waugh had ordered five survey officers to investigate the question of naming the peak. Four of the five had replied in time for Waugh to submit the results to the Asiatic Society along with his own August letter.[44]

W.H. Scott, the department's chief draftsman, was the first to reply. Waugh had noted that Scott had 'spent a quarter of a century in unravelling more intricate geographical problems than this'. Waugh was not disappointed in Scott's conclusions. Scott thought that Hodgson, the author of several dictionaries, had been so confused by the polyglottic nature of the area that he had mistaken Deodhunga for Peak XV. In fact, Scott asserted, there was 'no evidence' that the two peaks were identical.

The notion that Deodhunga was not Mount Everest was further articulated by J. Hennessy, the Trigonometrical Survey's head geodetic computer. Hennessy argued that Peak XV could not be seen from the Kathmandu valley, as claimed by Hodgson, but was instead blocked by Peak XVIII, proving that Deodhunga, which could be seen from the confines of the valley, was not Peak XV.

The third officer to reply was J.W. Armstrong, a civil assistant in the Trigonometrical Survey, who had first spotted Peak XV in 1846. He, too, claimed that Hodgson's evidence was conjectural and based on the 'vague information of untrained travellers', and not on personal observation. Moreover, Armstrong asserted that Mount Everest was entirely 'fitting' since the name served to 'stamp' the mountain's greatness.

European recognition of Mount Everest was a concern of the

last member of Waugh's committee. J.F. Tennant, in charge of the Jogi Tila Meridional Series, noted that Hodgson's choice of name would be unpronounceable by Europeans and that, in any case, the only thing Hodgson had demonstrated in his letter and memoranda to the Asiatic Society was that there existed a pass called Bhairava Langur.[45] Beyond that, Hodgson had proved nothing, especially since he had relied so heavily on travellers' accounts—'nothing is more fallacious,' Tennant wrote, 'than names given from a distance, even when an object is conspicuously visible.'

Despite their insistent tone, Waugh's letter and the committee's responses were not the last words on the subject. Murmurs of discontent with the name of Mount Everest were occasionally heard, most especially from the president of the Royal Geographical Society and from the German explorer, Hermann Schlagintweit.[46] Schlagintweit was one of three brothers who had travelled extensively in the Himalayan region—one of his brothers, Adolphe had been beheaded in central Asia—and when he returned to Europe he published views of his travels. One of his panoramas featured what appeared to be Peak XV drawn from Kaulia, a distance of just over 100 miles (Schlagintweit-Sakünlünski 1869–80, see Vol. II 1871: 253). He had been told by those he had asked that the mountain's name was Gaurisankar. Although Schlagintweit supported Hodgson's claim that local names did exist for the mountain, the controversy did not resurface until the mid-1880s.

From British Name to Universal Symbol, 1886–1931

Thirty years after Waugh's declaration that Peak XV would have a British name his decision once more became the subject of debate. Even though many of the elements remained the same—focusing on whether the mountain had a local designation—the terms of and reasons for the controversy had altered. One of the most important changes was the injection into the disagreement of a form of internationalism. The debate was no longer concerned with George Everest, the man. It seems that by the late nineteenth century he had become an almost forgotten figure. As a result, the name of the mountain was no longer about British scientific supremacy and accuracy. The name was no longer a reflection of what the British could achieve and discover through their methods of observation. Rather, and this is perhaps the most important shift in focus, the significance of the name of Everest for professional surveyors was that its foreignness was a symbol of universality. As a Survey officer noted, 'Mount Everest stands between the Aryan and Mongolian races. It belongs to no people, to no nationality' (Burrard 1931: 4). For detractors, who happened to be mostly mountaineers and explorers, the fact that the debate was less about Everest's surveying abilities or British scientific and imperial achievement, made a foreign name irrelevant and incongruous.

The man who re-ignited the argument over Mount Everest was Douglas W. Freshfield—an avid mountaineer and, for many years, the secretary of the Royal Geographical Society and president of the Alpine Club. There he edited *The Alpine Journal: A Record of Mountain Adventure and Scientific Observation.*

The debate over Mount Everest resurfaced in *The Alpine Journal* of 1886 and included three important papers. One was a critical evaluation of the performance of the Survey of India by Emil Boss and Douglas Freshfield (1886); the second was an extract from a narrative report by Colonel H.C.B. Tanner (1886) which included a comparative study of various peaks of the Himalayas; and the last was a reply by Freshfield (1886a), which explicitly addressed the issue of Peak XV. All three papers may be treated together since they provide a context for the renewed interest in the name of Mount Everest.

Emil Boss was perhaps the most outspoken critic of the Survey's maps; he dismissed them as unscientific, and even characterized some of them as 'nursery pictures'. He also informally invited them to Switzerland to see first-hand the proper manner of drawing mountain maps. Freshfield was only slightly less critical. His advice to the Survey was to train better, slow down, and concentrate on quality over quantity. Their evaluation of the Survey was one of the first occasions when the work of the Survey was openly criticized in Europe and provides the backdrop for the subsequent disagreements over Peak XV. Throughout the nineteenth century the Survey had been little noticed in Europe, let alone criticized. William Lambton, for example, had announced to the Royal Society, somewhat absurdly, that 'it may be satisfactory to the mathematicians in Europe to know, that I am now advancing through Hindoostan' (1823: 33). However, with the rise of mountaineering, greater numbers of unofficial men began to scrutinize the Survey's maps of mountainous regions. Scrutiny led to comparison and to a discussion concerning the accuracy and value of Indian survey maps.

In addition to the criticism offered by both Boss and Freshfield, *The Alpine Journal* also included a report on Himalayan peaks by Colonel Tanner, which provided a different perspective on the work of the Survey of India. Tanner had been in charge of the Darjeeling and Nepal boundary surveys and had developed an appreciation for mountainous terrain. His account of the highest and most prominent peaks in the Himalayas was among the first to provide a systematic and comprehensive description of each peak. Tanner furnished his readers with a table containing nine Himalayan mountains, together with an additional European mountain (Mont Blanc). Each peak was ranked according to its picturesque quality, defined, according to Tanner, by the amount of slope exposed to view compared with the height. The object of the table was to persuade the reader that although Mount Everest was generally accepted as ranking first, its true rank should be fifth, while Nanga Parbat, or Deo Mir, in Kashmir, deserved first place.

Tanner thought that Everest was only a 'very moderate hill, not in the least imposing and hardly picturesque'. In comparison to Nanga Parbat, the view of which 'baffles description', Mount Everest was 'only commonplace'. Tanner's re-appraisal of Mount Everest based on its unpicturesque aspect (at least as seen from either Purnea district or from near Darjeeling), provides an indication of how surveyors were re-evaluating the importance of Mount Everest. A relatively unknown peak (Nanga Parbat) was promoted due to its aesthetic appeal and the difficulty of its approach (it is observed after a 'frightful journey over cliffs, rocks, torrents'), while the famous mountain was deprecated. But, whereas previous generations would have regarded the mountain as a mirror, signifying their own greatness as a conquering and enlightened nation, Tanner viewed the peaks as representing not national triumph, but natural triumph. To view Nanga Parbat was to transcend the quotidian, the mean, and the ephemeral human world, and to glimpse an enduring and stupendous realm. 'It is quite overwhelming in magnitude,' he wrote, 'it is in fact one of the grandest spectacles that nature offers to the gaze of man.' Gone is the notion that meticulous observation could stamp greatness on the peak; instead, it is a privilege to view the 'spectacle', and to be 'overwhelmed' by greatness—a transcendent experience. Tanner's description of the Himalayan peaks prompted Douglas Freshfield to submit an essay in which he took issue with Tanner's unflattering portrayal of Mount Everest. As a mountaineer, Freshfield was particularly concerned with viewing peaks as expressions of local topographical and sociological features, rather than as entities suitable for inter-regional and international comparison. One of Freshfield's practical suggestions to the Survey of India was to compile a table of local words used in mountainous districts to describe the landscape, and, in addition to believing that Peak XV was an impressive sight, he also advocated changing the name to Gaurisankar.

Freshfield's suggestion that the name Everest should be discontinued once again raised the ire of high officers in the Survey. A retired Surveyor General of India, J.T. Walker, read Freshfield's notes and replied immediately, although instead of submitting his letter to *The Alpine Journal*, he chose the more widely read *Proceedings of the Royal Geographical Society* (Walker 1886a). While his predecessor, Waugh, had chosen to dismiss Hodgson's suggested names because he feared that those names represented other peaks, Walker adopted a different strategy to ward off 'Gaurisankar'. 'I propose to show,' he wrote, 'how the peak acquired the name of Everest in the first instance, and subsequently that of Gaurisankar' (ibid.: 88). He then proceeded to examine Schlagintweit's evidence that Peak XV was known as Gaurisankar, and concluded that Schlagintweit had misidentified both Peak XV *and* Gaurisankar. According to Walker, Schlagintweit had seen Peak XIII, Makalu, and had mistaken it for Peak XV. Such a confusion was possible since heights and even positions are distorted by distance; Makalu and Everest were both in Schlagintweit's line of view, but Everest, although higher, was out of sight behind Makalu. Walker did concede, however, that the name 'Devadhunga' was a possible true designation, but only of the undefined and little-known 'mountain masses' occupying areas close to Everest.

The debate was joined in earnest when Freshfield replied to Walker's spirited support of 'the invention of that curious hybrid,

Mont Everest.[47] Freshfield countered Walker's claim that Hermann Schlagintweit had seen Makalu, but never Everest, by referring to a manuscript, which had been sent to Freshfield by Hermann's brother, Emil, and which contained a description of the mountain in question. This description, according to Freshfield, could not be reconciled with Makalu. However, Freshfield had his own concession to give— Schlagintweit may indeed have misplaced Gaurisankar in his sketch of the part of the Himalayan range, but Freshfield was certain that the peak identified as the highest, and computed by Schlagintweit at 29,196 feet, was without doubt the 29,002 feet Peak XV. But Freshfield asserted that this 'confusion' did not mean that Peak XV was wrongly named Gaurisankar or Devadhunga (Deodhunga).

In fact, Freshfield pointed to another Schlagintweit sketch of the Himalayas which was executed from a different vantage point. In this sketch, Freshfield admitted, some of the 'minor' peaks had been placed to the left of Peak XXI, when they should have been located to the right. But this mistake did not surface in a more elaborate map, which, when viewed next to official survey maps, indicated that Peak XV was clearly visible, and not hidden by Peak XVIII, as Walker claimed must be the case. Although Freshfield assented that 'a public school education has ill fitted me to discuss questions of geometry with skilled surveyors', he still embarked on an elaborate proof that Schlagintweit had seen Peak XV and had correctly identified it as Gaurisankar. He concluded his article with two points. The first was that he trusted Hodgson and Schlagintweit because one was knowledgeable about the area while the other was a mountaineer—'many mountaineers learn to recognise individual summits ... (they) could never for a moment from any distance confuse appearances so far as to mistake the "silver spearhead" of a great mountain for a "very moderate hill".' His second point was that an anonymous 'lady pioneer' had seen what she described as Mount Everest, but which her attendants identified as 'Deodunga' and 'Gaurisankar'.[48] Freshfield wondered whether her story was 'fact or feminine fiction', but offered it as further evidence that Peak XV was not without a local name.

Freshfield's article was not to go unanswered. Walker submitted yet another paper to the Royal Geographical Society, which rehearsed the same arguments, while clarifying his previous observations

(1886b). He noted, for example, that the central question was whether Waugh had been justified in calling the peak Mont Everest. He concluded that since many observers had suggested a variety of local names, and since none could be exclusively and conclusively attached to the peak, Everest was a suitable choice. Walker also referred to a passage written by the anonymous 'lady pioneer', who claimed to have seen Mount Everest. 'Whilst I stand alone,' she wrote in a transcendent vein,

amidst this infinitude of Nature, the sun, beginning to ascend on his triumphal car of crimson cloud, tips the highest pinnacle with an aerial glory. In an instant it dawned upon me that I was at last gazing on Mount Everest, the highest mountain in the world. I could not be mistaken (quoted in Walker 1886b: 261–62).

Walker claimed that she had, in fact, been mistaken and had committed the same error as Hermann Schlagintweit—she had seen Makalu and assumed it was Everest. But what about the cries of 'Gaurisankar' and 'Deodunga' which she had heard so clearly? Walker explained that they were most probably invocations to the gods associated with those mountains and that all the names suggested, from Bhairavathan to Gaurisankar, were 'generic and not specific'.

The story of the name of Mount Everest, however, did not end with Walker's 'final note'. There was also disagreement over whether the mountain was a mount or a mont. Waugh's unexplained adoption of 'mount' in place of 'mont' was perhaps an indication that he wanted the name of this surveying discovery to be as memorable as possible. Waugh's successor later claimed that the reason why Mont was initially chosen over Mount was that it referred only to the peak, or mont in French, and not to the 'general mountain mass', or montagne. This claim however, was made thirty years later, when it was conceded that Deodhunga might indeed refer to the mountain mass, if not to the mountain (Walker 1886a: 92). Nevertheless, the prefix Mont did still ruffle some feathers nearly fifty years after Waugh had chosen it. In a letter to a German journal, reproduced in *The Alpine Journal*, a historical geographer complained that many were wrongly attaching 'Mount' to Everest! He applauded the 'unusual' use of Mont and noted that it helped to make the mountain, in his words, 'remarkable'. He ended his letter proclaiming that 'it would be petty pedantry to degrade it into an ordinary Mount' (Ruge 1903: 34). Douglas Freshfield, himself, provided another interpretation— that the Mont in Waugh's original 1856 letter to the Royal Geographical Society was a typographical error (1903a: 34–35).

Although there were disagreements over whether Mount or Mont was more accurate as a prefix to the name, most of the attention remained on the appropriateness of the name Everest. At the end of the nineteenth and the beginning of the twentieth century German and French editors maintained an interest in the affair, although they tended to report what had already been written in the London mountaineering and geographical journals.[49] The most intriguing and telling of these debates were the contributions of Major L.A. Waddell in 1898, Douglas Freshfield in 1903, and Sven Hedin and Sidney Burrard in 1923 and 1931 respectively. In all of these contributions the role of the mountain as a symbol of British scientific advancement and personal achievement was superseded by arguments over whether an almost-forgotten foreign man's name should be attached to the world's highest mountain which, even surveyors grudgingly acknowledged, may have local names.

L.A. Waddell informed the fellows of the Royal Geographical Society that, as a result of his own expedition to the region, he could find no person who lived within sight of Everest, who identified the peak or the mountain range as Gaurisankar, Bhairab [sic] Langur, or Deodhunga (1898: 565). Waddell asserted that the confusion in names resulted from a 'looseness of the Nepalese in their nomenclature', which complicated the task of identification. However, he then added that the Tibetans are more precise in their designations and that his researches tended to confirm an observation made by a Survey of India 'Pundit' while on a secret exploration in Tibet. In a journal which was later published, Sarat Chandra Das had described a mountain range 'of which the culminating point is Lapchhyikang (called Mount Everest in English maps)' (1885: 5). Waddell reported that he had been told that the Everest range was known to some in Tibet as 'Lapchi-Kang', and that the highest peak was 'Jomo Kang-kar', or the white glacier lady. Other Tibetans did not recognize the latter name, although all seemed to associate Lapchi-Kang with the Everest mountain mass, if not with the peak itself. Waddell also included a transliterated copy of a Tibetan picture map of the Everest range, which included the names of two passes, 'Laskyi Kang' and 'Chi-tsi', which he claimed were 'somewhat suggestive of Lap-chi Kang'.

Waddell's confirmation of Das' claim that Jomo Kang-kar and Lapchi-Kang were Tibetan names for Mount Everest was noticed by none other than Douglas Freshfield.[50] Freshfield had read a work by Kurt Boeck (1907) which included photographs of the Everest range. These photographs had been taken from the locations where Hermann Schlagintweit had drawn his sketches and they clearly showed (according to Freshfield) both Peak XV and Makalu. Freshfield admitted that Schlagintweit and others may have misidentified Peak XV, but that did not mean that Peak XV had not been visible from places where it had been characterized as Gaurisankar. To bolster his claim, Freshfield referred to Boeck's assertion that the peak, presumably Peak XV, had been called Gaurisankar by his guides. He acknowledged that 'Chomokankar' had been suggested as the Tibetan name but added that he hoped to see the Indian name, Gaurisankar, 'win the day'.

However, while Gaurisankar remained a contender for the name of Peak XV, mountaineers and explorers of Central Asia increasingly favoured Tibetan names. In 1926, according to a review by Sidney Burrard, Sir Sven Hedin noticed a very curious feature on an old Jesuit map of Tibet.[51] Hedin reminded his readers that only five years earlier, the first Mount Everest Expedition, led by Colonel Howard-Bury, had been told that the name 'Chomo Lungma' represented Mount Everest. Hedin then drew attention to a map published in 1733 by Jean D'Anville, based upon a sketch drawn in 1717 by Jesuits living in Beijing, who had instructed Chinese Lamas to survey Tibet in 1711. It may be remembered that D'Anville's map indicated that the Ganges originated above Mapama lake, far beyond Gangotri. Of still greater significance for Hedin, however, was the fact that at the very bottom of the map, at latitude 27° 20' and longitude east of Ferro 103° 50', D'Anville had inserted the words 'Tchoumour M'.[52] Hedin noted that both the name and the location were similar to the Chomo Lungma of the expedition, which, if identical to Mount Everest, would be at 27° 59' latitude and 104° 55' longitude east of Ferro. In a belligerent move, Hedin belittled not only the name Everest but also the man. Everest was 'able but not outstanding. By sheer accident without a trace of want of breath, he has become undying' (Burrard's translation).

Colonel Burrard of the Survey of India wrote a long and detailed reply to this contention (1931). There is an assumption throughout his narrative that hard labour (one of the first surveyors of the Himalayan peaks 'was found dead in his dooly') combined with scientific rigour (Everest had been the first to advocate 'greater accuracy of observation') resulted in a discovery embodying a larger and more noble endeavour ('the highest peak in the world is beyond reach of nationalism'). Moreover, Burrard wished to use the particulars of the debate, as well as the incidences and minutiae leading to the naming of the mountain, as a way of transcending disagreements, nationalism, and even the British Raj.

To discredit Hedin's announcement that D'Anville had been the first to represent Peak XV to Europe, Burrard compared the river systems depicted in the 1733 map with the same rivers as shown in a 'modern' map. Rather than dwelling on 'the identity of names', which only led to confusion, Burrard hoped that 'the identity of topographical features' would disabuse readers of the idea that Chomo Lungma was the Tibetan name for Mount Everest. Whereas D'Anville had shown two rivers (the Nutchou and the Yo Tsanpou, which Burrard identified as the Sun-Kosi and Arun rivers) emanating from mountains further to the north of the mountain Tchoumour Lancma, Burrard insisted that, if indeed this mountain was Peak XV, then these rivers should be seen to originate from that very mountain.

Burrard's triumphant conclusion was that there was no possibility that the Tibetan name referred to Mount Everest. He was even au-dacious enough to request Sven Hedin to use his influence to push the Tibetans to recognize the name Mount Everest over 'an indefi-nite regional name'. He suggested that such an acknowledgment by the Tibetans would further the prospect of 'world-wide unanim-ity' (ibid.: 18). By the 1930s, then, Mount Everest had become a universal symbol and was no longer a symbol of British scientific supremacy as it had been eighty years previously. For officials in the Survey of India the foreignness of the name Everest was what ena-bled the mountain to belong to nobody and to be recognized by all as unique. For detractors, its foreignness of name, together with the probability that numerous local names existed, made 'Everest' incongruous. The desirability to provide a local name was, no doubt, also heightened by the fact that the terms of the debate no longer focused on the mountain as a symbol of British supremacy.

Conclusion

What is it about names that makes them appropriate? In the eighteenth century, two hills in Berkshire, England, now called the Wittenham Clumps, were known as Mrs Dunch's Buttocks, in reference to the local landlady (Thomas 1983: 85). A landfill at Virginia Beach, USA, is named Mount Trashmore, and I have even been informed that a gently rolling cemetery in Florida styles itself Mount Ever Rest! Does irreverence make these names less appropriate?[53] Often the most incongruous names are attached to physical objects— Rennell thought that Gangotri, or the Cow's Mouth, was a misleading and inappropriate name designating the source of the Ganges, and yet Hodgson had no compunction in naming the peaks above Gangotri after four Christian saints. More than any other activity, naming gives voice to vision; a name encapsulates our understanding of what we see. Mount Everest or Gaurisankar, Mont Everest or Devadhunga, all articulated perspectives and defined perception. Viewed 'correctly', observed 'closely', the unnoticed could be made remarkable. And that which was recognized as unique by laborious, repetitive, and rigorous means could be appropriately termed great.

Why should the heights of mountains be an object of continuous speculation and calculation? What does it matter that Peak XV of the Survey of India should be named Mount Everest? Certain minutiae and ephemera of the nineteenth century were made monumental and momentous by being accorded histories and names. Certainly, Mount Everest, as the tallest peak in the world, is neither minute nor ephemeral, but, after all, Mount Everest is only a mountain—it does not speak for itself. And yet there are reasons why its height was considered important and why it was worth being named and being made remarkable.

Beginning in the second half of the nineteenth century, the debate over the naming of Peak XV exhibited the priorities and principles of what I have called reverential cartographic history.

Appropriateness lay in truth, and truth lay in perception. How could the most famous British geographer be duped by a common survey forgery? How could the most respected Orientalist scholar be induced to write a glowing foreword to an article on the source of the Ganges by a man who had never even seen the source? How could a British public be convinced, by men who had only peered from a distance, that Everest was an appropriate and dignified name for a mountain said to have many local names? I have argued that recognition is determined by formulas of perception and guides to observation, which, although seemingly true, are often charlatanic. Rennell understood Hearsey's map and words because of the manner of presentation, which, in seeming to be true, belied the manner of construction. Colebrooke read in Raper's rhetorical control of the *munshi's* perspective his own knowledge of and power over Indian understanding, and thus believed the details of the narrative. Many heard the name Mount Everest and thought it appropriate since it was represented to them that, according to 'scientific' criteria, it could not be proved that local perception correctly identified a certain peak observed by the Survey from a distance of over 100 miles.

Therefore, both the way of acquiring and of presenting information determined legitimacy. What made the name Everest acceptable to the surveying departments and to the government of India was the argument that the manner of identifying and locating Peak XV was more important and appropriate than the search for local names. The belief that George Everest embodied the principles of mathematical and geographical science and that his name could be recognized as a symbol of the triumph of British science in the colonies and around the world were the core arguments that had prompted the Survey of India to propose the name. The reverence paid to Everest, a retired surveyor, by naming a mountain after him was considered an appropriate way to celebrate British national triumph, colonial control, and scientific success.

By the end of the nineteenth century, however, the debate had altered to the extent that the name Everest was no longer associated with British political or scientific exceptionalism. Instead, it was thought to indicate, by its very foreignness, the idea that the mountain belonged to no nation.

Notes

1. BL Addl MSS 26,653.
2. There are disagreements as to his parentage. See entries in Dictionary of Indian Biography (DIB), Dictionary of National Biography (DNB), and Phillimore 1950 Vol. II. His middle name had originally been 'Jung'.
3. Tieffenthaller, sometimes spelled Tieffentaller, travelled widely in India and published several works on Indian geography and religion. The Ganges map is entitled: 'Carte Generale du Cours du Gange et du Gagra, dressee sur les Cartes particuliers du P. Tieffenthaler, J. Missionaire Apostolique dans l'Inde. Par M. Anquetil du Perron ... Paris, 1784.' Tieffenthaller's large collection of geographical material, including maps, is thought to have been burned at Lucknow during the 1857–58 war. For more information on Tieffenthaller, see Blunt 1911: 51–52.
4. D'Anville's map is included in du Halde 1735. This map will be important later in the chapter when we discuss the naming of Mount Everest, since it purportedly shows the Tibetan name for the peak.
5. In his celebrated 1752 map of India, D'Anville noted that no details were known about the upper course of the Ganges. Nevertheless, he added that even though the source of the Ganges had been thought to be at Gangotri, 'it is more distant in Tibet'.
6. Robert Orme echoed Rennell in saying that the Ganges is said by Indians, 'who look very little abroad', to travel through a pass and into 'Indostan' very near to a rock which resembles the head of a cow. OIOC Orme MSS 176, p. 38.
7. NAI, DDn Vol. List, Old No. SGO 53 (A), Sl. No. 81, Garstin to Lt. James Tod, 8 February 1809.
8. NAI, DDn Vol. List, Old No. SGO 364, Sl. No. 82, p. 202, Letters to Surveyor General, 1807–10, Webb to Garstin, 4 July 1809.
9. Charles Allen has written a full narrative of the journey (1982: 57–77).
10. While travelling to Afghanistan, Raper contributed to a route survey of the march of Elphinstone's embassy which was incorporated into a memoir and map. See OIOC, X/3029/2, (Old MSS 1, Vol. 2), p. 1.
11. *The Quarterly Review*, Vol. XVII, London: John Murray, April and July 1817: 403–41. The *Edinburgh Review* (Vol. XXI: 313) mentioned that 'there are but few of the most enlightened cabinets in Europe which can boast of an expedition equally disinterested and meritorious'.
12. For the complete Instructions given by R.H. Colebrooke to W.S. Webb on 21 March 1808, see NAI, DDn Vols Old No. SGO 53 (A); Sl. No. 81, pp. 131–32, Letter Book, continued, 1806–10 Surveyor General's Office.

13. NAI, DDn Vols Old No. SGO 53 (A); Sl. No. 81, p. 191.
14. NAI, DDn Vols Old No. SGO 364; Sl. No. 82, p. 59, Letters to Surveyor General, 1807–10; W.S. Webb to Garstin, 23 November 1808.
15. J.A. Hodgson, 'Astronomical Observations in various parts of Hindustan and a Journal of the Survey of the Sources of the Rivers Ganges and Jumna', OIOC X/1332 (formerly MSS 22). This essay is also printed in Vol. 14 of the *Journal of the Asiatic Society of Bengal* (see p. 118).
16. *The Quarterly Review*, Vol. XXIV, London: John Murray, October and January, 1821: 126.
17. The river's actual starting point is difficult to determine since it seems to begin under a glacier which is retreating up a valley above Gangotri.
18. One of the more accessible copies is in the library of the Royal Geographical Society. Readers are permitted to take notes but not to make photocopies.
19. NAI, Catalogue of the Memoirs of the Survey of India, Field Book 74 (M. 330), p. 5, *Astronomical Observations* ... by J.A. Hodgson, 1815.
20. OIOC MSS Eur. D. 1200, *Letters dated 1806–15 from Lt. (later Maj-Gen.) John Anthony Hodgson*, Seckipour, 4 August 1812.
21. OIOC X/1332 (formerly MSS 22), p. 109.
22. NAI, DDn Vol. List, Old No. 23/14, Sl. No. 566, p. 12.
23. NAI, DDn Vol. List, Old No. 16/3; Sl. No. 666, Letters sent to Deputy Surveyor General and Chief Computer, 1858. Letter to Thuillier from Waugh, 13 July 1858.
24. Waugh noted to his deputy that 'without maps of the country our troops would have been embarrassed in their movements'. NAI, DDn Vol. List, Old No. 16/3, Sl. No. 666, p. 36, Waugh to Thuillier, 23 May 1859. Soon after the British had regained control of northern India, the Governor General wrote to Waugh to congratulate him on his department's work during the Mutiny: 'It is a real pleasure,' he noted, 'to find that a gigantic work of permanent peaceful usefulness, and one which will assuredly take the highest rank as a work of scientific labour and skill has been steadily and rapidly progressing through all the turmoil of the last two years.' NAI, DDn Vol. List, Old No. SGO 226, Sl. No. 675, p. 101, Canning to Waugh, 18 July 1859.
25. NAI, DDn Vol. List, Sl. No. 665, pp. 146–48. The Government of India has restricted access to this volume.
26. *Proceedings of the Asiatic Society of Bengal*, Vol. XXV, No. 5, 1856: 437–39.
27. *Proceedings of the Asiatic Society of Bengal*, Vol. XXV, No. 5, 1856, 439. Colonel Waugh also wrote a letter to the Royal Geographical Society in which he repeated his claim that the peak had no known local name. He also explained his reasons for naming the mountain after his

predecessor. The Society published his letter together with B.H. Hodgson's complaint that there did indeed exist known local names for the peak (*Proceedings of the Royal Geographical Society of London*, Vol. I, 11 May 1857: 345–50).

28. *Proceedings of the Royal Geographical Society of London*, Vol. I, 11 May 1857: 350–51.
29. *Proceedings of the Asiatic Society of Bengal*, Vol. XXVI, No. 4, 1857: 312.
30. *Proceedings of the Royal Geographical Society of London*, Vol. I, 11 May 1857: 350.
31. A glimpse of his personality can be seen in an essay written by his niece, Mary Everest Boole, which was published in Bombay in 1905, and has been reproduced in J.R. Smith (2000: 156–60). She presents him as a less ferocious, more well-loved man than is perhaps apparent in the records of his time in India.
32. NAI, DDn Vol., List, Old No. 23/15, Sl. No. 671, p. 119, Departmental Order, 12 March 1861.
33. NAI, DDn Vol. List, Old No. 23/15, Sl. No. 671, p. 84, Waugh to Chief Computer, 25 August 1856.
34. NAI, DDn Vol. List, Old No. 1/5, Sl. No. 90, p. 275, Copies of Letters from Court of Directors, 1788–1859, Military Letter No. 61, 2 January 1857 (para. 24).
35. *Proceedings of the Asiatic Society of Bengal*, Vol. XXV, No. 5, 1856: 467–70. This letter was also published by the Royal Geographical Society, in its *Proceedings*, Vol. I, 11 May 1857: 347–50.
36. The words 'exhaustive enquiry' were written by Colonel Sir Sidney Burrard in his defence of Waugh's choice of name (1931: 1).
37. See *Selections from the Records of the Government of Bengal*, No. XXVII, Calcutta: 1857.
38. The words are by the Company's Resident at Kathmandu, Major Ramsey, who wrote to H.L. Thuillier in June 1855, praising Hodgson's knowledge. It might also be noted that the Survey included a sketch of the Himalayan basins by Hodgson in its new map of Nepal. See NAI, DDn Vol. List, Old No. 14/15, Sl. No. 663, pp. 4–7.
39. The president of the Royal Geographical Society asked George Everest, the former Surveyor General of India, to transmit the medal to Waugh. A week after the award ceremony, Everest wrote to the Secretary of the East India Company stating that, on a more 'appropriate' occasion, he would have told the Society that Waugh's success was in large measure due to the 'enlightened principles' of the Company. The Company's generous support had ensured that this 'Colossal series of Operations, without parallel perhaps in the history of mankind, was not long ago

crushed or so enfeebled as to be worse than worthless, instead of being
an achievement of which any country may well be proud'. NAI, DDn
Vol. List, Old No. 1/5, Sl. No. 90, Copies of Letters from Court of
Directors, 1788–1859, pp. 279–80, containing a letter by Everest to James
Melvill, 1 June 1857, p. 280.

40. *Proceedings of the Asiatic Society of Bengal,* Vol. XXVI No. 4, 1857: 297–313.
41. *Proceedings of the Asiatic Society of Bengal,* Vol. XXVI, No. 4, 1857: 298.
42. *Proceedings of the Asiatic Society of Bengal,* Vol. XXVI, No. 4, 1857: 297.
43. *Proceedings of the Asiatic Society of Bengal,* Vol. XXVI, No. 4, 1857: 300.
44. The fifth member of the geographical committee was Lieutenant
    Montgomerie, the survey officer in charge of the Kashmir trigono-
    metrical series. The mutiny of that year prevented him from replying.
    Waugh included all four responses in his August letter to the Asiatic
    Society of Bengal. *Proceedings of the Asiatic Society of Bengal,* Vol. XXVI,
    No. 4, 1857: 303–12. Waugh's Department Order No. 10267, was dated
    22 April 1857 and may be seen in manuscript form in NAI, DDn Vol.
    List, Sl. No. 648, p. 328. Waugh's letter to the Asiatic Society, which
    included his Departmental Order, may also be seen in manuscript in
    NAI, DDn Vol. List, Old No. 48/7, Sl. No. 718, p. 432. This letter was
    originally written to the Deputy Surveyor General, Major Thuillier, who
    then forwarded it to the Society.
45. All the members of the committee had reviewed Hodgson's original
    letter in the journal of the Asiatic Society, No. 5, 1856. They had also
    reviewed the following papers, published in the society's journal, No. 6,
    1856: 'Routes of two Nepaulese Embassies to Pekin, with remarks on
    the Watershed and Plateau of Tibet'; 'Systematic summary of the route
    from Kathmandu to Pekin', by Kaji Dalbhanjan Pande, 1822–23;
    'Abstract of Diary from Kathmandu to Pekin', by Chountra Pushkerash,
    1817; and 'Memorandum on the Seven Cosis with Sketch Map', originally
    published in the journal of the Asiatic Society, December 1848.
46. Sir Roderick Murchison, the president of the Royal Geographical Society,
    responded to the committee in a lukewarm fashion: 'I cannot conceive
    military engineers performing any duty more grateful to themselves
    than that of testifying to the merit of their former chief by attaching
    the name of Everest to the highest mountain in the world' cited in *The
    Alpine Journal,* Vol. XII, London: Longmans, Green, and Co., 1886:
    454.
47. *Proceedings of the Royal Geographical Society* (1886b).
48. See *The Indian Alps and how we crossed them: being a narrative of two years'
    residence in the eastern Himalaya and two months' tour into the interior. By a
    lady pioneer.* (New York [London, printed]: Dodd, Mead, and Company,

1876), 366. The volume includes a sketch of 'Deodunga or Mount Everest'.

49. Of particular interest are two articles written by Emil Schlagintweit, Hermann's brother: 'Der Name des höchsten Berges der Erde', in Pertermanns *Mitteilungen* (1890) and another article under the same title in 1901. For the French articles see, *Annales de Géographie*, Paris: Armand Colin et Cie, Vol. 11, No. 60, 1902: 470–71, Vol. 12, No. 63, 1903: 279, Vol. 14, No. 74, 1905: 186–87. In the last volume the editor announced the end of the debate: A Capt. Wood had determined that there were indeed two peaks and that Gaurisankar was a mountain whose highest peak (initially Peak XX of the Survey of India) had been identified by the Survey as Sankar!

50. Douglas Freshfield's article appears in both *The Alpine Journal* (1903) and *The Geographical Journal*, Vol. XXI, No. 3: 294–98.

51. My discussion of Hedin's book, *Mount Everest*, is based on Sidney Burrard's (1931) review, *Mount Everest and its Tibetan Names*.

52. The title of D'Anville's map is 'Carte Generale du Thibet ou Bout-tan et des Pays de Kashgar et Hami, dressée sur les Cartes et Memoires des RR PP Jesuites de la Chine ... Avril 1733'. A copy is available in the OIOC, reference X642. Hedin included a rough sketch of part of the map in his book (1923: 73).

53. For a general discussion of place names see Derek Nelson 1997.

FOUR

History, Romance, and the Survey of India

S urveyors in the second half of the nineteenth century turned some of their attention to the problem of how best to gain greater knowledge of the territories lying beyond the boundaries of India. There had always been a desire by Company surveyors to expand their topographical knowledge to foreign lands. However, these earlier surveyors were preoccupied with a number of objectives that necessarily diverted their attention away from making too many inquiries into the topography of countries lying outside of India. The trigonometrical, topographical, and revenue surveys that the Company authorized were not just confined to Company-controlled areas but often extended into the territories of princely states. However, apart from military surveys into Afghanistan, observations of Himalayan peaks, or the occasional traveller to Central Asia who was able to provide some written account of the location and description of towns and land that he encountered along his way, the Company's surveyors had neither the time nor the opportunity to gather much geographical information about areas to the north of Kashmir or beyond the boundaries of Nepal. Circumstances changed after the defeat of the Mutiny in 1857–58, when the Company was dissolved and political authority was transferred to the British Crown. Although surveyors were still largely focused on the routine surveying and mapping of India, occasional and loosely-coordinated attempts were made to push surveys into Central Asia. Several practical considerations prompted these efforts, including a fear of rapid Russian encroachment and an interest in the Central Asian trade routes. But, one additional and particularly intriguing aspect of these northern surveys conducted by the Survey of India, and one that may have contributed to their continuation over several decades, is that they were often regarded as romantic.

For much of the nineteenth century, 'romance' was a preoccupation for many British elites. It was at once an attitude, a demeanour, and a trait which helped bridge a growing gap between the increasingly discrete spheres of the public and the private. The invocation of romance helped Victorians exhibit private emotion, desire, and fantasy in a public forum or setting. In politics, the Tory Party's sponsorship of both medieval pageants and the Primrose League encouraged an exuberant and visceral enactment of their otherwise dry and unromantic principles. In poetry, the Pre-Raphaelite Movement or Tennyson's themes of courtly love, suggested a world where emotion and feeling were noble precisely because they were experienced and shared openly and without guile. In children's literature, the novels of G.A. Henty, and others, invented a world in which the young reader could imagine himself a hero on an imperial stage. In design, the patterns and philosophy of William Morris sought to recapture a pure artisanal expression. In virtually every public endeavour of the nineteenth and early twentieth century, romance was alluded to as a means of permitting the safe and circumscribed public expression of private emotion.

In South Asia, the Survey of India touted its trans-Himalayan and central Asian surveying forays as romantic. They were romantic because they encouraged a British public to envision the surveying of India as an activity that combined manly physical vigour with the high ideals of colonialism. Sentiments such as a pride in the adventurous spirit of the British, an admiration for British daring, and a deep desire to keep the British empire safe from Russian expansionism were all reflected within the stories of surveyors risking their lives to map beyond the safety of India. These surveys helped to raise the profile of the Survey of India, which chose several means to disseminate the results from its trans-Himalayan surveys, including publishing narrative reports of surveys and providing précis to the Royal Geographical Society in London.

Beginning in the mid-1860s, then, and lasting for twenty years, Fellows of the Royal Geographical Society were periodically regaled with heroic tales from the Survey of India. These stories often centred on the Survey's use of geographical spies. Indian surveyors, known as 'pundits', were employed to travel through the countries bordering India's northern frontier. The manner of surveying—rudimentary route surveys—and the information gathered were largely useless for a department that prided itself on its meticulous practices and verifiably accurate results. Indeed, even James Rennell, the great eighteenth-century advocate of military traverses and route surveys might well have found the pundits' surveys inadequate since they were usually not provided with the means to fix their positions astronomically. Nevertheless, the supposedly secret trans-Himalayan explorations were of great propaganda value for the Survey of India. Reports and narratives of the pundits' journeys were regularly published as official documents and as part of the *Journal of the Royal Geographical Society*. These public recordings of outdated, but secret, practices performed by Indian agents of the Survey fashioned a myth of romance which brought unprecedented attention to the department and its officers. The fact that these surveys were not conducted in the same scientifically rigorous manner as all other official surveys in India, but were throwbacks to the practices of the earliest Company surveyors, lent them the very antiquarian aspect that was so important in the creation of romance.

Another principal reason for the general popularity of the romance of the anachronistic trans-Himalayan surveys may have been that they were often expressed as examples of the thoroughness of British control over Indian, or 'native', agency.[1] The ability of British surveyors to direct and, especially, to train Indians to survey in a 'modern' fashion was the first indication of both the entrenched and enlightened nature of British power in India. Furthermore, the fact that these surveying agents were surveying not their own land but relatively unknown areas beyond India was a second sign that Britain had established sufficient stability within India for it to have the luxury of surveying beyond the northern boundaries. At a time when British colonial officials and an increasingly empire-conscious British public were still reeling from the psychological effects of experiencing the power of 'native insubordination', or mutiny, the fact that British officers could train and control Indians to do the Survey's bidding in lands where no British officer could even travel must have been satisfying. It was also evidence that British colonialism was simultaneously improving Indians, expanding knowledge, and demonstrating the pre-eminence of British scientific ingenuity.

Thus, the trans-Himalayan surveys might have been considered romantic because they enacted widely-held fantasies of teaching Indians to act in a manner that approached the self-definition of Europeans as manly, scientific, and intrepid. It is important to emphasize that this new image of Indians pictured them as only *approaching* a British ideal, because the romance of these surveys depended on the reassuring assumption that Indians could never *be* British, but they could be controlled and made to act in a British and scientific manner. It would appear, therefore, that anachronism and incongruity were important ingredients in this nineteenth-century surveying romance: the Survey employed Indians as topographical surveyors (though they termed them Pundits, or 'explorers')— an apparently incongruous practice—and they were instructed to survey in an antiquated manner which would furnish barely adequate geographical information. Nevertheless, these practices and their results were considered by the Royal Geographical Society to be visionary, even brilliant, because the Survey portrayed these odd and old-fashioned methods as both ingenious expedients and normal practice for an alert scientific organization.

This chapter will review why these pundits' anachronistic surveys were initiated and subsequently made public. The focus will be on the twin ideas that their romantic character was fashioned by their old-fashioned nature, coupled with the pleasure that was afforded by watching Indian agents mimic European practice. The possible rewards for the Survey of India in projecting itself as initiating a romantic survey were that they might have attracted some British public attention away from central African explorations and in doing so, they could have projected an image of a flexible department doing its best to protect India's frontiers.

Although several pundits' journeys will be mentioned in the chapter, only one will be examined in some depth. The surveys of K-P, or Kintup, are particularly revealing since they demonstrate the absurd nature of his anachronistic methods, in terms of providing accurate geographical data, and the British desire to control him as an instrument, even long after his retirement. The aura of romance that was drawn around K-P and many of the other pundits provides an insight into how and why the otherwise scientifically savvy Survey of India incorporated outdated practices.

Nineteenth-century Romance

Romance is a term that has many connotations, ranging from languages that either relate to or have developed from Latin to a class of medieval prose literature, to a love affair. Romance may also be a tale, often fictitious but also often about a remote time in the past. It is perhaps this combination of an untrue story made seemingly true by its location in a historical era that allows a romantic tale to capture a reader's imagination. Romantic tales may also have the characteristics of exaggerated storylines and characters, and the goals or intentions of these characters may appear to be noble and chivalric. It is perhaps this mix of hyperbole and idealized behaviour that permits a romantic tale to become, in part, social or political commentary on present-day affairs.

One example of how romance was used in nineteenth-century Britain to induce and calibrate certain kinds of political behaviour may be seen in the rise in popularity of 'medievalism'. Historians have argued that the revival of purportedly medieval traditions, and the increasing interest in pre-industrial ways of life, coincided with the onset of new imperialist ideology. It has been suggested that medieval pageantry and ceremony presented an escape from increasingly dismal industrial cities and lifestyles (see Boos 1992).[2] The Tory Party itself was at the very heart of the attempts to resuscitate medieval traditions. One such organization was the Primrose League, established in 1883 by leaders of the Conservative Party and named in honour of Disraeli—at his funeral, Queen Victoria had sent a wreath of primroses with the inscription: 'His favourite flower'. The league was formed for the explicit purpose of encouraging interest in the Empire.[3] The original declaration, for example, required that members pledge to maintain the religion, 'Estates of the Realm, and ... the Imperial Ascendancy of Great Britain', while keeping secret everything they learned as members of the league (see Robb 1942: 38).

Although supposedly secretive, the league organized public meetings, performances, and fairs to attract members and maintain interest in the Empire. One pantomime featured 'Britannia weeping over the fate of General Gordon', the tableau being 'worth far more as general party propaganda than a two-hour tirade by a paid lecturer on some weighty pronouncement of Mr. Gladstone's' (ibid: 105). Moreover, the league involved its own members in a continual pageant or chivalric show by transforming prosaic organizational forms into exciting 'medieval' customs. Thus, league dues were called 'tribute', local offices were known as 'habitations', official notices were recognized as 'precepts', and members became 'knights and dames', except children, who were 'buds', and the working class who were simply 'associate members' (ibid.: 51). At habitations all wore primrose badges and pins and processed under league banners and flags. The Primrose League was only one of several societies or organizations, all more or less political, which strove to apply to modern social and political life so-called medieval customs, titles, and forms. This medievalism, a form of 'invented tradition' also evident in literature and the monarchy (see Cannadine 1983), may be considered romantic because it was a publicly acceptable indulgence in an idealized past.

The Victorian preoccupation with romance was somewhat paradoxical, therefore. On the one hand, it was a form of idealistic and fanciful fiction—Walter Scott's novels being a good example—and yet it was also a form of history. Even though antonyms for romantic may include historical, truthful, unimaginative, or precise, wistful Victorian romance was often built around a mythical moment of the past. And it was the seeming antiquity given to these historical myths and traditions that gave them weight and meaning.

With regard to India, nineteenth-century scholarly analyses were occasionally written from a romantic perspective. The identification of village and caste as the two essences of Indian social, religious, and political life exemplified the tendency among administrators to see tradition, rooted in ancient practice, as the country's guiding principle (see Inden 1990). The invention of feudal ties binding the princely states to the queen empress was another expression of British reminiscences on the moment of conquest and the establishment of treaty relations.[4] Indeed, it could be argued that the reason for the deliberate retention of the princes after their subjugation was that they personified a condition—that of justified defeat. Considered despotic, debauched, and dissolute, the princes continued to represent the very reason for and moment of British paramountcy. And thus the romance associated with a visit to one of their gorgeous palaces was the safe fulfilment of a fantasy of living in an era of capricious power, fabulous wealth, and erotic indulgence.

Nineteenth-century romantic associations with India, therefore, were often orientalist and, as such, were expressed in the language of stereotypes. Their idealized conception of history relied on the notion that there existed in the past a moment worthy of repetition. Homi Bhabha has asserted that a stereotype is a form of knowledge 'that vacillates between what is always "in place", already known, and something that must be anxiously repeated' (1983: 18). If we continue with the example of the princes, they may have been seen as an emblem of past Indian decline and present British power. That, indeed, was their history—fixed and always known, yet incomplete without the addition of British paramountcy. The dark moment of Indian history which the princes represented was the catalyst for British conquest. Most British tourists and administrators knew the princes only as a stereotype and it was through the seemingly endless repetition of that stereotype in diaries, travelogues, darbars that the history of British dominion was explained and understood.

The use of romantic stereotypes and myths was not limited to descriptions of or attitudes towards the princes. Anthropological surveys, for example, regularly brushed their subjects with the stigma of the stereotype, arguing that Indians represented a lesser and older stage of civilizational development. Both knowledge and superiority were asserted through the categorization of certain 'types' of Indians.

The Survey of India's choice of using old-fashioned techniques and stereotyped Indian agents to raise its visibility in Britain may, therefore, be placed within a sociological and political context that existed in both Britain and India. In both countries, medievalism and orientalism were linked to the new imperialist ideology in such a way that both pride in Britain and a sense of superiority were generated through the possession of Empire.

The Romance of the Survey: Controlling Indians and Defending Borders

At the beginning of the twentieth century a retired surveyor, T.H. Holdich, gave a speech about surveying in India to the Royal Society of Arts. The talk was later published under the title 'The Romance of the Indian Surveys'. Holdich described some of the more 'stirring incidents' of selfless devotion to duty, noting, for example, that at one time, a surveyor, when trying to determine the effect of the Himalayas on the force of gravity, was at the same time placing 'the spout of a boiling kettle near his mouth, (and) inhaling steam to check the pneumonia which killed him'. However noble and selfless this act may have seemed, Holdich believed that of even greater romantic interest to the public were the 'extraordinary achievements' of the 'specially trained native agents'. He praised the Indian surveyors for their devotion to their duty and, going further, implied that, in contrast to the unfortunate British surveyor who had died, their exertions on behalf of the department were 'romantic' in large measure because they were *trained* to be loyal and to provide information which the Survey regarded as useful. 'It is not easy,' he said, 'to train the Asiatics to habits of close observation in unaccustomed fields. Heredity and instinct alike make him intensely conservative in habits of thought' (Holdich 1916: 180–81).[5] The Survey, therefore, not only trained Indians as they had never been trained before but what was even more gratifying was the fact that it appeared that its pundits were willing and loyal agents. It is this control over trained Indians that contributed to the romance of the surveys.[6]

Several scholars have written about the trans-Himalayan explorations and, together with the official reports published by the Survey of India, they document the journeys undertaken by the Indian surveyors.[7] Their perspectives have generally been those of astonishment and admiration for the Survey's ingenuity and the surveyors' pluck. The most comprehensive account is by Derek Waller (1990). Waller's history explains how the Survey first began to consider employing Indians as secret surveyors and documents how, over a thirty-year period, numerous explorations were authorized in Afghanistan, Central Asia, and, especially, in Tibet. Although there is some positive assessment of the importance of the pundits' surveys in the British construction of the geography of inaccessible regions, Waller devotes himself to writing the first and only narrative history of their journeys. In fact, most of the other literature on the pundits (except Raj 2002) also tends to concentrate on retelling the narratives of a select number of journeys and highlighting the fact that the surveying was conducted in secret. There has, therefore, been an inadequate analysis of the meaning of the Survey's training and control over the pundits.

When writing about the pundits, the political and social context for their employment should be borne in mind. Even though the Mutiny of 1857–58 had been suppressed in a brutal and, in the end, effective manner, many British officials, who were faced with the problem of ensuring 'native' loyalty and subordination, remained anxious. As one of the major colonial departments, the Survey employed large numbers of Indians as porters, messengers, and even revenue surveyors. It appears, though, that its officers were able to maintain control during the rebellion. For example, in 1859, the Secretary to the Government of India sent a letter to the Deputy Surveyor General congratulating the department on its record over the previous two years. In particular, the secretary commended the Survey's 'work of science and peace'. The secretary also pointed out Captain T.G. Montgomerie, a surveyor in the trigonometrical department in charge of the survey of Kashmir, and congratulated him for having succeeded 'in retaining the loyal and willing services of the Natives of Hindostan'.[8] In fact, there is further indication that Montgomerie had gained the respect of his superiors in the department. After his retirement, Andrew Waugh, the former Surveyor General, announced to the Royal Geographical Society that Montgomerie was renowned for having surveyed Kashmir throughout the mutiny without any of his party rebelling.[9] Controlling Indian subordinates was clearly a mark of success. It appears, therefore, that through the employment of Indian explorers the Survey was contributing to the imperial project of producing loyal and dutiful subjects, willing to risk their lives for the good of the empire. Just as the princes personified their own defeat, the pundits, as a stereotype of the 'intelligent native', represented a condition of subordination. It is no accident that the man praised by the colonial government for his control over Indians would become the main force behind the formation of the trans-Himalayan surveys.

The Survey began to consider using 'native agency' in positions of some authority during the mid-1850s. In a letter to the British officer in charge of trigonometrical operations along the Indus river, the Surveyor General pointed out that the department had recently conducted an experiment whereby two Indians, Radhanath Sickdhar and Ramdial De, had been promoted from the subordinate agency to sub-assistantships, positions which had until then been held only by British or Anglo-Indian officers. Although De had 'failed', Sickdhar had achieved 'brilliant success' because he had become 'thoroughly Europeanised' and had 'surrendered his caste and prejudices'.[10] Theoretically, every Indian in the department was eligible for appointment to the position of sub-assistant, although that had never transpired. The Surveyor General's proposition was to create 'a subordinate agency under the class of Sub Assistant ... on a lower scale than would render them eligible to Sub Assistantships'. In other words, the Surveyor General wished to make use of Indians, who were 'suited to the climate', without having to integrate them into the main officer corps of the department. Moreover, these new sub-assistants would be paid significantly less than their British and Anglo-Indian counterparts—a welcome economical arrangement.

Indians were first employed as trans-Himalayan surveyors in the early 1860s, when the triangulation of India was nearing completion and greater attention was being directed towards cadastral and topographical surveys.[11] Surveyors who were assigned to the northern Indian mountains were also intrigued by the possibility of knowing the locations of towns beyond the borders of British India. One such surveyor was Montgomerie, the prominent surveyor within the department who had been one of five experts asked by the Surveyor General, Andrew Waugh, to comment on the appropriateness of the name Mount Everest.[12] On that occasion he had been unable to reply in time because of the ongoing conflict. However, in looking for ways to include non-accessible but contiguous areas within his maps, Montgomerie was quick to find a solution. He was especially keen to fix the much-travelled and important trade route between Kashmir and Yarkand, a town lying fifteen marches to the north of

British-controlled territory. However, any attempt by a European to travel towards Yarkand would have brought the surveyors, in Montgomerie's words, 'within range of the Khirgiz hordes who infest that road'. Not wishing to cause any 'political complication' by his capture or murder, Montgomerie searched for more palatable solutions to his dilemma. He thought that 'if a sharp enough man could be found he would have no difficulty in carrying a few small instruments among his merchandise, and with their aid I thought good service might be rendered to geography' (Montgomerie 1866: 157).

Montgomerie was able to find suitably sharp men with the help of Edmund Smyth, an explorer and, at the time, education officer in Kumaon. Smyth was well-acquainted with the hill regions of northern India and in a good position to suggest candidates for the job. Later, when he looked back on his role in the training of the pundits, Smyth wrote:

In 1862–3 I was in correspondence with Colonel (then Captain) Montgomerie of the Survey of India—I think it was about an expedition I was going to make into Tibet—and hearing he wanted some trustworthy men to train as explorers in that region I strongly recommended to him to engage some of these Bhotias, both on account of their sound knowledge of the Tibetan language and also because they had the entrée into the country. He asked me to select two and send them to him to be trained. I accordingly chose our friend Nain Singh, who was then employed as a Pundit (or schoolmaster) ... and the second man I chose was his cousin Manee or Maun Singh (cited in Allen 1982: 138).

Taking Smyth's advice Montgomerie ordered their transfer and instructed them in the techniques of route surveying. Others were also selected later. All but one of the new pundits came from the hills, which was considered vital if the new surveyors were to pass unobtrusively into Tibet, and many were all given *noms de guerre*, often the first and last initials of their first name. One exception was Sarat Chandra Das, a Bengali, whose pseudonym was S.C.D. He was the only 'native explorer' to write his own report (Das 1885). All other Indian surveyors had their reports translated into English by a clerk and then edited by a British surveyor.[13] Although Das displayed an intimate knowledge of Tibetan language and culture, eventually becoming a language teacher to British surveyors, Holdich thought the 'Bengali Babu' was of little scientific help and could not rank among the finest pundits. 'He is, however, a living witness to the fact that a certain amount of enterprise (combined with much learning) is to be found in the ranks of the Bengalis. As a rule, the best explorers have been men of action rather than of the pen' (Holdich 1906: 227).

Holdich's reservations regarding Das were based on the prevailing stereotypes of Bengalis as either too bookish or obstreperous. Turn-of-the-century racial theories claimed that men from the hills would be hardier and more disciplined than Bengalis, and that for tasks requiring physical exertion, these men would be more pliable. Nevertheless, the fact that Das was a Bengali and still a pundit added to the romance for Holdich, since even he could be moulded, much in the same way as Radhanath Sickdhar had been 'Europeanised'.

This absolute control over the pundits was made even more exciting for British officers and, ultimately, for British audiences with the knowledge that they were to survey in secret and to use the most rudimentary techniques. To facilitate their passage over the border passes, the surveyors disguised themselves as pilgrims and adapted religious instruments to suit their purposes. A small compass and bearings written on paper were concealed in a prayer wheel, while a rosary, which usually contained 108 beads, now only contained 100, with every tenth bead being slightly larger than the others. Montgomerie, in a paper published in the Royal Geographical Society's journal, noted that the beads were made of a coral-like substance as well as of seeds. 'The rosary was carried in the sleeve,' he wrote, and 'at every hundredth pace a bead was dropped, and each large bead dropped, consequently, represented 1000 paces. With his prayer-wheel and rosary the pundit always managed in one way or another to take his bearings and to count his paces' (Montgomerie 1868: 140). Not having a theodolite, not having a chain, not being extensively trained in astronomy, and not being able to keep a proper journal, the pundits' journeys were a poor imitation of those their British colleagues were conducting in India.

Thus, the instruments, methods, and rationale were outdated; indeed, the route survey, had long been superseded by the introduction of trigonometrical surveying.[14] Yet the Survey went to some trouble, if not expense, to train their pundits to survey in a manner which would yield highly suspect scientific results. A scientific survey, however, may not have been the most important object of these explorations. In an essay on the textuality of empire, Chris Tiffin and Alan Lawson (1994: 3) suggest that although Europeans used 'native' guides and explorers for their surveys, travels, and discoveries, the knowledge these guides imparted was considered 'pragmatic rather than conceptual and strategic'. The 'pundits' were not expected to rationalize, compute, protract, or even narrate their surveys—all these tasks were to be accomplished by British Survey officers, using the explorers' raw and pragmatic information. It was the ability to train Indians to gather information, together with the foolhardy, almost reckless, nature of their journeys, that lie at the heart of why their surveys were considered romantic. As Charles Allen has noted, 'From the Survey of India's point of view Nain Singh's journey was a triumphant vindication of Western scientific method and training, even though it owed far more to resourcefulness and courage than anything else' (1982: 142).

The pundits were also useful to the Survey because they helped to generate a sense that the department was, through its secret mapping, an active participant in the defence of India. Throughout the nineteenth century, departments of survey in India had desperately sought international acclaim. The adoption of trigonometrical mapping, the exploration of river sources, and the naming of Mount Everest were, in part, attempts to attract attention and support from European audiences. The East India Company and then the Government of India had never neglected their surveying departments, but the surveyors themselves had always felt isolated, if not excluded, from European scientific bodies. George Everest, for example, wrote that the Royal Society's meddling and uninformed conduct regarding the appointment of a Surveyor General of India was 'illustrative of the habitual spirit of monopoly and selfishness of the Royal Society, and of the tendency of that spirit to blind the learned Fellows to the labours and performances of their own countrymen in the East, which they are as unwilling as unable to appreciate' (1839: 16).[15]

If not all surveyors were as embittered as Everest, many may have nevertheless felt a need to be heard by the European scientific community. One of the most effective means of communication was through the journal of the Royal Geographical Society, an organization which prided itself on its sponsorship of central African, South American and, later, Antarctic explorations. Certainly, a glance at the submissions to the journal for the second half of the nineteenth century reveals that discovery and adventure were indispensable to any narrative or report. It is perhaps as a result of this kind of exposure that the stories of the pundits became widely known.

It may also have been the case that the papers and conversations published by the Society provided Rudyard Kipling with the idea to write a fictional account of the secret trans-Himalayan surveys. *Kim* is the most renowned example of the romance of the Survey set in a 'great game' context. The novel is not only concerned with issues of controlling the young surveyor, it is also about the ability of the Survey to defend India from external threats. Both of these messages contribute to its romance.

Kipling's novel is perhaps the most prominent example of the Survey's public relations success. In fact, the popularity both of *Kim* and the journeys have continued to the present, with a recent television documentary highlighting the explorations.[16] The characters sweep across northern India and participate, with evident good humour and panache, in international espionage and intrigue. One of the central characters in *Kim* is Colonel Creighton, an elevated and arcane Captain Montgomerie, who trains the lost and orphaned son of an Irish soldier in the arts of clandestine survey; our hero must learn 'to make pictures of roads and mountains and rivers—to carry these pictures in thy eye till a suitable time comes to set them on paper' (Kipling 1901: 187).' In fact, many of the characters in *Kim* are based on real individuals—the Creighton-Montgomerie connection being the most important and evident. In *Quest for Kim*, Peter Hopkirk has attempted to locate and identify the models of as many of the novel's places and characters as possible (1997).

Although some of the characters, especially the male characters, may have historical models, one of the striking features of the novel is that the explorer and spy, Kim, is not Indian, although for much of the book he is mistaken by many to be a particularly acute 'native'. Colonel Creighton is undoubtedly the mastermind behind the spying but the success of the mission is wholly dependent upon Kim's wit and intelligence. In fact, even though Kim is respectful of authority, both Indian and British, he is portrayed as being beyond direct control and manipulation. He escapes from his various chaperones and always follows his own immediate agendas. This capricious and spontaneous behaviour, permitted because of his unique position of being neither wholly British nor wholly Indian, may be contrasted with the more historical narratives of the pundits' journeys, where control of information and its presentation were key concerns. Nevertheless, Kim's ability to blend into and be accepted by any social group, British or Indian, Catholic or Anglican, was a romantic expression of widely-held British fantasies of omniscience, mobility, and voyeurism. For much of the novel, Kim searches for his identity, caught as he is between being British and Indian. In the end, Kim shows himself to be truly British by solving the riddle of his father's identity and demonstrating, through his heroic deeds, his duty to the defence of the empire. Nevertheless, the prominence that questions of identity, loyalty and duty to the empire, and control have in the novel mirror the Survey's preoccupations with stereotyping pundits as either hardy hill men or bookish Bengalis, its anxiety over their loyalty, and its desire to demonstrate its control over their loyalty and actions. The wonder in *Kim* is that the young hero accomplishes so much while remaining so free; the wonder of the pundits is that they were so well trained as to be still fettered to the Survey, even when in the heart of Tibet.

Kipling's story also suggests that, with the help of such departments as the Survey of India, the Government of India was vigilant and active in protecting India's sovereignty and territorial integrity. Indeed, much of the romance of both the novel and the Survey's accounts of its pundits' journeys revolves around the notion that these trans-Himalayan surveys should be set within a great game political context. However, as Charles Allen has written, 'the Pundits were never "players in the Game" in the political sense, whatever Kipling and British public opinion in India may have wanted to believe' (1982: 137). Moreover, despite the messages of Kipling's novel and the Survey's narratives, the pundits were hampered by their inadequate training, lack of scientific instruments, and the solitary nature of the surveys. Once the pundits had left India, the Survey provided no material help whatsoever and seemed to just wait for their return. It is perhaps no surprise, therefore, that the cartographic benefits of these surveys were minimal, especially when weighed against the great risk the journeys posed to the lives of the pundits. Also, despite the impression conveyed by *Kim*, the Survey's use of the pundits provided little additional security to India. The limited results of the surveys are evident in the story of one pundit's journey. What is also apparent is the degree to which the pundits themselves, together with their surveys and narratives, were controlled and co-opted, and how that control made the Survey's trans-Himalayan reconnaissances romantic.

The Explorer K-P and the Control over His Person and Story

Explorer K-P, or Kintup, began his most famous survey into Tibet in August 1880.[17] The first public documentation of his journey appeared in the general report of the Survey of 1886–87, but the full text of the exploration—which had been translated by 'Norpu', a department employee, and subsequently compiled by Colonel Tanner—did not appear until 1889 (Thuillier 1889). Kintup had been selected to accompany a Lama into Tibet in 1880 by Captain Harman, Montgomerie's successor, in charge of trans-Himalayan explorations, with a mission to survey eastern Tibet and Bhutan and obtain conclusive evidence that the Tsangpo river became the Brahmaputra.[18] The journey took Kintup four years to complete, largely because shortly after their departure the Lama disappeared, but not before selling Kintup into slavery. Kintup, however, managed to escape and, after having tried in vain to contact the Surveyor General through another explorer, Nimsring (alias G.M.N.), who was acting as the interpreter at the court of Darjeeling, he threw into the Tsangpo, over a period of ten days, five hundred specially marked foot-long logs, hoping that at least one would be noticed floating down the Brahmaputra into the Bay of Bengal. Such a log, if discovered in the Brahmaputra, would have been incontrovertible proof that the Tsangpo was the Brahmaputra. Unfortunately, none was ever spotted. Moreover, Kintup was illiterate (the department had intended that the Lama should survey) and, therefore, his narrative report covering four gruelling years of travel seemed hardly scientific, even if his account was, to quote the Survey's records, a 'bona fide story' (Hennessey 1891: 3).

It appears that Kintup's story was more remarkable for his sufferings and continued loyalty to duty than it was for its geographical information. His report was published but there seems to be no evidence that the Survey relied upon many of his observations in the construction of their maps. In fact, the very truth of his journey was only vouched for later when British survey and political officers retraced some of his steps and were astonished at his accuracy. Their reports on his survey and on their efforts to rehabilitate his name indicate the continuing need to use him as a way of signalling the close and loyal bonds connecting the British officer with the Indian agent.

Thirty years after Kintup's survey, George Dunbar, a Political Officer, followed many of Kintup's routes during the Abor military campaign in Eastern India.[19] He was struck by Kintup's accurate geographical descriptions, noting that 'he was more often than not the complete Baedeker', and puzzled that he had not been accorded the same recognition as other explorers, who had been given land and titles by the government, and gold watches by various scientific societies, including the Royal Geographical Society (see Dunbar 1930: 256). One pundit, for example, Nain Singh, had received from the Great Trigonometrical Survey of India a surveying instrument. As an indication of his worth to the Survey, his superiors had inscribed on the instrument the words 'For Bravery and Devotion' (Waller 1990: in the illustration following page 136).

Dunbar was impressed by Kintup's report of his survey, especially since it had been recited from memory, and wanted to amend the record. 'It was a great personal pleasure,' he wrote, 'to have been one of those who proved Kintup to have been right, and to have vindicated one of the greatest explorers in the whole Survey of India during his lifetime. When we got back to India,' Dunbar continues, 'steps were taken to get the old man a pension, so that he could end his days in comfort. He was found in very poor circumstances in Darjeeling, trying to make a living at his old trade as a tailor, and every one who knows his story must be glad that this "romance" had, at long last, a happy ending' (Dunbar 1930: 257).

It is important to note that Dunbar's deliberate modesty and his effusive praise of a surveyor who had just been 'vindicated' are not rhetorically innocent. The silent subject is not Kintup, but Dunbar, who, by virtue of his large-hearted and valiant search for the truth, manages to apply for and procure a pension for a man dying in penury. Nor is it insignificant that Dunbar considers his verification necessary to prove the accuracy of Kintup's survey. Even with regard to the truth, Kintup was dependent upon and still subordinate to British officers. What made Kintup's journey romantic was, first, its seeming-accuracy, its seeming-truthfulness, all set in an almost mythical past time and in an unknown world. Its romance was also derived from the ultimate control exercised over Kintup by both the Survey (to whom he was presumably 'devoted') and Dunbar who, along with his colleagues, was able to verify the truth of his statements.

But, the topic of Kintup's vindication does not end with Dunbar's account. In his speech to the Royal Society of Arts Holdich praised Kintup's courage and blamed his temporary obscurity on politicians who had no appreciation for adventurous travel. He noticed, however, that 'thanks to the exploits of that splendid young traveller Bailey, Kintup now lives in honoured retirement with the halo of truthful adventure crowning his scanty grey hairs. His was a live romance' (Holdich 1916: 181).

F.M. Bailey was, like Dunbar, a Political Officer who, after the same 1914 Abor campaign, decided to travel west along the poorly mapped Tsangpo.[20] His travelling companion was Henry Morshead, a surveyor, and one of their principal objectives was to verify Kintup's route. They were particularly intrigued by Kintup's observation that there were 100-foot falls at Singdam, along the Tsangpo (Hennessey 1891: 10). The height was exaggerated in Survey lore to 150 feet (see, for example, Bailey 1957: 279), meaning that the falls could provide an Indian equivalent to Africa's 200–300-foot-high Victoria Falls, and were, therefore, an exciting discovery—that is, only if they existed. After a long and arduous march, Bailey and Morshead determined that Kintup had been correct in most of his observations although the height of the falls had been greatly exaggerated by a clerical error while Kintup's narrative was being copied and translated in the offices of the Survey of India.

The mediated nature of Kintup's report, its distortion and vindication for the purposes of fashioning a myth of romance become apparent upon reading Bailey's account of his journey up the Tsangpo. In his book, he notes that after completing the exploration he wished to contact Kintup and congratulate him, belatedly, for compiling such an accurate report on the villages and terrain along the river. Bailey acknowledges that the department clerk had mistranslated Kintup's report, thereby suggesting that the falls at Singdam were higher than in reality. More importantly, Bailey comments on how he, and not Dunbar, had managed to contact Kintup, and on the circumstances which led to the government's grant of a 'pension'. 'As far as the Survey of India was concerned,' he begins, 'Kintup was lost. ... I wrote to my friend Gyaltsen Kazi, a Sikkimese landlord with excellent sources of information, and asked him if he would institute a search. Very soon he sent me news that Kintup had been found ... I pestered the Indian Government to give Kintup a pension in recognition of his services to Tibetan exploration. But they were adamant. "We can't give the man a pension," they said. "That is an indefinite financial commitment. He might live to be ninety"' (ibid.: 279–80).

As it was, Kintup lived only a few months after having been given a lump sum of Rs 1,000, but his vindication was complete. As was the case with Dunbar, Bailey implied that it was only on his account that the truth of Kintup's survey had been established. Henry Morshead's son, for example, wrote that as a result of his father and Bailey's efforts, Kintup could henceforth be considered 'probably the greatest Himalayan explorer of them all' (Morshead 1982: 47). Moreover, by virtue of Bailey's efforts, the bond of dependence and patronage between colonial government and Indian surveyor had been reinstated.

The perspectives of Dunbar, Holdich, and Bailey, all foregrounded their commitment to the rehabilitation of Kintup's name, the colonial government's duty to maintain Kintup in a state of dependence, and the Survey's ability to exact from its pundits unquestioned loyalty and dedication. The subtle variations in the presentation of Kintup's exploration indicate that Kintup was never really the subject of the reports. He might have told the first narrative but the real story was about the government, the Survey, and their British officers. As Holdich wrote, public approbation ought to be given, first and foremost, to the Survey. 'When we read the marvellous records ...

of those painstaking, unresting native explorers who had been trained to use certain simple instruments to perfection, we must always remember who was behind them. They were the agents, but theirs was not the plan' (1906: 225).

Tibet was a terrain of instruction. It was the location where the Survey of India taught antiquated techniques in order to instil in Indians a myth of loyalty, while projecting to Europe a sense of romance. The public secrecy surrounding their activities was a contrived hoax. Easily broken pseudonyms, published narratives of clandestine explorations, papers presented before the Royal Geographical Society, all were attempts by the Survey to honour its imperial duty to inculcate science and loyalty, all the while preserving its integrity as an important and reliable participant in the government's efforts to defend a mapped and known India.

Conclusion

The mediated story of K-P provides insight into how British surveyors attempted to portray themselves as staunch and moral imperialists. On the one hand, K-P's journey was viewed as part of an effort to defend the boundaries of India by gaining knowledge of what existed beyond them. On the other hand, his stirring story and the attempts to resuscitate his name by validating his observations reveal a patronizing desire to demonstrate mastery over his survey. The twin need to be valiant and colonial informs much of the language that was used to describe the pundits' surveys.

The pundits seem to have provided a form of light relief for the Survey of India, an organization that was otherwise preoccupied with more mundane and systematic mapping. I have called their foray into trans-Himalayan exploration 'romantic', partly because that was a term that T.H. Holdich and others used to describe the pundits' journeys, but also because their surveys combined in an almost fanciful manner both anachronism and social control.

Romance is commonly associated with a chivalric past and noble endeavour. If that past is considered mythical, romance may derive its sentimental force from its contrast to current behaviour and practice. To call someone a romantic, for example, often means that he or she is charmingly old-fashioned and somewhat out of touch with modern ways. The use of pundits to survey beyond India in such a rudimentary fashion that virtually no dependable geographical information could be gleaned sufficient to justify the great risk to their lives suggests that the Survey of India wished to project itself and its relations with Indians in an almost mythical light. While one reality was that the Survey spent most of its time prosaically mapping India, the myth or romance of the pundits was that it was part of the great game, playing its part in defending the boundaries of the empire. The other reality was that, following the upheavals of the 1850s, there was an anxiety among many British officials concerning Indian loyalty and devotion; very few Indians were given responsible positions within the Survey, for example. The most prominent was considered a success because he had allayed fears that his sympaties were not with the empire by becoming Europeanized. The myth or romance that was expressed by the publication and discussion of the pundits' journeys was that Indians could indeed be trained, not only to survey in however an antiquated way it may have been, but also to devote themselves to completing the mission for their colonial employers, even if the journey would take years, and even at the risk of death.

Notes

1. In an essay on these trans-Himalayan surveys Kapil Raj (2002: 156–88) argues that Indians were made into reliable instruments because their journeys were replicable and they were deliberately given titles, such as pundit and munshi, that lent authority and credibility to their accounts. The relationship between British officers and Indian trans-Himalayan surveyors was highly paternalistic, especially in the nineteenth century. Peter Hansen (1999: 210–31) examines the changes in this relationship and suggests that by the mid-twentieth century Indians became partners to British explorers.
2. In the essay 'Alternative Victorian Futures', Florence Boos (1992: 13) writes that interest in the medieval arose because there was 'a sense of the "medieval" as *alternate culture* (at least for men)—alternative both to contemporary capitalist and imperialist *realpolitick*, and to the unrealities of their conventional classical education.'
3. John Mackenzie (1986: 7) notes that the British government had always had difficulty in educating the public about its colonies. In surveys

conducted by the Colonial Office as late as 1948–51, 'fifty-nine per cent of those interviewed could not name a single British colony. One man suggested Lincolnshire'.

4. David Cannadine's *Ornamentalism: How the British Saw their Empire* (2001) argues that ties of class were particularly important in the British Empire.

5. He also wrote that if the Indian surveyor 'had the bad luck to fall on evil times, to be sold as a slave, or to be robbed and maltreated, his records, concealed in the lining of his coat, in his turban or his waistband, would usually be all there, and his keenness in the evolution of the resulting map work would be absolutely absorbing' (Holdich 1916: 181).

6. George MacMunn's *The Romance of the Frontiers* (1978) is another example of the link between the idea of romance and exploration.

7. These include Derek Waller 1990, Peter Hopkirk 1982, John Keay 1993, Douglas W. Freshfield 1903, Charles Allen 1982: 121–45, and Indra Singh Rawat 1973.

8. R.J.H. Birch to Deputy Surveyor General, 19 July 1859. NAI, DDn Vol., Old No. SGO 36, Sl. No. 649, p. 157.

9. 'Discussion on Captain Montgomerie's Paper', in *Proceedings of the Royal Geographical Society*, Vol. X, 1866: 164.

10. NAI, DDn Vol. List, Old No. 56/3, Sl. No. 709, pp. 268–69, A.S. Waugh to J.T. Walker, 27 October 1856.

11. The first documented use of Indians as surveyors for the Company was in 1774, when Jacob Camac sent Ghulam Mohammed, a sepoy officer, to explore the country between Bengal and the Deccan. In cadastral operations Indians were particularly prominent, although their role was always considered subservient to that of British officers (see Phillimore 1945 Vol. I: 289). A good example of how Indians were employed as surveyors by government officials prior to the 1850s may be found in the OIOC. 'Mahomed Sadicks Journal' is a translated manuscript of an Indian spy who was asked by John Malcolm to report on geographical and statistical matters in Afghanistan (OIOC MSS Eur. F. 228/90).

12. For brief biographies of Thomas George Montgomerie, see the *Dictionary of Indian Biography* and Henry Yule, 'The Late Col. T.G. Montgomerie, R.E. (Bengal)', unpublished paper, 1878, British Library 10804.bbb.17 (2).

13. See, for example, *Report on the Explorations in Great Tibet and Mongolia, Made by A-K in 1879–82*, prepared by J.B.N. Hennessey, 1891.

14. The Survey's official manual of surveying indicated that route surveys 'do not come under the head of scientific or accurate works' since they are 'usually done by the eye, instead of being a continued series of angles

and measured lines, as in the more elaborate surveys' (Thuillier and Smyth 1875: 441–42).

15. The Society, thinking Everest had retired, petitioned the Company to appoint Major T.B. Jervis.

16. *The Shape of the World*, Granada Television Ltd. and PBS. The book of the same title by Berthon and Robinson (1991) is based on the six-part television programme. Other works which praise the pundits' explorations include Hopkirk's *Trespassers on the Roof of the World* (1982) Misra's *The Unification and Division of India* (1990), and an essay in *Congrès International des Sciences Géographiques, 1875*, Vol. II, 1880: 161–72.

17. A map of his four-year journey may be found in Derek Waller's, *The Pundits* (1990: 218).

18. The source and course of the Brahmaputra, Irrawady, and Tsangpo rivers had been a subject of much debate among European cartographers ever since D'Anville identified the Tsangpo as being another name for the Irrawady, while Rennell claimed that it was really the Brahmaputra. See, for example, E. Roux 1896.

19. Dunbar remembered that very little fighting occurred during the campaign, or perambulation, as it was euphemistically called, and that 'the active people were the scientists, who wanted the Abors alive and in sufficient numbers for an anthropological series, or (who) went out bug-hunting with a small escort' (1930: 167).

20. In addition to being a Political Officer, Bailey considered himself an amateur botanist. On their expedition up the Brahmaputra he collected over 2,000 butterflies, one of which was named *Lycaenopsis morsheadi*, after Henry Morshead. Years later, one Mary Rowlatt wrote to Morshead's son to inform him that she had asked to see the Morshead butterfly at London's Natural History Museum and had been shown two, 'both small and somewhat dingy, but apparently of the greatest interest to experts' (Morshead 1982: 42). Bailey was not to be forgotten, either. A blue poppy was named *Meconopsis baileyi*, while a shrew is known as *Scorculus baileyi* (Bailey 1957: 9 and 45).

FIVE

Mapping Nostalgia in Late-Victorian India

By the end of the nineteenth century the practice of history was in large part directed towards generating a nostalgia for original moments. This nostalgia exhibited by historians was didactic and often displayed graphically in the form of surveys, maps, or atlases. However, whereas a century earlier the writing of history was dependent upon cartographic notions of territory, the second half of the nineteenth century witnessed a reversal of roles; surveying, map making, and geography were all pressed into the service of history. Thus, history's preoccupation with a certain kind of past became cartography's mission.

History may be called a practice because in order for the past to live as shared memory it must be re-enacted or represented. This deliberate repetition, although always modified, contributes to patterns of expression and action which, when recognized as meaningful in a contemporary setting, constitute a regulated approach to the past. What is particularly fascinating about late-nineteenth-century history is its use of nostalgia as a way of encouraging participation and awareness. In what may be called the democratization of history the polemical and targeted writings of the eighteenth century were transformed into universally accessible, educational, and uncontroversial narratives. This chapter will examine the narratives of the new democratic history and demonstrate that its reliance upon correct progressions of events made the representation of origins especially significant. Much of what defined a late Victorian history—extended parables and moral tales embedded within a story of derring-do—was most effectively communicated when suffused with a nostalgia for beginnings.

Late-nineteenth-century nostalgia may be defined as a longing for a pure, but lost, moment. A moment might be a date, 20 June 1756, for example, or an era, such as the Roman Republic, but the significance of a moment was that it was always regarded as temporally discrete. Although historians wrote narratives which involved progressions, suggesting that movement was more important than static moments, two crucial features of these histories stand out. First, facts and events were given such weight that no understanding of history was possible without recognizing that events themselves were the catalyst for historical movement. It should be made clear that this chapter is primarily concerned with colonial historians, the majority of whom did not subscribe to a Hegelian idealism or a Marxist materialism. For the ordinary British historian of India, whether a retired administrator or a professional historian, events led to events, and facts created facts. For these historians causality was uncomplicated.

The second aspect of these histories was that the indispensable progression of events, sometimes even a teleology, was more often directed *backwards* in time than forwards. Even with histories which progressed, by means of a succession of events, to morally satisfactory conclusions, the original moment was all-important—it created the narrative and provided the moral. In an essay on the problems of writing history, Janet Abu-Lughod points out that because historical accounts are written 'after the fact', beginnings assume a heightened importance (1989: 112). Even the terms 'outcome' or 'conclusion' suggest that the end must be envisioned and comprehended in the beginning. Of great interest, therefore, is why beginnings are chosen and how they are depicted.

Nostalgia is commonly described as either a sentimental or an overly positive retrospective. British nostalgia for the Raj, which reached its height in the 1980s, is a good example of viewing the past through rose-tinted lenses.[1] Susan Stewart has written that in being hostile to history, 'and yet longing for an impossibly pure context of lived experience at a place of origin, nostalgia wears a distinctly utopian face, a face that turns toward a future-past, a past which has only ideological reality' (1984: 23). However, these ideas of nostalgia, which often involve an indictment of present conditions while searching for an impossible re-experience of what has passed, are far removed from the original meaning of the word.

The term 'nostalgia' was first used by Johannes Hofer, a Swiss doctor, in 1688, to describe a debilitating and potentially life-threatening disease afflicting young Helvetians who lived abroad.[2] Derived from two Greek words, *nosos*—to return to the native land and *algos*, meaning grief or suffering, nostalgia was defined as 'the sad mood originating from the desire to return to one's native land' (Hofer 1934: 380). Hofer suggested that in case nostalgia was not an acceptable term, doctors might wish to use either 'nosomanias' or 'philopatridomania' to describe the pathology of homesickness. Symptoms of the disease included 'continued sadness, meditation only of the Fatherland, disturbed sleep either wakeful or continuous, decrease of strength, hunger, thirst, senses diminished, and cares or even palpitations of the heart, frequent sighs, also stupidity of the mind' (ibid.: 386). Rapid repatriation was prescribed as the most effective cure.

Fred Davis has noted that nostalgia is no longer considered a pathology, nor is it widely associated with homesickness—'it is much more likely,' he writes, 'to be classed with such familiar emotions as love, jealousy, and fear than with such "conditions" as melancholia, obsessive compulsion, or claustrophobia' (Davis 1979: 5). He argues, moreover, that our understanding of nostalgia should be distinguished from an indulgence in an antiquarian feeling; that an affinity with the general past is different from a sentiment or an attachment for a past which we have experienced but now consider lost. His example is that, according to current usage, we may not be nostalgic for the Crusades, a period of time so remote from our own. Rather, it is best to regard any such longing as an antiquarian emotion.

Although I accept Davis' characterizations of present-day nostalgia as neither a disease nor an overriding desire to return home, I wish to use the term in a way that approaches its original meaning. Throughout this chapter, nostalgia refers to a cultural pathology— a compulsive obsession with returning to an idealized home and a sense of belonging through the staged experience of a foundational moment. What I wish to stress here is that the homesickness demonstrated in the construction and use of maps involved the imagination of a pure moment in the colonial past which was equated with a national homecoming. In other words, in obsessing over a foundational moment, colonial tourists, administrators, and map makers were reinforcing the pervasive sense of what it meant to be British, and, possibly, Indian. I do not follow Davis' distinction between nostalgia, which he defines as a fond remembrance of an event or period from a lived experience, and an antiquarian feeling, which he regards as an affinity for a time long since past. Instead I argue that the nostalgia exhibited by late-Victorian colonial tourists and officials was an effort to make a moment in the distant past of ultimate meaning in the present-day understanding of the British nation and its relation to its Empire. Without a ritualized return to these foundational moments, commentators, tourists, and administrators reported feelings of inadequacy and displacement often coupled with a desire to return to the physical home of Britain, Europe, or the West.

This chapter looks at an original moment to show how nostalgia was mapped, literally, into its history. This mapped moment exemplifies an aspect of nostalgia and enables an examination of the didactic and inclusive nature of nostalgia. Throughout the chapter there is an emphasis on the curious relationship between the late-Victorian colonial state, cartography, and the past. It is suggested that maps dissimulate when they seem impartial. They often mask social relations and always naturalize the perspective of the cartographer. Deployed by the state, maps seem all that the state is not—visible, inclusive, comprehensible, and useful. My use of maps in this chapter, however, is deliberately expansive. For example, specific directions in a guide book or lines in the ground designating the limits of a building are considered maps. Such a wide use of the term indicates that cartographic perspectives and directives may be effectively and beguilingly presented in a form other than a traditional map.

The chapter examines the various histories of the Black Hole deaths and pays particular attention to the manner of representation and the structures of the narratives. The argument is that cartography, in its widest sense, was a convenient resource for educating a British and Indian public and, importantly, an effective tool for including visitors in a touristic re-enactment of the events of 1756. The Black Hole of Calcutta (now renamed Kolkata) is perhaps the single-most important (non-)event in the British colonial imagination. History books alluded to it with the formulaic phrase 'as every schoolboy knows', and yet the gruesome narrative of the night of 20 June 1756 was invariably retold in a breathless and mock-horrified fashion. Thomas Babington Macaulay, for example, a notorious colonial official and historian known for his staunch anti-vernacular stance in mid-nineteenth century education debates, wrote that, regarding the Black Hole, 'nothing in history or fiction, not even the story which Ugolino told in the sea of everlasting ice, after he had wiped his bloody lips on the scalp of his murderer, approaches the horrors which were recounted by the few survivors of that night' (quoted in Firminger 1909: 1). The Black Hole was *the* event of British colonial histories of India.

Late-Victorian interest in the Black Hole was stimulated by the publication of *Echoes from Old Calcutta* in 1882, in which H.E. Busteed lamented the fact that the crumbling monument to those who died, erected by John Zephaniah Holwell, the chief survivor and publicist of the event, had been demolished in 1821, following years of neglect, and never replaced (1888: 49). Lord Curzon read Busteed's book on the boat out to India—later presenting his daughter with a copy— and decided that one of his first acts as Viceroy would be to remedy the situation by delineating with thin brass lines the walls of old Fort William, the last remnants of which had been torn down in the early nineteenth century.[3] Curzon was one of the most historically-conscious and imperially-minded viceroys, and the Black Hole gave him the opportunity to express both his interest in the exercise of British power in the past and also his desire that there should be a general appreciation for how and why Britain had won an empire.[4] Thus, with the help of the researches of R. Roskell Bayne, who in 1863 first located portions of the old fort while laying the foundations of the new East India Railway Company's offices, H.E. Busteed, and C.R. Wilson, Curzon placed black marble over the exact location of the Black Hole prison within the fort's walls, made a scale model of the fort and prison for the Victoria Memorial Exhibition, and constructed a replica of Holwell's monument on the original site.

Fig. 10. *View and Map of Old Fort William, showing the location of the Black Hole (Busteed 1888: 20).*

This mapping of the Black Hole onto the pavement of Calcutta was an expression of the need to explain contemporary political circumstances with reference to an original moment. Cartography was important in this regard because it enabled Curzon to educate and illustrate the relevance of the Black Hole in an appealing and beguiling fashion. Indeed, it was the very manner of representing the Black Hole—as a public exhibit, as a tourist site—which fused the event into the exhibit, and permitted the projection of nostalgia onto the site. In turning a moment into a monument, Curzon hoped to locate the origins of British rule in a place, while at the same time making that location of universal significance.

Since so much was dependent upon this original moment, including the justification for British dominion over India, it was crucial that it be represented correctly. The difficulty, of course, was that as a representation it could never be the truth itself, although it could help to formulate several true perspectives. Ian Hacking has argued that the conception of reality, as a human creation, is dependent upon the practice of representing (1993: 136). A tree may exist independently from our thought but our idea of a tree relies on representation; we know and recognize a tree based on an idea of what constitutes its correct colour, shape, and size. Similarly, the truth (or truths) about the Black Hole existed only insofar as it could be understood through its representation. Suffocation may or may not have occurred, but our knowledge of and reactions to the Black Hole are wholly dependent upon subsequent representations. It was, therefore, by means of Curzon's statist recreation and mapping of the Black Hole that an early-twentieth-century audience may have been persuaded that it was a viewing participant in the foundational event of British rule in India. We shall see that the longing to recapture the moment was simultaneously whetted and satisfied by the representation.

Curzon's mapping may also have helped to build a sense of Britishness among the expatriate community in Calcutta. A sense of belonging to a nation was one of the possible reactions to the voyeuristic participation in the reliving of the Black Hole. By the end of the nineteenth century, the nation-building processes that had begun more than a century earlier were sufficiently successful for many British men and women to feel a strong emotional attachment to 'home'. Moreover, living in the colonies might have been an alienating and somewhat lonely experience—one that gave rise to homesickness or nostalgia. This nostalgia could have been assuaged by their reliving the original and founding moments of British colonial rule, moments which encapsulated the military explanation and moral rationale for the continued British presence in India. In providing that link to the past and in making that history accessible to a mass audience, Curzon's map seemingly strengthened the value and sense of being British.

The Black Hole: A Historical Imagination

The Black Hole had long been a figment of imperial historical imagination. Young East India Company cadets during their training at Addiscombe, near Croydon in south London, for example, were physically, graphically, and rudely introduced to the Black Hole. Unruly cadets were often confined in a small room, fifteen feet by eight feet, located, of all places, just beneath the vestry. This punishment room was known as the Black Hole, and a cadet was forced to spend hours in solitary confinement with the single window locked and the doors bolted. On one occasion a cadet played a trick and pretended to have committed suicide by hanging. When the sergeant opened the door and saw what he supposed was a dead cadet hanging by a rope, 'he called the cadet by name twice in a most terrified voice, and then rushed from the "Black Hole"' (Vibart 1894: 126). Turning a terrible national memory into a facetious schoolboy prank might have been tasteless, yet the ritual re-enactment of the Black Hole imprisonment served to remind and reinforce the significance of the original prison.

The horror of the school punishment cell was made legendary by its association with the Black Hole prison. Although only one cadet was confined at a time as punishment, the use of the name Black Hole exaggerated the need to escape from a suffocating and inhumane dungeon. But, while there might have been a desire to flee, there was also an urge to visit, even experience, the Black Hole. The fascination of the Black Hole was in the (safe) experience of its horror; after all, the cadet at Addiscombe did not die, but merely suffered an inconvenient detention.

Midway through his travels around the world, Mark Twain hoped
to feel that same *frisson* of terrible pleasure when he visited Calcutta
(see Twain 1897: 519). His anticipation and excitement were so great
that his very first outing was to the site of the Black Hole prison. The
Black Hole represented to him 'the Foundation Stone, upon which
was reared a mighty Empire'. Nothing remained, however—no 'ingots
of historic gold', no 'accounting for human beings'. Twain wanted
the experience of the Black Hole, to touch and see and imagine, but
without a wall to feel, without a monument to admire, without a map
to guide him, he felt cheated. Twain's disappointment is reminiscent
of Timothy Mitchell's (1991) observations on nineteenth-century
European exhibitions of Egypt and the Middle East. Mitchell points
out that the exhibitions that were held in European capitals created
representations and expectations that were invariably different from
the 'real' subjects of the representations. Travellers to the 'Orient'
who had visited these exhibitions and had been influenced by their
depictions were often disappointed in what they subsequently saw.
Similarly, Twain had an expectation, based on its infamous character,
that the Black Hole would still be standing, perhaps as a monument
to Oriental cruelty and as a reminder of the original cause for British
colonial control.

By the early part of the twentieth century, tourists to Calcutta were
more fortunate than Twain. They might have read, for example,
Thacker's Guide to Calcutta (1906), written by the famous scholar W.K.
Firminger. A year after this guide appeared H.E.A. Cotton wrote a
similar history book for tourists, entitled *Calcutta Old and New* (1907),
in which he also devoted a chapter to retelling the Black Hole story.
Although I will refer occasionally to Cotton's book, I will mainly
concentrate on *Thacker's Guide*. The guide's second chapter, entitled
'In Search of the Old Fort and Black Hole', takes the visitor on an
archaeological journey to downtown Calcutta. As with all guides,
Firminger wants his readers to use his book and not just peruse it—
it is a manual for viewing. The manner of approach is explained,
the order of seeing 'the sites' is coordinated with a narrative, and the
suitable emotional response is anticipated and encouraged.

The guide is written in a scholarly style, although the choice of
topics and the manner of presentation are similar to other guides
of India, such as John Murray's, and the intended audience is the

British tourist. It contains two maps of Calcutta—one depicting the city in 1906; the other a larger-scale map of the old town showing a section around the old fort as it was in 1756 and in 1906. The superimposition of the later city onto the original town becomes a particularly effective means of making the past recognizable in a contemporary setting, especially since the map is to be read in conjunction with the text. Lord Curzon would later also publish a map that superimposed the new city onto the old in order to show which portions of the old fort walls he had demarcated on the pavement of the city.

Firminger begins his chapter on the Black Hole by suggesting an itinerary. The route chosen is designed to help the tourist 'realise the proportions' of the old fort, locate the site of the Black Hole within the fort, imagine the occurrences on the night of 20 June 1756, and finally notice Curzon's replica of the monument. By designating a specific tour, to be repeated by visitor after visitor, the guide transforms the journey into a pilgrimage, the very term used by Lord Curzon to describe a tourist's approach to the Black Hole site (see Curzon 1906: 157). A visitor unfamiliar with Calcutta and relying on *Thacker's Guide*, is led on a tour where every stop and perspective manipulates emotion and leads towards the appropriate and anticipated response—that of nostalgia.

What is particularly curious about Firminger's tour of the fort and the Black Hole is that there are almost no original ramparts or monuments or ruins to see! Apart from two lines of twelve arches from Fort William, one of the oldest buildings is Curzon's 1902 replica monument. In fact, the most important sites of the Black Hole— the prison itself and Holwell's monument—had been demolished by 1821, and so Firminger has little to show. It was that very lack of monumentality which so irritated Mark Twain. Nevertheless, tourists with their new guide were shown monuments of the imagination which Twain might well have enjoyed. The tour began in the compound of the post office, where two white marble tablets were on view. These tablets were placed by Curzon to draw the visitor's attention to brass lines in the stone pavement, which demarcated the walls of the old Fort William, and to the fact that the Black Hole was formed by bricking up two arches, similar to the ones which were still standing. A note in the guide stated that 'in order to get a clear notion of the site of the Old Fort' it was preferable to follow the tablets, as they presented a story by linking the events with a site (Firminger 1906: 16).

Having acquainted the tourists with the dimensions of the fort, the guide provided a colourful history—Macaulay's version of the Black Hole. Macaulay was one of the most widely read and respected commentators on Indian affairs and history. Most of his essays on India appeared in the *Edinburgh Review* and, in January 1840, having recently returned from serving on the Governor General's Council, he submitted a biography of Robert Clive (Macaulay 1907). This essay contained a narrative of the events of the Black Hole and rapidly became the most compelling and authoritative popular history of the founding of the British Empire in India. It was a story of triumph over adversity, of victory after defeat, of British virtue above Oriental dissipation.[5] But embedded in the biography was a moment which both began the narrative and encapsulated the meaning, reason, and end of the story. That original moment was, of course, the Black Hole.

Macaulay's history was lurid and sensational. Siraj-ud-Daula, the Nawab of Bengal, was depicted as a caricature—'it is said he had arrived at that last stage of human depravity, when cruelty becomes pleasing for its own sake'—and the narrative was set up as a simplistic, Manichaean good-versus-evil story (ibid.: 36). The Black Hole was introduced as 'that great crime, memorable for its singular atrocity, memorable for the tremendous retribution by which it was followed'. Macaulay recounted how Calcutta was stormed by the troops of the Nawab of Bengal and how, subsequent to the British defeat, 146 prisoners, including the Acting Governor, J.Z. Holwell, were shut up in the Black Hole prison for the night. Only 23 were said to have survived.

Holwell's original account highlighted three aspects of the narrative which were common to most later renditions—there was a gruesome, almost perverse pleasure in recounting the (momentary) humiliation and death of British power in Bengal; there was an acknowledgment that the 'crime' deserved 'retribution' in the form of conquest; and there were horrible images and phrases which were repeated ad infinitum. One recurring image was Holwell's enigmatic sentence declaring that after the night of 20 June, all survivors were set free except Holwell, two officers, and a Mrs Carey 'who was too young and handsome'. The thought that an Englishwoman should have been immured within a harem was disturbing enough for it to be recited by, among others, Macaulay, Busteed, Cotton, Curzon, and Firminger. Indeed, Firminger noted with some relief that Busteed had conducted research on the subject and had concluded that Mrs Carey, who had been widowed in the Black Hole, had never been sent to the harem at Murshidabad at all, but had remained only in Calcutta and had remarried (1906: 22).[6]

One of the reasons why the guide presented Macaulay's version of the Black Hole rather than the original account by Holwell might have been that, although each was rhetorically powerful, Macaulay provided a mediating voice, creating a distance which permitted the viewer to place the Black Hole within the larger context of British conquest. As we shall see, Holwell's narrative was about himself; Macaulay's, on the other hand, was about the building of an empire, phoenix-like. The very fact that Macaulay's version was part of a biography of Clive suggested that the Black Hole should be understood as the event which induced the Company's army, under Clive, to invade Bengal. In fact, it was generally taken for granted that the Black Hole provided the Company with the moral legitimacy to establish its own temperate and enlightened rule. George Curzon, for example, noted that the English 'martyrs' on 'that night of doom ... had laid the foundation stone of British Dominion in Bengal' (1925, Vol. 2: 150). However, Firminger was not content simply to provide a seemingly dispassionate historical perspective. His book was a guide, meant to inform and teach through its use; he thus attempted to animate the site and aid his readers to envision the events of the Black Hole.

Visitors using *Thacker's Guide* were directed around the post office compound in Calcutta and told to follow brass lines in the pavement. At numerous points along the walk tablets drew their attention to particular spots which were once part of old Fort William. The authoritative voice of a prominent historian explained the story and the significance of the Black Hole, and at last, having walked and read and anticipated, the tourist was led to the area of the prison. Various kinds of maps had been employed to bring the tourist to the Black Hole. Maps in the guide compared contemporary Calcutta to the city as it existed in the mid-eighteenth century; brass lines led the tourist around a now-demolished fort; and a scale model of the fort and prison, 'to make the subject intelligible to the modern student', Curzon wrote, were even on display in the newly completed Victoria Memorial Hall Exhibition (ibid.: 157). The model, in fact, was based on William Wells' map of 1753 and was of particular interest since the top had been removed to allow a spectator to peer down into the Black Hole. What was important about these maps was that they both fostered a nostalgia for the moment of birth of the British Empire and taught that nostalgia by encouraging an inquisitive and imaginative participation in the events of the Black Hole.

Late-nineteenth-century nostalgia tended to focus on momentous happenings, occurrences which originated a sequence of events which could be clearly traced back to those original moments. One of the ways in which Lord Curzon hoped to revive memories of the Black Hole was by helping tourists gain a better understanding of the site's dimensions by investing that space with special significance. When visitors reached the site of the Black Hole they would see a polished black marble slab, surrounded by an iron railing, covering the exact location of the prison. Above the slab was an inscription in gilt letters on a black marble tablet—contrasting with the white marble tablets denoting other buildings of the fort—which announced that the marble had been placed by Lord Curzon to mark the site of the Black Hole. Unfortunately, a building stood over about a third of the prison, so the black marble could not cover the whole length of the site. However, Curzon was quite prepared to rearrange structures; he ordered a brick and plaster gateway to be demolished since it obscured the site from the street—he called it an 'obstruction'—and he replaced the gateway with open railings, which made the slab and tablet visible to passers-by.[7] The site was intended to attract attention; the sombre nature of the marble, the visibility from the street, the inaccessibility to the black slab due to the railings, all added a sense of permanence and monumentality to a building which no longer existed.

Curzon, however, was not content with simply tracing in the pavement the outlines of the old Fort William, placing marble slabs and tablets at important locations, and demolishing gateways. He also conjured up images of the Black Hole and built a monument to those who died. Curzon wanted to impress upon visitors the historical significance and contemporary relevance of the Black Hole deaths, and as part of that effort he attempted to make his exhibits of personal interest. For example, in a chapter he wrote on the Black Hole which appears as part of a two-volume work on British government in India, he noted, 'for the benefit of any visitor', that close to the Black Hole there existed 'a low apartment used as a kitchen by the native employés of the Post Office' which reminded him of what he imagined the prison might have looked like (Curzon 1925, Vol. 2: 153). Indeed, once the prison had been mapped onto Calcutta, the imagination could be stimulated. In an address at the unveiling of the Holwell Monument in December 1902, Curzon said that he never passed by 'without the Post Office and Custom House and the modern aspect of Writer's Buildings fading out of my sight, while instead of them I see the walls and bastions of Old Fort exactly behind the spot where I now stand.'[8]

But just as Curzon had to resort to allusions to cramped kitchens and imagined walls, since he had no original buildings to display, *Thacker's Guide* had to rely on what Firminger called the 'historical imagination'. Tourists were to imagine themselves entering the east gate of the fort. If they were to turn to the south, climb onto a veranda, and look to the left they would notice a row of arches, the last portions of which would form the Black Hole. 'To enter it,' the reader was told, 'we must pass through the adjacent Barrack Rooms, and we mentally note that the door opens inwards into the Prison—a circumstance which will delay the removal of the survivors when the dead block the way' (Firminger 1906: 22). The rhetorical 'we' serves to heighten the sense of participation and inclusion, while the detail of the door, reported in a matter-of-fact manner, helps the imagination calculate dimensions. An important aim for both Curzon and the guide was to foster a historical awareness by encouraging an experience of space which was shared by all who visited the Black Hole: the reverence and awe expected from every visitor was taught through the use of the maps—asking tourists to imagine themselves in an eighteenth-century world, while simultaneously involving them in an archaeological hunt for the exact location of the Black Hole, pulled the prison out of all historical contexts and placed it within a tourist's itinerary. In other words, the hope that tourists would project acceptable emotions onto the monument was aided by the mapped and directed manner of approach. The brass lines, the tablets, the model, and the guide book, all led the tourist on a journey where what mattered was the discovery and revelation of the Black Hole site and not the sequence of events that June evening. Even the inclusion of Macaulay's historical account was in aid of and subservient to the need to find the prison and appreciate its importance as an emblem.

The site of the Black Hole, therefore, acquired an additional consequence since, in part, the mystery of the precise location was resolved through the search. Late Victorians invested much emotion into monuments, and the transformation of the Black Hole site and its narrative into a monument worthy of a tourist's attention was an indication of the degree to which Curzon wished to impart a sense of respect for momentous occurrences and achievements. But what was it about the past and the Black Hole that he wished to honour? What did the prison represent?

The Monument and the Transformation of the Meaning of the Black Hole

The twin focus of the tour of the Black Hole was the monument, a memorial to those who had died. The monument was first built by Holwell but was reconstructed in 1902 by Lord Curzon, who paid for the materials and donated it to Calcutta, as his personal gift. The argument in this section of the chapter is that the use of a variety of maps enabled the expression of nostalgia, or the longing to recapture an original moment, and that often, nostalgia was orchestrated in such a fashion—through mapped tourist itineraries, for example— that a moral lesson was taught. The monument was a conventional way of channelling emotion so that the anger or guilt or indignation which might have been evoked when viewing the Black Hole site was transformed into the more noble and useful virtues of patriotism and gratitude.

While explaining the central idea of the Victoria Memorial Hall, which he termed a 'historical museum', Curzon suggested that such memorials were not frivolous whimsies but utilitarian creations—

'There is no more practical or business emotion,' he said, 'than patriotism. ... I believe that it will teach more history and better history than a study-full of books.'[9] Indeed, the didactic use and meaning of mapped sites was not limited to Calcutta. In fact, Curzon had instituted a programme whereby all major buildings which once housed famous Indian or British personalities were to be commemorated with an inscribed terracotta medallion. In a resolution written by H.H. Risley, the Secretary to the Government of India, it was stated that fixing historical plaques to buildings would be 'not only interesting but instructive'. Moreover, since 'authentic history is beginning to pass, in some cases into tradition, in others into legend', directing the public's attention to these plaques would 'arrest and crystallize' the public's declining knowledge and appreciation of important men.[10] The monument, therefore, was an aid to help teach the historical importance of the Black Hole.

The original memorial, John Zephaniah Holwell's Monument, was self-serving, vengeful, and venomously didactic. The brick and plaster obelisk was erected by a 'Surviving Fellow Sufferer' and inscribed to the memory of those 123 persons who were, by 'tyrannic violence', suffocated in the Black Hole prison 'and promiscuously thrown the succeeding morning' into a ditch (Curzon 1925: 160). The inscription on the reverse was triumphant: 'This Horrid Act of Violence was as Amply as Deservedly Revenged on Surajud Dowla By his Majesty's Arms ... .' The idea that the Company's victories over the Nawab of Bengal were in retribution for despotic outrages was not necessarily Holwell's. Seven months after the loss of Calcutta, Admiral Watson justified his declaration of war against the Nawab by citing the fact that many had been 'deprived of their lives in the most barbarous and inhuman manner' (Hill 1968 Vol. II: 86). Even though this may or may not have been a reference to the Black Hole deaths, a tradition was established very soon after the recapture of Calcutta which asserted that the military operations exacted just punishment.

However, the idea of punishment and the desire for revenge were not laudable late-Victorian public values. For Curzon, the rebuilding of the monument was not an exercise in exciting overt racial animosities. He noted, for example, that it would be 'undesirable' to repeat Holwell's inscriptions, and so, instead, he ordered that six tablets be inscribed with a more complete listing than Holwell had provided of the names of those who had died both in the prison and in the previous days' fighting. By shifting the focus away from vengeance and towards individual valour, Curzon hoped to encourage both gratitude and patriotism: 'They were the pioneers of a great movement,' he said at the unveiling of the reconstructed monument in 1902, 'the authors of a wonderful chapter in the history of mankind; and I am proud it has fallen to my lot to preserve their simple and humble names from oblivion and to restore them to the grateful remembrance of their countrymen' (1906: 7).

Despite Curzon's diplomatic but patronizing words, the Black Hole complex—the brass lines, the model, the tablets, and the marble slab—was a location for the projection of national humiliation and racial hatred. Macaulay, for example, had repeated a widely held belief that 'from a child Surajah Dowlah had hated the English' (1907: 36). The claims, too, that Mrs Carey had been abducted and that the dead bodies had been thrown 'promiscuously', or without regard to national origin or class, into a mass grave, were designed to impassion a British audience. Even Curzon told his listeners that 'if there be a spot that should be dear to Englishmen in India, it is that below our feet which was stained with the blood and which closed over the remains of the victims of that night of destiny' (1906: 9). The macabre pleasure of sitting above their graves was enhanced by the knowledge that their deaths were not in vain. Nevertheless, while the Black Hole complex guided the tourist to an original moment, prompting a curious mixture of horror and satisfaction, the viewing of the monument provided an opportunity to express those emotions as patriotism and gratitude. The horror which gave way to anger and a desire for vengeful conquest was muted and given appropriate expression by the reconstruction of the monument. Mapping, therefore, became important in locating the Black Hole complex so that tourists were positioned in such a way that they themselves became amenable to nostalgia. Mapping provided an avenue of approach, helping to tell a story and taking the occurrences out of historical context. This meant that there was a complete focus on the site, which became emblematic of British conquest over adversity and a symbolic of British fortitude.[11] The site was about race, nationality, and malicious bitterness. However, the spite and anger mixed with racial pride, although deliberately prompted by Firminger's tour and Macaulay's account, were converted into nostalgia by the viewing and reading of the monument.

The Holwell and Curzon monuments should be compared with the Patna monuments honouring those who were massacred in October 1763.[12] William Ellis, the chief of the Company's Patna factory, had been engaged in a long-running feud with Mir Kasim, and when Mir Kasim succeeded Mir Jafar as the Nawab of Bengal, the tension between the two men erupted into conflict. The upshot of it was that Ellis, along with his staff and supporters, was captured and confined in a house owned by Haji Ahmed. Mir Kasim then ordered them killed in revenge, it is said, for the capture of his fort at Monghyr. The execution of the fifty-three prisoners was conducted by Walter Reinhardt and the bodies were buried in the garden or thrown down a well. Two years later, the garden was turned into the Patna City Cemetery.

There is some disagreement as to when the first monument was erected. Vincent Davies (1989: 7–8) claims that the monument was nearly contemporaneous with the massacre and that it was rebuilt in the late nineteenth century. Sir John James notes (1930: 2), more persuasively, that the monument was first built in 1880 and that it was subsequently rebuilt in the early twentieth century. What is curious, and strikingly similar to the Holwell and Curzon monuments, is that the Patna monuments were also reinscribed. The first inscription begins 'In memory of Captain John Kinch' and, after naming twenty-four men associated with the Company's military, closes by stating that the Company's civil servants, including Ellis and other prisoners, were 'brutally massacred near this spot by the troops of Mir Kasim, Nawab Subadar of Bengal, under command of Walter Reinhardt, alias Samru, a base renegade, E dedecore hostium nata est gloria eorum' (ibid.: 17).

The central question is: Why was this dedication altered? Clues to the answer exist in the order of names, in the choice of words, and in the Latin inscription. The early-twentieth-century dedication begins with the words 'Sacred to the memory of the prisoners of the Nawab Mir Kasim who were massacred near this spot in October 1763 under the direction of the Alsatian renegade Walter Reinhardt alias Somru' (ibid.: 91). The list of names starts with the civil servants, beginning with William Ellis and his second, Henry Lushington, and only then are the names of the military servants included. The list is more complete than the 1880 dedication, providing the deceased's official titles, and it also includes those killed as prisoners or in battle in the months preceding the October massacre. The later dedication also does not include the original Latin inscription. The alterations and omissions in the second dedication indicate that the focus of indignation and anger were to be shifted away from the incident as a national military debacle and towards the killings as a personal tragedy and crime. The original dedication chose to focus on the names of the officers, noting that they were killed by the 'troops' of the 'Nawab Subadar of Bengal', who were 'under [the] command of Walter Reinhardt'. Moreover, the Latin inscription may be literally translated as 'from the shameful conduct of their enemies their glory was born', all of which suggests that the conflict was military in tone and that their defeat was a humiliation for the nascent British administration. This view is reinforced when we consider that the Latin word used for enemies ('hostium') refers to enemies of the state, or public enemies, as opposed to 'inimicus' which suggests a personal foe.[13]

By examining the changes to the original inscription, therefore, it becomes apparent that by the twentieth century the sponsors of the new Patna Memorial wanted to downplay the military defeat and national humiliation, and instead couch the massacre as one in which vulnerable 'prisoners' were killed as a result of the Nawab's and Reinhardt's personal vendetta. The new monument may suggest that the viewer see the massacre as a historical incident, and not as a defeat requiring retribution.

With regard to the Calcutta memorials, Firminger and Curzon were also particularly interested in a didactic nostalgia—a reverence for a foundational event which, through an orchestrated and mapped approach, could provide the basis for learning and disseminating an acceptable morality. Thus, the new phrases in both the Patna and Calcutta memorials reflect changes in what it meant to be both colonial and British, and in how the past was used to explain present-day affairs.

However, before we examine how and why Curzon altered the meaning of the monument when he ordered its reconstruction, it might prove instructive to examine Holwell's original account. As the first to provide a comprehensive narrative of what happened, Holwell's story helped make the Black Hole a public concern. Although there were newspaper notices and other contemporary references to the brief confinement of Europeans by Siraj-ud-Daula following the loss of Calcutta (see Hill 1968 Vol. III Appendix II), the details became public knowledge only after Holwell's publication of his Black Hole narrative. Among some of the Company's Bengal servants, Holwell seems to have been an unpopular member of the Calcutta Council (see Busteed 1888: 3, 39). Robert Clive, for example, wrote to a friend that Holwell 'is a deceitful and ungrateful Knave for he has taken the whole merit of the late Revolution to himself and left the Blameable Past entirely upon Vansittart'.[14] Outside of Bengal, however, Holwell was well respected, with Robert Orme even going so far as to consider him 'the gallant defender of the Fort and the asserter of the reputation of the nation'.[15] Busteed called Holwell 'the historian *par excellence* of the Black Hole' and cited a glowing obituary. Holwell's own reputation rested on his account of what occurred immediately after the fall of Calcutta.

What is astonishing is that his narrative should have become, to use Kate Teltscher's (1996: 30–51) phrase, a 'foundational myth' of the British Empire, whereas other accounts of capture or torture, such as emerged from the wars against Haider Ali and Tipu Sultan,[16] were not accorded such reverence, authority, or importance. The veracity of Holwell's narrative, however, has been examined more than once. William Lindsay was perhaps the first to question Holwell's motives for writing his account. In a letter to Orme, Lindsay noted that Holwell was a reluctant defender of Calcutta, remaining only because his boat had been stolen. 'I mention this,' he remarked wryly, 'as I understand he made a merit in staying when he found he could not get off'.[17]

Making a virtue of necessity seems to have been Holwell's *métier*. During the World War I, J.H. Little published two revealing articles in *Bengal Past and Present* which argued that Holwell had substantially invented his account and that he had very likely not constructed a monument to the dead.[18] For many years there had been whispers that Holwell had lied and invented, and these rumours were so powerful that even H.E.A. Cotton felt compelled to write that 'professional white-washers' were trying to brush away the true horror of the Black Hole (1907: 463). Cotton included several arguments as to why Holwell's story was true, noting, for example, that several contemporaries, such as Robert Orme, one Captain Mills, and William Tooke, some of who were in Calcutta during that time, corroborated Holwell's claim that many died of suffocation in the Black Hole prison. Despite this and other defences of Holwell's veracity and narrative, Little marshalled evidence that Holwell was an inveterate liar, pointing to the fact that Holwell's 'discovery' and partial translation of an ancient Sanskrit *sastra* (religious text) was pure nonsense. Holwell's translation is indeed curious, containing Urdu phrases and terms such as *hazaar par hazaar* (which he translates as thousands upon thousands), *mhurd* (man) and *oustmaan* (air). Moreover, the substance of the text reads more like Milton's *Paradise Lost* than a Hindu treatise, with angelic bands rebelling against God and subsequently being expelled from the heavenly regions (Holwell 1767 Vol. II: 9, 51). Little suggested that Holwell probably had exaggerated a brief imprisonment in order to exonerate himself from the charge of having lost Calcutta. He also noted in his second article that since there were so many contradictory prints, views, and descriptions of the monument, with no one who described it saying they had actually seen it, it was quite possible that there had never been a monument at all.

Curzon (1917) responded with venom, citing much of the same evidence which Little had relied upon, but from a different perspective, and declaring that he wished to demolish 'one of the most egregious absurdities which it has ever been sought to foist upon the public'. Nevertheless, the debate over the truth of the Black Hole continued into the second half of the twentieth century with, for instance, the publication of two books—the first by Noel Barber (1982), who vehemently supported Holwell's account, and the second by Iris Macfarlane (1975), whose careful analysis proclaimed the incident 'a nothingness' (see also Gupta 1966).[19]

Holwell's account is disarmingly entitled '*A genuine NARRATIVE of the Deplorable Deaths of the English Gentlemen and Others, who were suffocated in the Black Hole in Fort William, at Calcutta, in the Kingdom of Bengal; in the Night succeeding the 20th Day of June, 1756*' (1758).[20] It was written in the form of a letter to a friend—a common genre of literature throughout the eighteenth century, perhaps remaining popular since the pretence of intimacy suggested that readers were privy to secret information. This is not the place to rehearse the debates on the veracity of Holwell's narrative, a sketch of which has been outlined above. Rather, I will focus on one of its aspects which has rarely been mentioned in the scholarly literature on the Black Hole, but which forms an integral part of the account. Much of the account details the horrors of the night spent in the prison, and all the retellings and criticism have focused on both the style and substance of that section; however, roughly one quarter of his narrative describes the long march he was compelled to undertake, from Calcutta to Murshidabad, following his release from the Black Hole. This report of his forced journey, in the company of two other men, was particularly important since it provided a political and historical assessment of the consequences of the Black Hole debacle. Although the graphic first section was intended to elicit immediate sympathy, it was this second section, I will argue, which enabled a select British readership to understand the true meaning of the defeat.

Holwell was a political man. Throughout his life he participated in the factional and internecine battles which characterized mid-eighteenth-century Company politics, and he was the author of several tracts which advocated the swift acquisition of new territory and power. In *Interesting Historical Events* Holwell provided 'a Seasonable Hint' to the Company directors by declaring—'let us boldly dare to be Soubah *ourselves*' (1765: 183). Like many of his contemporaries, Holwell was ambitious and resourceful and, from his experience as a member of the Calcutta Council, he knew how to write letters which were at once ingratiating, self-serving, and seemingly true. Choosing an appropriate style of writing was a high consideration since only letters provided information of what was occurring half a world away. While the first section of the narrative 'letter' portrayed Holwell as both hero and victim, the second part provided a context within which it was possible to comprehend his valour and sufferings. But what is particularly interesting for this chapter is that Holwell decided to write in a style reminiscent of standard journals kept by military surveyors. His march north from Calcutta to Murshidabad was a military survey, but with a difference—the customary perspective, the usual observations, the standard behaviour, were all reversed, indicating how thorough the revolution had been.

Previous chapters have examined in detail the aesthetics and presuppositions of eighteenth-century route surveys. It was suggested that, among other features, surveys began at a centre of power, were reported from the perspective of a representative of that power, and were undertaken with the express intention of providing geographical, social, and political information which would be materially useful for administrative and military purposes. Holwell began his narrative of the journey to Murshidabad—'where I think you have never been'—with an invitation to 'take this trip with us likewise' (1758: 39). As with any route survey, Holwell meticulously noted the date, the temperature, and the hour when significant events occurred. He also remarked on the manner of travel, the difficulties encountered, the important towns, and how authority was demonstrated and yielded to along the way. 'When we came near the Cutcherry of the district,' he wrote, 'the Zemindar with his pykes, was drawn up ready to receive us; but as soon as they presented me to him as a prisoner of state, estimated ... at four lack of rupees, he confessed himself sensible of his mistake, and made no further shew of resistance' (ibid.: 43). Surveyors' journals are full of similar remarks, except that it is usually the Company surveyor who commanded authority and acquiescence. In this case, the zamindar, the local administrator and upholder of the law, when given a choice, opted to side with the Nawab. It is a telling indication of how the Company's defeat was a catastrophe at the most local level. Experiencing the new authority of the guard, surveying the political scene in the country beyond Calcutta, Holwell wrote a journal which gave the same strategic and geographically-oriented information as any surveyor would have provided. His survey was the assessment of the cost of the loss of Calcutta.

Even though Holwell acted the surveyor, his route was the opposite of what one would have expected from a survey and march. For his guards, the journey was a saturnalia of sorts and a perversity or reversal of the right order; those in charge were cruel and exploitative; the *zamindar*, usually a figure of administrative responsibility, was easily swayed in favour of the Nawab's forces (remember that Holwell was himself a fellow zamindar of the 24 Parganas); the English, being no longer in charge, were degraded, oppressed, and forced to take orders—'I was obliged to crawl: they signified to me, it was now my business to obey' (ibid.: 42). Moreover, the guards plundered, even stealing his plantains, while the English were deprived of adequate transport and decent nourishment. The river became a conduit for prisoners rather than a route for trade, and, interestingly, the direction of travel was away from Calcutta, renamed Alinagar, and towards Murshidabad, the new centre of power in Bengal. Moreover, when they finally arrived at the capital, it was Holwell, the 'felon', who became the observed: 'The immense crowd of spectators ... so blocked us up from morning till night, that I may truly say we narrowly escaped a second suffocation, the weather proving exceeding sultry' (ibid.: 47). Such a reversal of expectations and roles presented, nevertheless, in a recognized and conventional fashion, would signify to those in Britain whose business it was to cultivate authority, that the disaster in Calcutta had ramifications well beyond the city's limits.

Holwell had written several letters to his superiors after his release from custody, although in one of them he claimed to have 'barely strength to hold the pen'.[21] These letters, together with his published narrative letter, constituted Holwell's attempt to rehabilitate his name. What is of interest is that Holwell should have decided to present part of his account in the form of a survey journal; indeed, it was precisely the use of a surveyor's perspective that helped Holwell's narrative of the Black Hole become the original moment of a myth of punishment and empire. The reason why the report of his march north to Murshidabad was so important for understanding the significance of the loss of Calcutta is that the narrative was highly ironic. Dictionaries define 'irony' as the use of words to signify the opposite of what they would usually express, and, in this case, the disingenuous nature of his account and the fact that it was published after the recapture of the Company's possessions in Bengal, suggest that Holwell was deliberately positioning his personal sufferings, which were also identified as the Company's, as sufficient reason for the subsequent revolutions in Bengal. The power of Holwell's irony is that even as his narrative was being published, everybody knew that Calcutta had been recaptured. Why did Holwell write his account and why was the survey a crucial component of it? As an ironic survey journal, Holwell's narrative was as much a rationale for a *fait accompli*, meaning the death of Siraj-ud-Daula following his defeat by Clive, and a plea for further revolutions, as it was an excuse for his disgraceful loss of Calcutta.

Those who were likely to read Holwell's account at the time of its publication—and Holwell, who had written political tracts and was to publish more, was no doubt especially keen to attract the attention of the Company directors—would have noticed the irony— the man who had suffered most and who recognized the magnitude of the loss to the Company, was also the man to be appointed Governor of the recaptured Presidency. In fact, Holwell did become Governor for a short period, but as memories of the loss of Calcutta faded, Holwell's account was no longer read as ironic but at face value. Considered as an innocent and apolitical description, the *Narrative* is a story of horrible despair, national fortitude, and Oriental tyranny. It is this ahistorical and uncontextualized reading which Busteed and Curzon chose when they co-opted his account for their own nostalgic and didactic recreation of the Empire's original moment.

While Holwell's survey was a political tract, full of ingratiating deception and subtle irony, Curzon's mapping, by contrast, was devoid of conscious irony. As nostalgia, it could not be but an earnest attempt to recreate the conditions of 1756, sanitized and tempered, of course, in the face of modern political and social exigencies. In a speech at the unveiling of the Mutiny Telegraph Memorial in Delhi, Lord Curzon remarked that 'one ingenious gentleman' had written an extraordinary work to prove that the Black Hole tragedy had never occurred. In Curzon's eyes, the Mutiny and the Black Hole were clear and incontrovertible facts. Perhaps they were distasteful in some regards, tinged as they were with the 'racial element', 'but that is no reason for ignoring them', he pleaded: 'pass over them the sponge of forgiveness; blot them out with the finger of mercy and of reconciliation' (1906: 441). There is something rather astonishing in Curzon's speeches and writings on memorials and the Black Hole. By focusing on what he considered to be simple acts of courage, Curzon hoped to convey to Indians a fundamental British magnanimity and generosity of spirit. He wished not only to turn what had been symbols of revenge into signs of forgiveness, but he also attempted, seemingly without irony, to arrogate the discourse of race; it was not Indians who had been injured by the 'racial element', but the

British, who, having suffered, could now demonstrate their high moral standing.

Curzon's Black Hole complex, therefore, had two audiences—the British tourist, who was led on a mapped journey towards the rediscovery of an original moment, and the Indian subject, who was a mute, but indispensable, witness to the mapped and staged discovery. Furthermore, it was hoped that both would learn moral lessons through the use and viewing of the complex. However, the expected patriotism and gratitude evinced by both British and Indian viewers were not alike. The British were to transform their righteous indignation into an acknowledgment that the past sufferings of 'brave men' had 'cemented', in Curzon's words, 'the foundations of the British Empire in India' (ibid.: 5). And while the British tourists, busy thanking their forefathers for dying in such noble style, were cementing their own bonds with Britain, the complex was supposed to inspire in Indian passers-by an allegiance to the Empire. Indians, many of whom were threatening the colonial bureaucracy's control by legal, political, or violent actions, were to thank their rulers for undeserved leniency and forgiveness.[22]

Many Bengalis, however, saw the monument as a sign of enslavement. Subhas Chandra Bose, a prominent nationalist who headed the Indian National Army which fought against the British during the World War II, declared that on 3 July 1940 he would lead a *satyagraha*, or a non-violent campaign, to demand the monument's removal. That day, he wrote, would be observed by Bengalis as

Sirajuddowla Day—in honour of the last independent King of Bengal. The Holwell Monument is not merely an unwarranted stain on the memory of the Nawab, but has stood in the heart of Calcutta for the last 150 years or more as the symbol of our slavery and humiliation. The monument must now go (cited in Gordon 1990: 412).

The day before the campaign, however, Bose was arrested, and the monument was not immediately dismantled. Nevertheless, this is one clear instance of Bengali opposition to the Black Hole memorial. Although Curzon wanted to include Indians as spectators and to deliver a message to them, it would seem that the symbolic power of the monument might have been more successfully deployed as an aid in the construction of a colonial British identity. The tying of the colony to Britain, the making of a meaning for colonial control and British presence, and the expression of pride in being British, were all furthered by the mapping of the Black Hole complex.

In a speech before the Asiatic Society of Bengal in 1900, Curzon said that the Imperial Government had an obligation to patronize antiquarian inquiries. It was 'our duty,' he declared, 'to dig and discover, to classify, reproduce, and describe, to copy and decipher, and to cherish and conserve' (1906: 186). Vigorous and robust, manly and nostalgic, late-Victorian history was a way of teaching appropriate conduct and mores through the re-enactment of carefully selected past moments. The construction of the Black Hole complex, the manipulation of emotion by means of a mapped tour of specific locations, the disingenuous assumption of racial narratives, were all endeavours by the Government of India to fuse the Empire's needs for enthusiastic and loyal subjects with its prevailing preoccupation for detailed knowledge regarding facts, events, and original moments. Led by nostalgia, guided by maps, the tourist in search of the Black Hole became the quintessential colonial historian.

Conclusion

Timothy Mitchell has argued that late-nineteenth-century European exhibitions of Egypt had the effect of suggesting to a viewer, who had never visited Egypt that the exhibition's depiction of life on a Cairo street was so authentic and so authoritative that when that viewer subsequently journeyed to the East, the new experience of Cairo would necessarily disappoint and bewilder (1991). The idea of the Black Hole was similarly powerful and authoritative. Due to the writings of historians ranging from Macaulay to Busteed, due to its re-enactment in a mock-dungeon at Addiscombe, due to the argument that the Black Hole was, au fond, the very reason for the British conquest of India, the events of that night in June 1756 were impressed upon the imagination of many Western travellers to Calcutta. But the lack of any monument and the disappearance of the fort and the prison disappointed those who had expected to see what they could only imagine. The re-creation of the Black Hole complex was meant to satisfy the need to understand the origins and reasons for British rule in India.

The late-Victorian renewal of interest in the history of the Black Hole was not just a way for the British to reassert their belief in the legitimacy of colonial rule. It also had the effect of strengthening a sense of what it meant to be British. Manu Goswami has argued in an essay on mutiny tours in India that 'Englishness' was as much constructed in the colonies as it was 'at home'; that the process of visiting the sites of initial horror but ultimate victory, such as Lucknow or Delhi, encouraged the reactive and aggressive nationalism of the late nineteenth century. Moreover, the manner in which these tours were conducted—they were organized around spaces rather than temporal events—provided a context through which the occurrences were understood locationally rather than sequentially (Goswami 1996: 73). Thus the manipulation of monuments, graves, and perspectives evoked a particular kind of history, where national awareness was continually fashioned within and by specific colonial sites. As the 'original' site of British colonialism in India, the reconstructed Black Hole complex may have contributed to the making of a British identity in two ways. First, it satisfied a nostalgia or a desire to return home. The 'pilgrimage' that tourists took when they visited the site made them aware of a national bond that stretched from Britain to India, and from the distant past to the present. Second, it embedded colonialism within a national identity. Britain was Britain—seemingly strong, militaristic, manly, rich— because of her history and because of her empire.

The final lesson of the Black Hole complex was that the British empire was moral. The idea that the study of the past is a moral endeavour is nestled within the nineteenth-century assumption that the search for original moments would necessarily lead to an explanation for history. Lord Curzon and Busteed believed that a tourist-like experience of a recreated and mapped Black Hole narrative would prompt an anticipated and controlled response. Upon viewing the Black Hole, Indians would necessarily feel grateful and indebted to a righteous colonial race, while a touring British public would transform its anger into a more noble and dignified sentiment. An expatriate community would also feel closer to Britain and feel more British through sharing the re-experience of the Black Hole and knowing that a moment in the past gave meaning to the present. History, therefore, was as much concerned with teaching a morality and ensuring a stable and predictable future as it was with identifying significant events and facts in the past. Indeed, what made a nineteenth-century historical account particularly trenchant or memorable was the ability of its writer to project any number of political and moral agendas in such a beguiling manner that the reader was encouraged to recognize in the past the same ideas and feelings which preoccupied her or his generation. By ingeniously yoking cartography with history, nineteenth-century historians and map makers were able to give meaning to a British colonial identity.

Notes

1. Salman Rushdie discusses Raj nostalgia as a 'refurbishment of the Empire's tarnished image', in his essay, 'Outside the Whale' (1992).
2. I am grateful to Dipesh Chakrabarty for suggesting that I examine the history of the term.
3. In 1811, John Garstin, a Surveyor General of India, noted that he blasted with gunpowder the last walls of the old Fort. The experiment was 'so simple and easily managed' that he wished to apply the technique to the Jamuna River, where he wished to deepen the bed of the river. NAI, DDn Vol. List, Old No. SGO 53, Sl. No. 128, p. 23, John Garstin to C.H. Gardiner, 29 March 1811.
4. The best biography of Curzon is David Gilmour's *Curzon* (1995).
5. It is also a story of Macaulay over previous historians of India. He suggests that the reason that, in his words, 'every schoolboy knows' about the imprisonment of Montezuma but nothing of the Battle of Buxar is because of the 'tediousness' of previous historians, especially Orme, Mill, and John Malcolm (Macaulay 1907: 1–3).
6. Busteed's research on the fate of Mrs Carey is a good example of how the stories of the Black Hole intertwine suggestion, myth, and rumour, to produce the solid rope of history. Based on an interview with an anonymous descendant of Mrs Carey, Busteed claims that other women were present in the Black Hole, although no mention of any is ever made by Holwell.
7. Curzon's address at the unveiling of the Holwell Monument, December 1902. OIOC MSS Eur. D. 804, p. 4.
8. OIOC MSS Eur. D. 804, p. 2.
9. OIOC SB/XVIII/26, p. 16, *Extract from a speech delivered by His Excellency Lord Curzon ... at a meeting of the Asiatic Society of Bengal, on 26th February 1901.*

10. NAI, Home Department, Public A, No. 15, p. 21, Resolution 29 January 1904, Calcutta, H.H. Risley, Sec. to the Government of India.

11. In this regard, the Black Hole complex may be compared with the Residency at Lucknow. For a discussion on Mutiny tours see Goswami, 1996.

12. Rebecca Brown first alerted me to the existence of the Patna memorial and suggested there may be interesting comparisons with the Holwell memorial.

13. I am grateful to Jane Chaplin for this distinction.

14. OIOC MSS Eur. B.165, Letter from Clive to Major John Carnac, 26 September 1761.

15. Robert Orme, 'Account of the loss of Calcutta, composed by Robert Orme at Madras, 27 October, 1756', in Hill 1968 Vol. III: 130. In a letter to John Payne, written in November 1756, Orme acknowledged that Holwell was disliked, but that his conduct was without comparison. In a later letter Orme wrote that Clive 'joins the Vigilance of a Cat the Intrepidity of a Lion and either as Defender or Assailant is a dangerous Enemy'. OIOC Orme MSS 28, pp. 54 and 92.

16. See, for example, the minuscule and secret diary kept by Colonel Cromwell Massey as Haider Ali's prisoner from 1780 to 1784. The diary is only 4 1/2 inches by 2 1/2 inches and a magnifying glass is needed to read the writing. OIOC MSS Eur. B. 392. Another account was kept by Lieutenant Richard Runwa Bowyer, whose narrative includes a song about their imprisonment. 'Like Horses we're pent in a Shed, Like Felons we're loaded with Chains, And while Mother Earth is our Bed, We float in the times of the Rains. The Sentinels placed at the Door, Are for our Security Bail, With Muskets and Chawbuck secure They guard us in Bangalore Jail.' He explains that 'Chawbuck is a Leather Thong they beat us with'. OIOC MSS. Eur. A. 94. A Surveyor General of India published a lurid account of Tipu Sultan and his alleged cruelty, and attached it to reproduced drawings of Mysore (see R.H. Colebrook(e) (1805).

17. 'Letter from Mr. William Lindsay to Mr. Robert Orme concerning the loss of Calcutta, dated "Syren" sloop, off Fulta', in Hill 1968 Vol. I: 168.

18. See Little, 'The Black Hole—the Question of Holwell's Veracity' (1915) and 'The Holwell Monument' (1917), which includes a reply by Firminger, the author of *Thacker's Guide* (1906). See also Harvey Einbinder (1964: 184–87).

19. The most recent and rewarding analysis of Holwell's *Narrative* (1758) is Kate Teltscher's essay. One of her most trenchant arguments is that although colonial historiography had hoped to palliate the anxiety of

political and racial impotence by suggesting that Clive's victory was a punishment for gross wrongdoing, there remained a lingering and unresolved insecurity among the British (1996: 42).

20. The *Narrative* also appears in Holwell 1764 and in Hill 1968 Vol. III.

21. See 'Duplicate letters from Mr. J.Z. Holwell to Councils, Bombay and Fort Saint George, dated, Muxadavad, 17 July 1756' in Hill 1968 Vol. I: 114.

22. Bengali and Indian nationalist movements were of great concern to Curzon and the closer incorporation of Indians into the Empire was one of his priorities. In his study of Sir Arthur Conan Doyle, David S. Payne suggests that nostalgia is a 'means of dealing with too great or too swift (a) change' (1992: 20). Faced with Bengali hostility, for example, or an intractable Lord Kitchener in his Council, Curzon may have resorted to nostalgia as a means of fending off impending and unwelcome change.

Conclusion:
Maps and History

In 1800, William Faden published a third edition of a map of the peninsula of India. It was based on recent route surveys and provided good information regarding the direction of roads and rivers and the location of places. The map is certainly useful for the traveller. But the map is much more than a travel document; it is also a history of the recent Company wars against Tipu Sultan, the ruler of Mysore. As history, the map contains two very intriguing features. The first is that the map shows 'The Acquisitions of Great Britain and her Allies the Nizam and the Marhattas by the Partition Treaties of 1792 and 1799'. These territorial 'acquisitions' are indicated in the map by the date of their conquest. The powerful visual effect is to see a progressive and systematic British military encroachment on Mysore. The second feature is that a colour scheme shows the history of the wars' campaigns by tracing the marches of Lord Cornwallis, General Meadows, General Abercromby, and Captain Little's detachment. Both of these features are explained in references at the bottom of the map. Within the map itself, colour is also used to distinguish and delineate territories. The history of increasing British military control over the peninsula of India is clearly established by the map.

The map also indicates other histories of possession. Differences in typography, for example, alert the reader to what was (such as 'ANCIENT DOMINIONS') and what is (such as 'NAYRS COUNTRY').

Fig. 11. *Detail of William Faden's 'A M*

...ap of the Peninsula of India', 1800.

Moreover, the map not only identifies the names of districts, regions, or states, but also includes the names of select local rulers, thus reinforcing the map's other political and territorial messages. In an effort perhaps to de-legitimate the state of Mysore, the title cartouche explains that 'The Divisions of the Carnatack (Carnatick) into Talookeh Carnatack Bijapoor, Talookeh Carnatack Hyderabad and Sircar Carnatack, is according to the Registers of the Empire in use among the Natives. It is also to be observed that the Region or District of Mysore is not mentioned in those Registers'. The war that had just been concluded had destroyed Tipu Sultan's rule (he himself had been killed), and the map may be viewed as providing some justification for the war's prosecution.

Faden's map is a good example of how eighteenth- and nineteenth-century British maps of India incorporated history. Using dates, colour, typography, and references, the map suggests that Mysore was illegitimate as an independent state and was relentlessly destroyed in a series of campaigns that saw the Company act in concert with Indian allies. Four important points emerge from a consideration of the map that touch upon the major themes of this book. First, colonial control is established and presented. Second, the map draws a history of possession that allows for the legitimacy of that colonial rule. Third, large parts of the peninsula are shown as British territory (acquisitions). And, last, a British national identity is championed through the conquest and control of territory.

Eighteenth- and nineteenth-century British maps of India are about control—control over land, over access to locations, over names, over people, over representation, over the past. They exult in national victory and present British power in India as established, legitimate, protected by boundaries, and long-lasting. Being about control, the subject of the maps is Britain, and the narratives contained within them tell the story of the extension and consolidation of its rule over India. Rather than being about foreign rule in India, the maps are about making into British territory what was once foreign land. From this perspective, and considering that new forms of surveying were introduced to India to facilitate the extension of British power, it may be argued that a distinctive, colonial form of rule was founded in the mid-to-late eighteenth century. One of the challenges facing the British involved in colonial rule, from its inception in the mid-eighteenth century until the twentieth century, was to make that rule seem appropriate, natural, and responsible.

Establishing a history of possession was one of the most important ways maps helped make foreign rule seem legitimate. For cartographers and surveyors during the colonial era, though, history could be expressed in a variety of ways. In response to changing surveying techniques, increased geographical knowledge, or altered political circumstances, map makers adjusted their historical approaches and made their maps current political documents.

Five cartographic uses of history may be identified. In the late nineteenth century James Rennell adopted associative history in order to attach the name of a distinguished Company soldier or administrator to the map. Doing so made it seem as if the lands depicted were conquered and controlled in a responsible manner. By the early nineteenth century trigonometrical surveyors saw their new techniques and perspectives as superior to older route survey methods and, consequently, infused their surveys with a sense that their work was a symbol of the progress that accompanied colonial power. In the mid-nineteenth century the surveying establishment wished to revere its former head by naming a mountain after him. The reverence for the accuracy of his surveying methods made it seem appropriate to give his name to a mountain that, in all likelihood, had numerous local names. In the 1860s the Survey of India, while still lauding trigonometrical techniques, also reintroduced long-outdated route surveys in an effort to add adventure to their activities. A romantic history was adopted which involved the training of Indians to survey in circumstances reminiscent of the eighteenth century. The willingness of Indians to risk their lives for the empire and for geographical science was regarded by the Survey, in an atmosphere still preoccupied with memories of the Mutiny, as a sign of the thoroughness and correctness of colonial rule. By the turn of the twentieth century a nostalgia for the original moments of the British Raj led Lord Curzon to map the Black Hole onto the pavement of Calcutta. The display was an effort to instil in viewers a pride in the character of British rule and to reinforce the notion that India was British for legitimate reasons. In at least these five ways history was incorporated into the map.

In addition to transforming Indian history into British history, colonial maps made India part of British imperial territory. Several words were used in the eighteenth and nineteenth centuries to indicate ownership, including possessions, acquisitions, empire, and British India. The power of colonial maps was that they were able to show, in a beguiling way, that control was not just over people and rights of trade, but also over land. The control and ownership of land became the defining measure of the extent and greatness of the British Empire, and maps were particularly useful as a means of conveying the significance of land to power. In viewing shades of pink or red on maps of India or of the Empire, a viewer could readily comprehend Britain's economic, political, and military reach. Moreover, by drawing boundaries and indicating the extent of British power, the maps made territorial defence and protection overriding priorities.

Noticing the apparent strength and breadth of the Empire, together with the need for its defence, might also have helped fuel a pride in being British. In drawing maps of Indian possessions, cartographers also drew a British national identity. By inserting the British nation into the conquest of India, by insisting that British mathematical and scientific acumen was superior to that of Indians, by revisiting the sites of original national tribulation and triumph, cartographers buttressed a sense of satisfaction in being born British. British national sentiment, then, from the late eighteenth century until at least the early twentieth century, was inextricably involved in the creation and maintenance of an Indian empire. Empire was integral to national identity, and maps were crucial to the seeming legitimacy of the British Indian empire.

Bibliography

Principal Archival Sources

National Archives of India (NAI), New Delhi

> Catalogue of the Memoirs of the Survey of India
> Dehra Dun Volumes List (DDn Vol. List)
> Home Miscellaneous Series

Oriental and India Office Collections (OIOC), London

> European Manuscript Collections
> Orme Manuscript Collections
> Mackenzie Manuscript Collections
> Map Manuscript Collections

Public Record Office (PRO), London

> Colonial Office Collections (CO 54 and CO 55)
> War Office Collections

British Library (BL), London

> Manuscript Letters (Clive, Hastings, Rennell)

Published Primary and Secondary Sources

Abu-Lughod, Janet. 'On the Remaking of History: How to Reinvent the Past' in *Remaking History*, edited by Barbara Kruger and Phil Mariani. Seattle: Bay Press, 1989.

Abu-Lughod, Janet. *Before European Hegemony: The World System, AD 1250–1350.* New York: Oxford University Press, 1989.

Adas, Michael. *Machines as the Measure of Men: Science, Technology and Ideologies of Western Dominance.* Ithaca: Cornell University Press, 1989.

Akerman, James R. 'The Structuring of Political Territory in Early Printed Atlases' in *Imago Mundi* Vol. 47, 1995: 138–54.

Allen, Charles. *A Mountain in Tibet: The Search for Mount Kailas and the Sources of the Great Rivers of India.* London: Andre Deutsch, 1982.

Anderson, Benedict. *Imagined Communities: Reflections on the Origin and Spread of Nationalism.* London: Verso, 1987.

Anon. *The Indian Alps and How We Crossed Them: Being a Narrative of Two Years' Residence in the Eastern Himalaya and Two Months' Tour into the Interior. By a Lady Pioneer.* New York: Dodd, Mead, and Company, 1876.

Armitage, David. *The Ideological Origins of the British Empire.* Cambridge: Cambridge University Press, 2000.

Arnold, David. *Science, Technology and Medicine in Colonial India.* The New Cambridge History of India III. 5. Cambridge: Cambridge University Press, 2000.

Bailey, F.M. *No Passport to Tibet.* London: The Travel Book Club, 1957.

Baker, J.N.L. *The History of Geography.* Oxford: Basil Blackwell, 1963.

Barber, Noel. *The Black Hole of Calcutta.* New York: Collier Books, 1982 (1965).

Barnett, Richard B. 'Introduction' in *Rethinking Early Modern India,* edited by Richard B. Barnett. New Delhi: Manohar, 2002.

Bayly, C.A. *Rulers, Townsmen and Bazaars: North Indian Society in the Age of British Expansion, 1770–1870.* Cambridge: Cambridge University Press, 1983.

———. *Empire and Information: Intelligence Gathering and Social Communication in India, 1780–1970.* Cambridge: Cambridge University Press, 1999.

Berthon, Simon and Andrew Robinson. *The Shape of the World: The Mapping and Discovery of the Earth.* Chicago: Rand McNally, 1991.

Bhabha, Homi. 'The Other Question—Stereotype and Colonial Discourse' in *Screen* Vol. 24, No. 6, November-December 1983: 18–36.

Black, Charles E.D. *A Memoir on the Indian Surveys, 1875–1890.* London, 1891.

Black, Jeremy. *Maps and History: Constructing Images of the Past.* New Haven and London: Yale University Press, 1997.

Blunt, E.A.H. *List of Inscriptions on Christian Tombs and Tablets of Historical Interest in the United Provinces of Agra and Oudh.* Allahabad: Govt Press, United Provinces, 1911.

Boeck, Kurt. *Aux Indes & au Nepal.* Paris : Hatchette, 1907.

Bolts, William. *Considerations on Indian Affairs.* London: J. Almon 1772.

Boos, Florence S. *History and Communalism: Essays in Victorian Medievalism.* New York and London: Garland Publishing, Inc., 1992.

Boss, Emil and Douglas W. Freshfield. 'Notes on the Himalaya and Himalayan Survey' in *The Alpine Journal: A Record of Mountain Adventure and Scientific Observation.* London: Longmans, Green, and Co., 1886: 52–60.

Boswell, James. *The Life of Samuel Johnson.* London: Everyman's Library, 1978.

Bowen, H.V. *Elites, Enterprise and the Making of the British Overseas Empire, 1688–1775.* New York: St Martin's Press, Inc., 1996.

Bravo, Michael T. 'Precision and Curiosity in Scientific Travel: James Rennell and the Orientalist Geography of the New Imperial Age (1760–1830)' in *Voyages and Visions: Towards a Cultural History of Travel,* edited by Jas Elsner and Joan-Pau Rubiés. London: Reaktion Books, 1999.

Brohier, R.L. *Land, Maps and Surveys.* Colombo: Ceylon Government Press, 1950.

Buckland, C.E. *Dictionary of Indian Biography.* New York: Greenwood Press, 1969.

Buisseret, David (ed.). *Rural Images: Estate Maps in the Old and New Worlds.* Chicago: University of Chicago Press, 1996.

Burke, Edmund. *The Works of the Right Honourable Edmund Burke.* London: Henry G. Bohn, 1854.

Burnett, D. Graham. *Masters of All they Surveyed: Exploration, Geography, and a British El Dorado.* Chicago: The University of Chicago Press, 2000.

Burrard, Sir Sidney. *Mount Everest and its Tibetan Names: A review of Sir Sven Hedin's Book,* Survey of India professional paper No. 26. Dehra Dun: Survey of India, 1931.

Burrow, Reuben. *The Lady's and Gentleman's Diary or, Almanack: (1776-7-8-9).* London: T. Carnan and G. Robinson, 1776–79.·

Burton, Antoinette. *At the Heart of Empire: Indians and the Colonial Encounter in Late-Victorian Britain.* Berkeley: University of California Press, 1998.

Busteed, H.E. *Echoes from Old Calcutta: Being Chiefly Reminiscences of the Days of Warren Hastings, Francis and Impey.* Calcutta: Thacker, Spink and Co., 1888 (1882).

Cambridge, Richard Owen. *An Account of the War in India between the English and French on the Coast of Coromandel, from the Year 1750 to the Year 1760.* London: T. Jefferys, 1761.

Cannadine, David. 'The Context, Performance and Meaning of Ritual: The British Monarchy and the "Invention of Tradition," c. 1820–1977' in *The Invention of Tradition,* edited by Eric Hobsbawm and Terence Ranger. Cambridge: Cambridge University Press, 1983.

Cannadine, David. *Ornamentalism: How the British Saw their Empire*. Oxford: Oxford University Press, 2001.

Carter, Paul. *The Road to Botany Bay: An Exploration of Landscape and History*. Chicago: The University of Chicago Press, 1987.

Chatterjee, Partha. *The Nation and its Fragments: Colonial and Postcolonial Histories*. Princeton: Princeton University Press, 1993.

Chaudhury, Sushil. *From Prosperity to Decline: Eighteenth Century Bengal*. New Delhi: Manohar, 1995.

Clarke, G.N.G. 'Taking Possession: The Cartouche as Cultural Text in Eighteenth-century American Maps' in *Word & Image* Vol. 4, No. 2, April-June 1988: 455–74.

Cohn, Bernard. *An Anthropologist Among the Historians and Other Essays*. New Delhi: Oxford University Press, 1987.

Colebrooke, H.T. 'On the Sources of the Ganges, in the Himadri or Emodus' in *Asiatic Researches* Vol. 11, 1979 (1817): 429–45.

Colebrook(e), R.H. *Twelve Views of Places in the Kingdom of Mysore, the Country of Tippoo Sultan, from Drawings Taken on the Spot*, 2nd Edition. London: J. Nichols, 1805.

Colley, Linda. *Britons: Forging the Nation, 1707–1837*. New Haven: Yale University Press, 1992.

Cook, Andrew S. 'Major James Rennell and *A Bengal Atlas* (1780 and 1781)' in *India Office Library and Records: Report for the Year 1976*. London: British Library 1978.

_____. '"An Author Voluminous and Vast": Alexander Dalrymple (1737–1808), Hydrographer to the East India Company and to the Admiralty, as Publisher: A Catalogue of Books and Charts'. PhD thesis, University of St Andrews, 1992.

Cormack, Lesley B. *Charting an Empire: Geography at the English Universities, 1580–1620*. Chicago: University of Chicago Press, 1997.

Cotton, H.E.A. *Calcutta Old and New: A Historical and Descriptive Handbook to the City*. Calcutta: W. Newman & Co., 1907.

Curzon, Lord George N. *Lord Curzon in India: Being a Selection from His Speeches as Viceroy and Governor-General of India, 1898–1905*. London: Macmillan and Co. Limited, 1906.

_____. 'The True History of Holwell's Monument' in *Bengal Past and Present* Vol. XV, 1917: 11–12.

_____. *British Government in India: The Story of the Viceroys and Government Houses*, 2 vols. London: Cassell and Company Ltd., 1925.

Dalrymple, Alexander. *Essay on the Most Commodious Methods of Marine Surveying*. London, 1771.

_____. *A General View of the East India Company, Written in January 1769, To*

Which are Added, Some Observations on the Present State of Their Affairs. London, 1777.

_____. *General Remarks for the Use of Those Who Have Not Been Accustomed to Navigate Unfrequented Seas.* London: W. Ballantine, 1806.

Das, Sarat Chandra. *Narrative of a Journey to Lhasa in 1881–82.* Calcutta: Bengal Secretariat Press, 1885.

Davies, Vincent. *A Short History of Patna and Dinapore and their British Cemeteries.* Putney, London: BACSA, 1989.

Davis, Fred. *Yearning for Yesterday: A Sociology of Nostalgia.* New York: The Free Press, 1979.

Dirks, Nicholas B. 'Colonial Histories and Native Informants: Biography of an Archive' in *Orientalism and the Postcolonial Predicament: Perspectives on South Asia*, edited by Carol A. Breckenridge and Peter van der Veer. Philadelphia: University of Pennsylvania Press, 1993.

_____. *Castes of Mind: Colonialism and the Making of Modern India.* New Delhi: Permanent Black, 2003.

Dow, Alexander. *The History of Hindostan.* London: T. Becket and P.A. De Hondt, 1772.

Dunbar, George. *Frontiers.* London: Ivor Nicholson and Watson Ltd., 1930.

Edney, Matthew H. 'The Atlas of India 1823–1947: The Natural History of a Topographic Map Series' in *Cartographica* Vol. 28, No. 4, Winter 1991: 59–91.

_____. 'Mathematical Cosmography and the Social Ideology of British Cartography, 1780–1820' in *Imago Mundi* Vol. 46, 1994: 101–16.

_____. *Mapping an Empire: The Geographical Construction of British India, 1765–1843.* Chicago: The University of Chicago Press, 1997.

Einbinder, Harvey. *The Myth of the Britannica.* New York: Grove Press, 1964.

Everest, George. *An Account of the Measurement of an Arc of the Meridian.* London: Parbury, Allen and Co., 1830.

_____. *A Series of Letters Addressed to His Royal Highness the Duke of Sussex ... Remonstrating against the Conduct of that Learned Body.* London: William Pickering, 1839.

Firminger, Walter K. *Thacker's Guide to Calcutta.* Calcutta: Thacker, Spink and Co., 1906.

_____, (ed.). *The Diaries of Three Surgeons of Patna, 1763.* Calcutta: The Calcutta Historical Society, 1909.

Fraser, James Baillie. *Journal of a Tour through part of the Snowy Range of the Himalya Mountains and to the Sources of the Rivers Jumna and Ganges.* London: Rodwell and Martin, 1820.

Freshfield, D.W. 'Notes' in *The Alpine Journal: A Record of Mountain Adventure and Scientific Observation* Vol. XII, 1886a, 448–60.

Freshfield, D.W. 'Notes' in *Proceedings of the Royal Geographical Society* Vol. VIII, 1886b: 176–88.

_____. 'Mount Everest, or Jomo-kang-kar' in *The Alpine Journal* Vol. XXI, 1903a: 34–35.

_____. *Round Kangchenjunga: A Narrative of Mountain Travel and Explanation.* London: Edward Arnold, 1903b.

Gellner, Ernest. *Nations and Nationalism.* Ithaca: Cornell University Press, 1983.

Gilmartin, David. 'Scientific Empire and Imperial Science: Colonialism and Irrigation Technology in the Indus Basin' in *The Journal of Asian Studies* Vol. 53, No. 4, November 1994: 1127–49.

Gilmour, David. *Curzon.* London: John Murray, 1995.

Gole, Susan. *India within the Ganges.* New Delhi: Jayaprints, 1983.

_____. *Maps of Mughal India Drawn by Colonel Jean-Baptiste-Joseph Gentil, Agent for the French Government to the Court of Shuja-ud-Daula at Faizabad, in 1770.* Delhi: Manohar, 1988.

Gordon, Leonard A. *Brothers Against the Raj: A Biography of Indian Nationalists Sarat and Subhas Chandra Bose.* New York: Columbia University Press, 1990.

Goswami, Manu. '"Englishness" on the Imperial Circuit: Mutiny Tours in Colonial South Asia' in *The Journal of Historical Sociology* Vol. 9, No. 1, 1996: 54–85.

Gottmann, Jean. *The Significance of Territory.* Charlottesville: The University Press of Virginia, 1973.

Grant, James. *An Inquiry into the Nature of Zemidary Tenures in the Landed Property of Bengal.* London: J. Debrett, 1791.

Green, Nicholas. *The Spectacle of Nature: Landscape and Bourgeois Culture in Nineteenth-century France.* Manchester and New York: Manchester University Press, 1990.

Greet, Annie, Syd Harrex, and Susan Hosking (eds). *Raj Nostalgia: Some Literary and Critical Implications.* Adelaide: The Centre for Research in the New Literatures in English, 1992.

Guha, Ranajit. *A Rule of Property for Bengal: An Essay on the Idea of the Permanent Settlement.* New Delhi: Orient Longman, 1981.

_____. *An Indian Historiography of India: A Nineteenth-century Agenda and its Implications.* Calcutta: K.P. Bagchi & Co., 1988.

Gupta, B.K. *Sirajuddaullah and the East India Company: Background to the Foundation of British Power in India.* Leiden: E.J. Brill, 1966.

Hacking, Ian. *Representing and Intervening: Introductory Topics in the Philosophy of Natural Science.* Cambridge: Cambridge University Press, 1993.

du Halde J.B. *Description Geographique, Historique, Chronologique, Politique, et Physique de l'Empire de la Chine et de la Tartarie Chinoise*, 4 vols. Paris: P.G. le Mercier, 1735.

Hansen, Peter H. 'Partners: Guides and Sherpas in the Alps and Himalayas, 1850s-1950s' in *Voyages and Visions: Towards a Cultural History of Travel*, edited by Jas Elsner and Joan-Pau Rubiés. London: Reaktion Books, 1999.

Harley, J.B. *The New Nature of Maps: Essays in the History of Cartography*. Baltimore and London: The Johns Hopkins University Press, 2001.

Harvey, P.D.A. 'English Estate Maps: Their Early History and their Use as Historical Evidence' in *Rural Images: Estate Maps in the Old and New Worlds*, edited by David Buisseret. Chicago: University of Chicago Press, 1996.

Headrick, Daniel R. *The Tentacles of Progress: Technology Transfer in the Age of Imperialism*. New York: Oxford University Press, 1988.

Hedin, Sven. *Mount Everest*. Leipzig: F.A. Brockhaus, 1923.

Helgerson, Richard. *Forms of Nationhood: The Elizabethan writing of England*. Chicago: University of Chicago Press, 1992.

Hennessey, J.B.N. (prepared by). *Report on the Explorations in Great Tibet and Mongolia, made by A-K in 1879–82*. Dehra Dun: Trigonometrical Branch Office, 1891.

Herb, Guntram Henrik. *Under the Map of Germany: Nationalism and Propaganda 1818–1945*. London and New York: Routledge, 1997.

Hill, S.C. *Bengal in 1756–1757*. New York: AMS Press, 1968 (1905).

Hodgson, Brian Houghton. *Letters on National Education for the People of India, Styled Preeminence of the Vernaculars*. Serampore, 1837.

———. 'Route of two Nepalese Embassies to Peking with remarks on the water-shed and plateau of Tibet' in *Journal of the Asiatic Society of Bengal* Vol. VI, 1856: 473–86.

———. *Miscellaneous Essays relating to Indian Subjects*. London: Trübner & Co., 1880.

Hofer, Johannes. 'Medical Dissertation on Nostalgia or Homesickness' (translated by Carolyn Kiser Anspach) in *Bulletin of the History of Medicine* Vol. II. Baltimore: Johns Hopkins University Press, 1934.

Holdich, T.H. 'The Romance of the Indian Surveys' in *Journal of the Royal Society of Arts* Vol. 64, 1916: 173–85.

———. *Tibet the Mysterious*. New York: Frederick A. Stokes Publishers, 1906.

Holwell, J.Z. *A Genuine Narrative of the Deplorable Deaths of the English Gentlemen and Others, Who Were Suffocated in the Black Hole in Fort William, at Calcutta, in the Kingdom of Bengal; in the Night Succeeding the 20th Day of June, 1756. In a Letter to a Friend*. London: A. Millar, 1758.

———. *India Tracts*. London: T. Becket and P.A. de Hondt, 1764.

Holwell, J.Z. *Interesting Historical Events, Relative to the Provinces of Bengal, and the Empire of Indostan ... As also the Mythology and Cosmogony, Fast and Festivals of the Gentoos Followers of the Shastah.* London: T. Becket and P.A. De Hondt, 1767.

Hopkirk, Peter. *Trespassers on the Roof of the World: The Race for Lhasa.* London: John Murray, 1982.

_____. *Quest for Kim.* Ann Arbor: University of Michigan Press, 1997.

Hunter, William Wilson. *Life of Brian Houghton Hodgson.* London: John Murray, 1896.

Hutchins, Francis G. *The Illusion of Permanence: British Imperialism in India.* Princeton: Princeton University Press, 1967.

Inden, Ronald, *Imagining India.* Oxford: Blackwell, 1990.

James, John Francis William. *List of Pre-mutiny Inscriptions in Christian Burial Grounds.* Bihar Govt. Publications, 1930.

James, Lawrence. *Raj: The Making and Unmaking of British India.* New York: St Martin's Griffin, 1997.

Kalpagam, U. 'Cartography in India' in *Economic and Political Weekly* Vol. 30, No. 30, 29 July 1995: 87–98.

Kaviraj, Sudipta. 'On the Construction of Colonial Power: Structure, Discourse, Hegemony' in *Contesting Colonial Hegemony: State and Society in Africa and India*, edited by Dagmar Engels and Shula Marks. London and New York: British Academic Press, 1994.

Keay, John. *When Men and Mountains Meet: The Explorers of the Western Himalayas, 1820–75.* Oxford: Oxford University Press, 1993.

_____. *The Great Arc: The Dramatic Tale of How India was Mapped and Everest was Named.* New York: Harper Collins, 2000.

Kerr, Ian J. *Building the Railways of the Raj, 1850–1900.* New Delhi: Oxford University Press, 1997.

Khilnani, Sunil. *The Idea of India.* New York: Farrar, Straus, Giroux, 1999.

Kipling, Rudyard. *Kim.* New York: Doubleday, Page and Co., 1901.

Krishna, Shankaran. 'Cartographic Anxiety: Mapping the Body Politic in India' in *Challenging Boundaries: Global Flows, Territorial Identities*, edited by Michael J. Shapiro and Hayward R. Alker. Minneapolis: University of Minnesota Press, 1996.

Lafont, Jean-Marie. *Chitra: Cities and Monuments of Eighteenth-Century India from French Archives.* New Delhi: Oxford University Press, 2001.

Lambton, William. 'An abstract of the Results Deduced from the Measurement of an Arc on the Meridian ...' in *Philosophical Transactions* Vol. 108, 1818: 486–517.

_____. 'Corrections Applied to the Great Meridional Arc ...' in *Philosophical Transactions* Vol. 113, 1823: 27–33.

Lawson, Philip and Jim Phillips. '"Our Execrable Banditti": Perceptions of Nabobs in Mid-eighteenth Century Britain' in *Albion* Vol. 6, No. 3 Fall, 1984: 225–41.

Lemann, Nicholas. 'Atlas Shrugs: The New Geography Argues that Maps Have Shaped the World' in *The New Yorker,* 9 April 2001: 131–34.

Little, J.H. 'The Black Hole—the Question of Holwell's Veracity' in *Bengal Past and Present* Vol. XI, 1915: 75–104.

_ ___. 'The Holwell Monument' in *Bengal Past and Present* Vol. XIV, 1917: 275–95.

Locke, John. *Of Civil Government: Second Treatise.* Chicago: Gateway, 1955 (1689).

Macaulay, Thomas Babington. *Lord Clive.* Cambridge: Pitt Press Series, 1907.

Macfarlane, Iris. *The Black Hole; or the Making of a Legend.* London: George Allen & Unwin Ltd., 1975.

MacKenzie, John, M. *Propaganda and Empire: The Manipulation of British Public Opinion, 1880–1960.* Manchester: Manchester University Press, 1984.

_____. (ed.). *Imperialism and Popular Culture.* Manchester: Manchester University Press, 1986.

Mackenzie, W.C. *Colonel Colin Mackenzie: First Surveyor-General of India.* Edinburgh and London: W & R Chambers Ltd., 1952.

MacMunn, George. *The Romance of the Frontiers.* Quetta: Nisa Traders, 1978.

Macpherson, William Charles (ed.). *Soldiering in India, 1764–1787.* Edinburgh and London: William Blackwood and Sons Ltd., 1928.

Madan, P.L. *Indian Cartography: A Historical Perspective.* New Delhi: Manohar, 1997.

Mahomet, Dean. *The Travels of Dean Mahomet: An Eighteenth-Century Journey through India,* edited by Michael H. Fisher. Berkeley: University of California Press, 1997.

Markham, Clements R. *A Memoir on the Indian Surveys.* London: Allen & Co., 1878.

_____. *Major James Rennell and the Rise of Modern English Geography.* London: Cassell and Co. Ltd., 1895.

Marshall, P.J. 'Introduction' in *The Eighteenth Century in Indian History,* edited by P.J. Marshall. New Delhi: Oxford University Press, 2003.

Metcalf, Thomas R. *The Aftermath of Revolt, 1857–1870.* Princeton: Princeton University Press, 1964.

_____. *Ideologies of the Raj.* New Delhi: Cambridge University of Press, 1995.

Micheal, Bernardo Ammadeus. 'Separating the Yam from the Boulder: Statemaking, Space, and the Causes of the Anglo-Gorkha War of 1814–16'. PhD dissertation, University of Hawaii, December 2001.

Misra, B.B. *The Unification and Division of India.* Delhi: Oxford University Press, 1990.

Mitchell, Timothy. *Colonising Egypt.* Berkeley: University of California Press, 1991.

Mitchell, W.J.T. 'Imperial Landscape' in *Landscape and Power,* edited by W.J.T. Mitchell. Chicago: University of Chicago Press, 1994.

Montgomerie, T.G. 'On the Geographical Position of Yarkand, and Some Other Places in Central Asia' in *The Journal of the Royal Geographical Society* Vol. 36, 1866: 157–72.

_____. 'Report on the Route-Survey Made by Pundit—from Nepal to Lhasa, and thence through the Upper Valley of the Brahmaputra to its source' in *The Journal of the Royal Geographical Society* Vol. 38, 1868: 129–210.

_____. 'Report of the Trans-Himalayan Explorations during 1867' in *The Journal of the Royal Geographical Society* Vol. 39, 1869: 146–87.

_____. 'Report of The Mirza's Exploration from Caubul to Kashgar' in *The Journal of the Royal Geographical Society* Vol. 41, 1871: 132–83.

Moor, Edward. *A Narrative of the Operations of Captain Little's Detachment.* London: George Woodfall, 1794.

Morshead, Ian. *The Life and Murder of Henry Morshead: A True Story from the Days of the Raj.* Cambridge: The Oleander Press Ltd., 1982.

Mundy, Barbara E. *The Mapping of New Spain: Indigenous Cartography and the Maps of the Relaciones Geográficas.* Chicago: The University of Chicago Press, 1996.

Murdoch, Alexander. *British History, 1660–1832: National Identity and Local Culture.* New York: St Martin's Press, Inc., 1998.

Murray, Hugh. *Historical and Descriptive Account of British India, from the Most Remote Period to the Present Time.* New York: Harper and Brothers, 1836.

Nandy, Ashis. *The Intimate Enemy: Loss and Recovery of Self Under Colonialism.* New Delhi: Oxford University Press, 1991.

Nelson, Derek. *Off the Map: The Curious Histories of Place-Names.* New York, Tokyo and London: Kondansha International, 1997.

Newman, Gerald. *The Rise of English Nationalism: A Cultural History, 1740–1830.* New York: St Martin's Press, 1997.

Noyes, J.K. *Colonial Space: Spatiality in the Discourse of German South West Africa 1884–1915.* Chur, Reading: Harwood Academic Publishers, 1992.

Payne, David S. *Myth and Modern Man in Sherlock Holmes: Sir Arthur Conan Doyle and the Uses of Nostalgia.* Bloomington: Gaslight Publications, 1992.

Perlin, Frank. 'State Formation Reconsidered' in *Modern Asian Studies* Vol. 19, No. 3, 1985: 415–80.

Phillimore, Reginald H. *Historical Records of the Survey of India.* Dehra Dun: Survey of India, 5 vols, 1945, 1950, 1954, 1958, 1968.

Popper, Frank. *Art of the Electronic Age.* New York: Harry Abrams, 1993.

Pratt, Mary Louise. *Imperial Eyes: Travel Writing and Transculturation.* New York: Routledge, 1992.

Price, Uvedale. *Essays on the Picturesque, As Compared with the Sublime and the Beautiful; and, On the Use of Studying Pictures, for the Purpose of Improving Real Landscape.* London: Mawman, 1810.

Raj, Kapil. 'When Human Travellers Become Instruments: The Indo-British Exploration of Central Asia in the Nineteenth Century' in *Instruments, Travel and Science: Itineraries of Precision from the Seventeenth to the Twentieth Century,* edited by Marie-Noëlle Bourguet, Christian Licoppe, and H. Otto Sibum. London and New York: Routledge, 2002.

_____. 'Circulation and the Emergence of Modern Mapping: Great Britain and Early Colonial India, 1764–1820' in *Society and Circulation: Mobile People and Itinerant Cultures in South Asia, 1750–1950,* edited by Claude Markovits, Jacques Pouchepadass, and Sanjay Subrahmanyam. New Delhi: Permanent Black, 2003.

Raman, Shankar. *Framing 'India': The Colonial Imaginary in Early Modern Culture.* Stanford: Stanford University Press, 2001.

Ramaswamy, Sumathi. 'Catastrophic Cartographies: Mapping the Lost Continent of Lemuria' in *Representations* Vol. 67, Summer 1999: 92–129.

_____. 'History at Land's End: Lemuria in Tamil Spatial Fables' in *The Journal of Asian Studies* Vol. 59, No. 3, August 2000: 575–602.

Raper, F.V. 'Narrative of a Survey for the Purpose of Discovering the Sources of the Ganges' in *Asiatic Researches* Vol. 11, 1979 (1817): 446–563.

Rawat, Indra Singh. *Indian Explorers of the 19th Century.* New Delhi: Government of India, 1973.

Rennell, James. *A Description of the Roads in Bengal and Bahar.* London: printed by order of the Honourable Court of Directors, 1778.

_____. 'An Account of the Ganges and Burrampooter Rivers' in *Philosophical Transactions of the Royal Society* Vol. 71, 1781: 87–114.

_____. *A Bengal Atlas Containing Maps of the Theatre of War and Commerce on that Side of Hindoostan.* London, 1780, 1781.

_____. *Memoir of a Map of Hindoostan; or the Mogul's Empire.* London, 1783, 1785.

_____. *Memoir of a Map of Hindoostan; or the Mogul Empire.* London, 1788, 1792, 1793.

_____. *Memoir of a Map of Hindoostan; or the Mogul Empire.* Calcutta: Editions Indian, 1976 (1793).

_____. *Memoir of a Map of the Peninsula of India from the Latest Authorities.* London: sold by G. Nicol, 1793.

_____. *The Journals of Major James Rennell.* Calcutta: Baptist Mission Press, 1910.

Robb, Janet Henderson. *The Primrose League, 1883–1906.* New York: Columbia University Press, 1942.

Robertson, William. *An Historical Disquisition Concerning the Knowledge the Ancients had of India.* London: Cadell and Davies, 1805.

Roux, E. 'Les Sources de L'Irrawaddy' in *Annales de Géographie* Vol. V 1896: 483–95.

Ruge, S. 'Mont Everest' in *The Alpine Journal* Vol. XXI, 1903: 34.

Rushdie, Salman. 'Outside the Whale' in *Raj Nostalgia: Some Literary and Critical Implications,* edited by Annie Greet, Syd Harrer, and Susan Hosking. Adelaide: The Centre for Research in the New Literatures in English, 1992.

Sack, Robert David. *Human Territoriality: Its Theory and History.* Cambridge: Cambridge University Press, 1986.

Schlagintweit, Emil. 'Der Name des Höchsten Berges der Erde' in *Mitteilungen* Vol. 36, 1890: 251–52.

———. 'Der Name des Höchsten Berges der Erde' in *Mitteilungen* Vol. 47, 1901: 40–43.

Schlagintweit-Sakünlünski, Hermann Rudolph Alfred von. *Reisen in Indien und Hochasien.* Jena: Costenoble, 1869–80.

Scott, James C. *Seeing Like a State: How Certain Schemes to Improve the Human Condition have Failed.* New Haven: Yale University Press, 1998.

Sewell, William H. Jr. 'Historical Events as Transformations of Structures: Inventing Revolution at the Bastille' in *Theory and Society: Renewal and Critique in Social Theory* Vol. 25, No. 6, December 1996: 841–81.

———. 'Three Temporalities: Toward an Eventful Sociology' in *The Historic Turn in the Human Sciences,* edited by Terrence J. McDonald. Ann Arbor: University of Michigan Press, 1996b.

Skinner, Thomas. *Fifty Years in Ceylon: An Autobiography.* New Delhi: Asian Educational Services, 1995.

Smith, Adam. *An Inquiry into the Nature and Causes of the Wealth of Nations.* Chicago: University of Chicago Press, 1976 (1776).

Smith, Anthony D. *National Identity.* Reno: University of Nevada Press, 1991.

Smith, J.R. *Everest: The Man and the Mountain.* Latheronwheel, Scotland: Whittles Publishing, 1999.

Stein, Burton. 'State Formation and Economy Reconsidered' in *Modern Asian Studies* Vol. 19, No. 3, 1985: 387–413.

———. *A History of India.* Oxford: Basil Blackwell, 1998.

Stewart, Susan. *On Longing: Narratives of the Miniature, the Gigantic, the Souvenir, the Collections.* Baltimore and London: The Johns Hopkins University Press, 1984.

Stokes, Eric. 'The First Century of British Colonial Rule in India: Social Revolution or Social Stagnation?' in *Past and Present* Vol. 58, 1973: 136–60.

Styles, Showell. *The Forbidden Frontiers: The Survey of India from 1765–1949.* London: Hamish Hamilton, 1970.

Suleri, Sara. *The Rhetoric of English India.* Chicago: University of Chicago Press, 1992.

Sutherland, Lucy S. *The East India Company in Eighteenth-Century Politics.* Oxford: Oxford University Press, 1962.

Tallis, John. *The Illustrated Atlas and Modern History of the World.* London and New York: John Tallis & Company, 1851.

Tanner, H.C.B. 'Extract from the Narrative Report ... Season 1883–84' in *The Alpine Journal.* London: Longmans, Green, and Co., 1886: 438–48.

Taylor, E.G.R. *The Mathematical Practitioners of Hanoverian England, 1714–1840.* Cambridge: Cambridge University Press, 1966.

Teltscher, Kate. *India Inscribed: Europeans and British Writers on India, 1600–1800.* Delhi: Oxford University Press, 1995.

_____. '"The Fearful Name of the Black Hole". Fashioning an Imperial Myth' in *Writing India, 1757–1990: The Literature of British India*, edited by Bart Moore-Gilbert. Manchester and New York: Manchester University Press, 1996.

Thomas, Keith. *Man and the Natural World: A History of the Modern Sensibility.* New York: Pantheon Books, 1983.

Thuillier, H.R. and R. Smyth. *A Manual of Surveying for India.* Calcutta: Thaker, Spink and Co., 1875.

Thuillier, H.R. and George Strahan, (prepared under). *Report on the Explorations of Lama Serap Gyatsho, 1856–68; Explorer K-P, 1880–84; Lama U.G., 1883; Explorer R.N., 1885–86; Explorer P.A., 1885–86, in Sikkim, Bhutan, and Tibet.* Dehra Dun: Trigonometrical Branch, 1889.

Tidrick, Kathryn. *Empire and the English Character.* London: I.B. Taurus, 1992.

Tiffin, Chris and Alan Lawson, (eds). *De-scribing Empire: Post-Colonialism and Textuality.* London and New York: Routledge, 1994.

Trautmann, Thomas R. *Aryans and British India.* Berkeley: University of California Press, 1997.

Twain, Mark. *Following the Equator: A Journey Around the World.* Hartford: The American Publishing Company, 1897.

Verelst, Henry. *A View of the Rise, Progress and Present State of the English Government in Bengal.* London: J. Nourse, 1772.

Vibart, H.M. *Addiscombe: Its Heroes and Men of Note.* Westminster: Archibald Constable and Co., 1894.

Waddell, L.A. 'The Environs and Native Names of Mount Everest' in *The*

Geographical Journal, Including the Proceedings of the Royal Geographical Society Vol. XII, No. 6, 1898: 564–9.

Walker, J.T. *Account of the Operations of The Great Trigonometrical Survey of India, Volume 1 ... Also an Introductory Account of The Early Operations of the Survey During the Period 1800–1830.* Dehra Dun: Great Trigonometrical Survey, 1870.

_____. 'Notes on Mont Everest' in *Proceedings of the Royal Geographical Society* Vol. VIII, 1886a: 88–94.

_____. 'A Last Note on Mont Everest' in *Proceedings of the Royal Geographical Society* Vol. VIII, 1886b: 257–63.

Waller, Derek. *The Pundits: British Exploration of Tibet and Central Asia.* Lexington: University of Kentucky Press, 1990.

Washbrook, David. 'Law, State and Agrarian Society in Colonial India' in *Modern Asian Studies* Vol. 22, No. 1, 1988: 57–96.

Waugh, Andrew S. 'Communications Received' in *Proceedings of the Asiatic Society* Vol. XXVI, No. 4, 1857.

Welsh, James. *Military Reminiscences; Extracted from a Journal of Nearly Forty Years' Active Service in the East Indies.* London: Smith, Elder and Co., 1830.

Wilson, Kathleen. *The Sense of the People: Politics, Culture and Imperialism in England, 1715–1785.* Cambridge: Cambridge University Press, 1998.

Winichakul, Thongchai. *Siam Mapped: A History of the Geo-Body of a Nation.* Honolulu: University of Hawaii Press, 1994.

Wolpert, Stanley. *A New History of India.* New York and Oxford: Oxford University Press, 2000.

Yule, Henry and A.C. Burnell. *Hobson-Jobson.* Delhi: Munshiram Manoharlal, 1984 (1903).

Index